Douglas Kelly is a theologian who has studied science as well as the Bible and philosophy. He seeks to understand and explain the relationship between Genesis 1–2 and modern science. The result is this thoughtful, thorough, and well-researched book that will be valuable, not only to pastors and students, but to anyone wishing to dig deeper into many of the questions raised today concerning Genesis. I highly recommend *Creation and Change.*

Walter T. Brown
Director, Center for Scientific Creation,
Phoenix, Arizona

Dr Kelly is to be commended for a highly intelligent engagement with these crucial verses with which God opens the Bible, declaring himself to be a speaking God who is our Maker. The discussion is scholarly but accessible, a model of the kind of exegetical theology which the church of our day needs more than anything else.

Nigel M. de S. Cameron
Research Professor of Bioethics, Chicago-Kent College of Law,
Ilinois Institute of Technology, Chicago, Illinois

I greatly appreciate the content as well as the style of this book. It is the best work that I have read on this subject. The author's statements concerning the role of faith in science are very important; the subject is frequently misunderstood. With regard to his exegesis of the biblical text I hope that Douglas Kelly's courageous voice will be listened to.

Frederick N. Skiff,
Professor of Physics,
University of Iowa, Iowa City, Iowa

CREATION AND CHANGE

Genesis 1.1-2.4
in the Light of
Changing Scientific Paradigms

●

DOUGLAS F. KELLY

MENTOR

Copyright © Douglas F. Kelly 1997
ISBN 978-1-85792-283-7

10 9 8 7 6 5 4 3 2 1

First published in 1997
Reprinted in 1999, 2002, 2004, 2008 and 2010
in the
Mentor Imprint
by
Christian Focus Publications,
Geanies House, Fearn, Ross-shire,
IV20 1TW, Scotland, UK

www.christianfocus.com

Cover design by Alister MacInnes

Printed and bound by
Bell and Bain, Glasgow

Mixed Sources
Product group from well-managed
forests and other controlled sources
www.fsc.org Cert no. TT-COC-002769
© 1996 Forest Stewardship Council

FSC

Contents

PREFACE 9

1. CREATION: WHY IT MATTERS,
    AND HOW IT IS SCIENTIFICALLY VIABLE 15
    Technical and Bibliographical Notes 28
    Questions for Study 36

2. INTERPRETATION AND OUTLINE OF
    THE FIRST THREE CHAPTERS OF GENESIS 37
    Technical and Bibliographical Notes 43
    Questions for Study 49

3. AN ABSOLUTE BEGINNING 51
    Technical and Bibliographical Notes 58
    Questions for Study 66

4. DAY ONE OF CREATION: CREATION 'OUT OF NOTHING'
    AND THE BEGINNING OF THE FORMATIVE PROCESS 67
    Technical and Bibliographical Notes 79
    Questions for Study 82

5. CREATION OF ANGELS AND 'THE GAP THEORY' 83
    Technical and Bibliographical Notes 88
    Questions for Study 94

6. 'DAYS' OF CREATION – THEIR BIBLICAL MEANING 95
    Technical and Bibliographical Notes 107
    Questions for Study 119

7. THE AGE OF THE WORLD AND THE SPEED OF LIGHT 121
    Technical and Bibliographical Notes 135
    Questions for Study 139

8. THE AGE OF THE WORLD
    AND PHYSICAL CHRONOMETERS 141
    Technical and Bibliographical Notes 156
    Questions for Study 160

9. **DAYS TWO AND THREE OF CREATION:**
    SEPARATIONS RESULTING IN AIR AND DRY LAND **161**
    Technical and Bibliographical Notes 169
    Questions for Study 178

10. **DAYS FOUR AND FIVE OF CREATION:**
    ADDITIONS TO THE CREATED ORDER –
    LUMINARIES, FISH AND FOWL **179**
    Technical and Bibliographical Notes 188
    Questions for Study 189

11. **DAY SIX OF CREATION:**
    MANKIND, THE CROWN OF CREATION **191**
    Technical and Bibliographical Notes 205
    Questions for Study 208

12. **THE SABBATH DAY AND THE ORIENTATION**
    OF THE WHOLE CREATED ORDER
    TOWARDS WORSHIP OF GOD **209**
    Technical and Bibliographical Notes 217
    Questions for Study 222

BIBLIOGRAPHY **223**
SCRIPTURE INDEX **229**
PERSON INDEX **232**
SUBJECT INDEX **236**

This book is dedicated to
Angus Robertson Kelly III, my son,
with love and appreciation.

"Thou art worthy, O Lord, to receive glory and honour and power:
for thou hast created all things,
and for thy pleasure they are and were created"
(Rev. 4:11).

AUTHOR'S PREFACE

A Word About Theology and Science

This volume is a theologian's attempt to think through the relationship of the first two chapters of Genesis to the real world as described by various disciplines of modern science. I am a theologian and student of the Bible, and in no sense a scientist. Much as I have tried to read widely in the field of science for many years, I possess no professional credentials and lack any expertise in any of its demanding disciplines.

For that reason I am well aware that I have engaged in a very perilous undertaking, and I have done so with considerable hesitation. I am far more confident about the general validity of the portions of this volume that deal with Biblical interpretation and its theological implications, than I am about the sections where interaction with science seemed necessary. Many times during this project I have wondered, 'Should I even be doing this?'

The answer, I felt, was 'yes', because the truth claims of Holy Scripture directly impinge upon the actually existing world of space, time and matter. At the best, I may well have done a poor enough job of relating the two realms, but to refuse to look seriously at material reality in the light of the Word of God seemed to me even worse than making this fledgling attempt. At least I am aware of my limitations, and from the beginning have sought counsel, critique and advice from scientific professionals whom I respect, and who are respected in their own fields of research. (They are listed in the Acknowledgements).

It has been my desire throughout to present fairly points of view with which I disagree, and to deal charitably with all in the midst of critical assessment. Undoubtedly the most problematical sections of the book are the seventh and eighth chapters, which argue for the possibility of a young universe. I do know enough to realize that I am far from having proven that point, and also, I believe that the rest of the book stands on its own, regardless of one's assessment of theories concerning the antiquity or youth of the cosmos.

Perhaps I have been imprudent in dealing at all with a subject so difficult and controversial, especially when I am giving a minority reading of it. My response is this: while the time has *not* come when we can honestly claim incontrovertible proof of the youth of the solar system, I believe the time has come when we may properly raise foundational questions about the philosophical framework and methodologies said to establish its high antiquity beyond anyone's propriety to doubt.

This seems to be our current situation: the naturalist system of thought which radically questioned (and rejected) the authority of the truth claims of Scripture to describe the origins of the universe, is now an authority itself, and is receiving, willy-nilly, some of the same sort of sceptical questioning that it once put to the Biblical world and life view. The reasons why the naturalist world view and its attendant assumptions and methodologies appear more open than ever to radical questioning are listed throughout this book and need no repetition here. I may unwittingly be wrong in many of the answers I have given from a Christian believer's perspective, but I do not believe I am wrong to have raised sceptical and foundational questions about the established naturalist explanation of the origins, age and significance of the physical cosmos.

Let me say publicly that I will gladly correct any errors I can be shown, should there be future editions of this book. And in the meantime I am prepared to do the best I can in corresponding with those who may have suggestions or criticism about any of this material. It is my hope that other scholars who are more competent than I in science, will enter the discussion, and do a better job than I did, and that they in turn will encourage others, who will do an even better job than they, all in the good cause of advancing our understanding of truth.

A Word to Students

I have written this volume for the general public, but also with students in mind; whether High School, University, Seminary or perhaps Bible study groups. Younger students and Bible study groups may well wish to skip the first two chapters, and begin with chapter three (which is where I begin actually commenting directly on the Genesis text). Chapter One in particular is probably more demanding than the rest of the book. Those who find it (and Chapter Two) hard to handle, should still be able without much difficulty to cope with the expository sections of the other chapters, except perhaps for the seventh and eighth chapters on the age of the cosmos. These two chapters could also be skipped, as they are not essential to the rest of the volume.

The book is structured to assist those who wish to make it a text for personal or group study. Each chapter is divided into three parts: (1) Exposition of the Genesis text; (2) Technical and Bibliographical Notes for those who desire fuller details on various points raised in the Exposition; (3) Questions for Study. These questions deal only with the Expository part of each chapter, and thus students can skip Part 2 and go directly to the Questions, as they may wish.

Mrs. Bobbie Ames of Hoffman Christian Center in Montgomery, Alabama, has prepared a Teachers' Guide to assist teachers or leaders. She is a distinguished Christian educator with wide, deep and long experience of communicating truth to the next generation, and I am profoundly grateful for her help.

Acknowledgements

In completing this volume I feel very heavily the debt of thanks I owe to many people, who have significantly assisted me along the way. First, I am grateful to my family for the atmosphere of faith in which I was brought up. When we were about ten or eleven years old, our great-aunt Ethel (Mrs. Haynes Britt) and her daughter, Ethel Blue, used to take my cousin, Ray Hendrix, and me to their home in Southern Pines, North Carolina, for occasional weekends. During some of those times they discussed with us the importance of creation, and particularly evidences against evolutionary theory. Perhaps that is what started my interest in a subject that has continued to grip my attention all my days.

This book largely comes out of the research I did while teaching a large, adult Sunday School Class at First Presbyterian Church of Jackson, Mississippi, in the early 1990s on the subjection of Creation. 'The Young Seekers' (as they are called) gave me much stimulating interaction, and several of them encouraged my turning the spoken word into written form with a view to publication. Their friendship has been of the greatest significance to me for many years.

Part of what I gave 'The Young Seekers' came out of a series of sermons on Genesis 1-3 that I preached in my pre-professor days, while I was minister of First Presbyterian Church of Dillon, South Carolina in the mid-1970s. Part of it also came out of class material I have prepared over the last fourteen years for my students at Reformed Theological Seminary, first at the campus in Jackson, Mississippi, and recently at the campus in Charlotte, North Carolina.

When William MacKenzie of Christian Focus Publications suggested that I prepare a volume dealing with creation, it seemed a good time to draw together and rethink my work on this subject during the past twenty years. My secretary, Mrs Tari Williamson, took the cassette tapes of the Sunday School addresses and typed them soon after they were presented, and the First Presbyterian Church of Dillon also had the Sermons printed around 1977. Both of these resources have helped me, although I have laid scores of other books and articles under contribution since then, in addition to frequent conversations with various scientists and with theological, philosophical and historical colleagues.

Especially I must thank several scientists, who took time out from heavy duties to look over the manuscript and make suggestions and corrections, as well as answering enquiries by phone. Among them are Dr Cliff Hull, Jr., of Laurel, Maryland; Dr Frederick N. Skiff, Associate

Professor of Physics of the University of Maryland; Dr Walter T. Brown, Jr. of the Center for Scientific Creation in Phoenix, Arizona; and Dr Carl B. Fliermans, Senior Microbial Ecologist Fellow of the Westinghouse Savannah River Company, Aiken, South Carolina. Also Dr Hilton Terrill of the Family Medical Practice in Florence, South Carolina (and editor of *The Journal of Biblical Ethics in Medicine*) read over the manuscript with helpful critique. My Old Testament colleague of Reformed Seminary in Jackson, Dr John Currid, helpfully interacted with me on questions of Hebrew exegesis. Jean-Marc Berthoud of Lausanne, Switzerland, has encouraged me in several ways, not least by suggesting that I read the remarkable 1539 *Hexameron* of the Strasburg Reformer, Wolfgang Capito. I am grateful to them all, but do not claim their approbation for everything in this book. Certainly, any confusion and mistakes are all mine, not theirs.

While I was composing the substance of this volume last winter in our family home in Dillon, South Carolina, many friends there helped me with cooked food, fire wood and in many other ways! I wish to thank such friends as Jim Atkins, Harry and Betty Gibbons, F. E. and Alice Hobeika, William and Virginia Hobeika, Coble and Joanne Adams, Bruce Price, Bill King, Jimmy Renfrow, Dr John Baumgardner, Larry Horne and Charles O'Neal, Jr., Bill McNeill, Elmer McCallum, Charles and Sarah Lee, Sherrill Elvington, and our excellent domestic helper – Cookie Townsend Lighty. Architects Douglas Dale and Lynton Cooper of Jackson, Mississippi guided me in dealing with a leaky roof during book preparations, and David Bowling of Jackson sent me scientific material. Dr Michael Brown and Mrs Joanne Carr, of Dillon, and Tom Swaim, of Myrtle Beach, S.C., read over the material for comprehensibility. And not least I am grateful to the weekly prayer meetings of First Presbyterian and First Baptist Churches of Dillon, as well as the 'Fishers of Men' Prayer breakfast of Dillon. I also thank my friends and former students: Alan Webb of Gadsen, Alabama; Russ and Elizabeth McElroy of Birmingham, Alabama; and my friends, the Rev. William F. Fulton of the United Methodist charge in Thorndale, Texas; and the Rev. Jimmy Turner and wife, Ellen, of Jackson, Mississippi; as well as Tommy and Linda Peaster of Yazoo City, Mississippi; and my parents-in-law, Jeffery and Sheila Switzer of Cambridge, England; Buz Lowry of Jackson, Mississipi; Henderson Belk of Charlotte, North Carolina; and Linda Rogers of Florence, South Carolina. Also I thank Pastor Edward C. Roberts of Calvary Christian Church in Charlotte.

My former student, Robert Lucas, (now Ph.D. candidate of the University of Aberdeen in Scotland) has assisted me with some references, as have my colleagues, the Rev. Duncan Rankin of Reformed Seminary in Jackson, and Dr Ligon Duncan, now Minister of First Presbyterian Church, Jackson, Mississippi, and also Christian

Glardon, a student at the University of Lausanne, Switzerland. Various student assistants have rendered me much help in gathering books and articles. Among them are Murray Garrott (Ph.D. candidate of the University of Edinburgh), Bill Bradford, John Saffold, John Llewellen, Mark Harrington and Richard Alford. I am particularly grateful to my student, David Rea, and also to his mother, for helping me with printer problems at the last minute. Thanks to our head librarian at Reformed Seminary in Orlando, Florida, John Muether, and to our Seminary President, Dr Luder Whitlock of Orlando, and Vice-President, Dr Robert Cannada of Charlotte.

Two Christian ladies in Louisiana kindly helped formulate several of the questions included in this volume: Mrs Jackie Peacock of Monroe, and Mrs Mary Condit of Lake Charles. They are involved in the daily instruction of youth, and responded to the call of Pastor Steve Wilkins of Auburn Avenue Presbyterian Church in Monroe to assist my efforts.

I am grateful to have worked with Malcolm MacLean of Christian Focus Publications, whose comments have been an insightful guide in the process of preparing the manuscript for publication. My dear wife, Caroline, has constantly and cheerfully assisted me with looking over the English of the manuscript with clarity in view, and also with handling the computer. I appreciate all of these friends and loved ones, and am mindful of all they have done to make this book finally appear.

Douglas Kelly,
Charlotte, North Carolina
January 1997

Chapter One

Creation:
Why it matters, and how it is
scientifically viable

THE question of origins is one of the most significant that a person ever faces: where we came from is crucial to understanding who we are and where we are going. Whether the world was created or has evolved has been a major point of controversy in philosophy, religion, politics and science for the last 200 years. There is no doubt that the biblical vision of man as God's creature, whom he made in his own image, has had the most powerful effect on human dignity, on liberty, on the expansion of the rights of the individual, on political systems, on the development of medicine, and on every other area of culture. How different from the humanistic viewpoint of man as merely an evolved creature; not made in God's image because there is no God! Such a premise has enabled the Marxist totalitarian states conveniently to liquidate millions of their citizens because of the assumption that there is no transcendent person in whose image those citizens are created, no being to give those citizens a dignity and a right to exist beyond what the state determines.

This point has been explored at length by Baron Eric Von Kuehnelt-Leddihn of Austria, who is possibly our century's greatest scholar on questions of liberty and totalitarianism. In his magisterial *Leftism Revisited: From de Sade and Marx to Hitler and Pol Pot*, he shows that apart from the belief that mankind is created in the image of the transcendent God, the divinely derived dignity and liberty of human beings disappears. 'For the genuine materialist there is no fundamental, only a gradual "evolutionary" difference, between a man and a pest, a noxious insect.'[1] His research demonstrates that 'The issue is between man created in the image of God and the termite in a human guise.'[2]

Essentially, mankind has only two choices. Either we have evolved out of the slime and can be explained strictly in the materialistic sense, meaning that we are made of nothing but the material, or we have been made on a heavenly pattern. Modern events have forced upon us the reality that more than a biological debate is at stake here. Behind many of the most important military, political, and economic struggles now going on in the world has been a conscious commitment to the materialistic explanation of man's origin. Yet the fall of the Berlin Wall and other events that have occurred since 1989 in Romania, Hungary, Poland and elsewhere seem to illustrate people's increasing refusal to allow themselves to be treated as soul-less animals with no transcendent reference.

It is precisely because the debate moves inevitably from the merely biological arena into the area of morality that it has engendered intense emotional commitments, both among those who most claim scientific impartiality as well as among 'the religious'. How we choose to answer the question of whether or not we are created answers a larger question of, 'Who is in charge of all this and by whose rules should we play?'. Should society live by the Ten Commandments given by God, or by following human theories enforced because they are favored by a 51 per cent majority or even by an elite who controls that 51 per cent majority? The answer to questions such as these flow directly from one's understanding of creation bringing the whole issue squarely into our day to day existence.

The Bible is God's revelation of his Word to us and includes all we need to know concerning his will for our lives. Notice how God chose to begin this all important book. He initiated his whole revelation with a description of creation, demonstrating that it is not only primal in the historical sense, but primary for the understanding of other doctrines as well. This sense of primacy was well expressed by the Strasburg

---

1. Eric Von Kuehnelt-Leddihn, *Leftism Revisited: From de Sade and Marx to Hitler and Pol Pot,* Preface by William F. Buckley, Jr.(Regnery Gateway: Washington, D. C., 1990), 76.
2. *Ibid.,* xx. He shows what evolutionary views mean when applied to the concepts and practice of law, as in Chief Justice Oliver Wendell Holmes, Jr., of the United States Supreme Court earlier this century. Holmes wrote: 'Man is at present a predatory animal. I think that the sacredness of life is a purely municipal idea of no validity outside the jurisdiction' (*Ibid.,* 20). See also pp. 66, 187, 188, 325.

Reformer, Wolfgang Capito, in his 1539 *Hexameron*, when he stated that an understanding of creation is 'the head of divine philosophy'.[3]

Frances Schaeffer, in an interview toward the end of his life with Christopher Catherwood, stated the crucial evangelistic importance of a sound space/time doctrine of creation.[4] The author heard him remark in a discussion group at L'Abri in December of 1968 that if he had an hour with a person on a plane who did not know the Lord, he would spend the first fifty-five minutes talking about creation in the image of God and where that man came from, and the last five minutes on the presentation of the gospel of salvation. Schaeffer felt we are greatly mistaken to avoid the important subject of how we got here, why we are like we are, who is in charge, by whose rules we should play, and by whose rules we will be judged. Schaeffer thought that when one avoids those questions, which are deeply implanted in every human heart, and jumps immediately to salvation, one loses the major impact on those who are seeking the truth.

An understanding of the doctrine of creation is important for another reason: it helps us see that the Holy Bible is to be taken seriously when it speaks to the real world. If we avoid dealing with what the Bible says about creation of the material universe, then there is a tendency for religion to be disconnected from the real world, or to change the figure, there is a tendency to put Scripture and Christianity into a stained-glass closet that does not impact the space/time realm.

Scottish theologian, James Denney, made this point in the late 1890s: 'The separation of the religious and the scientific means in the end the separation of the religious and the true; and this means that religion dies among true men.'[5] Instead, if the church does seriously address creation, people immediately perceive that God is interacting with the real world where they live, in history, space, and time. The result is that the Bible can become very important to their daily life and to their personal destiny.

In other words, the doctrine of creation with which God's Word begins must be foundational because God starts here. It teaches that

---

3. Wolfgang Capito, *Hexameron, Sive Opus Sex Dierum* (Argentinae [Strasburg], 1539), 22 ('caput divinae philosophiae...').

4. Christopher Catherwood, *Five Evangelical Leaders* (Christian Focus Publications: Geanies House, Fearn, Scotland, 1994). He considered that creation was 'the first category that many churches either failed or refused to recognize'. He wrote, '... these people do not realise that they are lost evangelically. How could they?' ... He went on to elaborate his reply. 'This lostness is answered by the existence of a Creator. So Christianity does not begin with accepting Christ as Saviour, but with In the beginning God created the heavens and the earth... That,' he continued, 'is the answer to the twentieth century and its lostness (the original cause of all lostness) and the answer in the death of Christ' (pp. 135, 136).

5. James Denney, *Studies in Theology* (London, 1894), 15.

since God is the fountain of all reality, then His Word applies to our everyday life. To assume that the early chapters of Genesis are just 'religious' (and thus take the viewpoint of the origins of the world from unbelieving varieties of philosophy) is to relegate the Bible and 'religion' to the realm of the unimportant and the unreal, and eventually to empty the churches since they are no longer thought to deal with actual truth. That is what happened in much of Europe in the nineteenth century (and in America in the twentieth), as Michael Denton (not a professing Christian) has suggested in his recent critique of evolution.[6]

Although Western Society has become greatly secularized since the theories of Darwin confronted Genesis, still that is not the whole story of twentieth century thought. For science, particularly the new physics has, for most of this century, been turning away from many of the assumptions of mechanistic naturalism, which were so congenial to evolutionary theory.

Evolutionary thought has flourished in the world-view engendered by the 18th-century secularist Enlightenment. An important factor in this world-view was 'Deism', a theory that radically separates God from interaction with the real world. As part of this deistic philosophy, deep dualism was assumed: a separation between God and the world, between spiritual and physical, between Kant's noumenal and phenomenal, between the intelligible and sensible, between theory and practice. Although it has not yet entered into the popular consciousness, much of empirical or experimental science (or perhaps, 'operational science')[7] for most of the twentieth century has been functionally abandoning the various dualisms of eighteenth century secularist philosophy. The deistic philosophical assumptions which have kept the concept of God out of the natural realm since the eighteenth century have now themselves been deeply challenged by advances in physics. Thus the philosophical framework which has excluded divine creation and nourished materialist evolution for several generations, is now collapsing.

T. F. Torrance of Edinburgh University shows that the non-dualist or unitary outlook upon the universe brought about by relativity theory and quantum physics has displaced the older mechanistic view of the world as a closed materialist framework, from which God was deistically detached. He asks:

---

6. Michael Denton, *Evolution: A Theory in Crisis* (Adler & Adler: Bethesda, Md., 1986), 66.
7. This term is used by Charles B. Thaxton, Walter L. Bradley & Roger L. Olson in *The Mystery of Life's Origin: Reassessing Current Theories* (Philosophical Library: New York, 1984), 202-206.

How does such an approach look, in the context of the scientific revolution today, in which the dualist outlook on the universe, whether in its Ptolemaic or in its Newtonian form, has been overthrown, and a profoundly unitary outlook is in the process of establishing itself in which the formal and the ontological, the theoretical and the empirical, the structural and the dynamic, are held indivisibly together? Negatively, one can say that Christian theology is now liberated from the rigid framework clamped down upon it by the conception of the mechanistic universe...[8]

Perhaps over the next three or four decades Western Society may see what Thomas S. Kuhn in his book *The Structure of Scientific Revolutions* calls a 'paradigm shift'. Kuhn is a historian of science, who notes that science progresses not in an even uphill line but in terms that he calls 'revolutions' and 'sudden shifts'. For instance, the reigning world-view, which is what he means by paradigm (or explanation of a given set of facts) will be to the forefront for many years. But then this particular way of explaining things no longer seems to be entirely satisfactory, because many questions are raised which it is unable to answer. Suddenly someone comes up with another way of explaining it, another paradigm, another world-view, another hypothesis which challenges the old hypothesis. Then there is a struggle between the two, and eventually the new hypothesis (like a revolution overthrowing the government), takes over so that a new way of looking at things emerges and replaces the old paradigm. He calls this a 'paradigm shift'. For example, scientific research showed that the old phlogiston theory of light was no longer tenable and thus developed another way to approach it. Kuhn shows that this has happened frequently in science. He actually employs a word from spiritual experience to describe this profound change of viewpoint: conversion.[9]

Instead of science remaining the same and commanding universal consent over the generations, actually it proceeds in terms of challenges, in which new questions are raised, so that a new model replaces an old model (when the pressure is sufficiently compelling). Today, many of the central assumptions of the evolutionary framework are being seriously challenged by the new physics, as well as by scientific advocates of 'intelligent design' in biological studies, who have mounted an empirically based challenge to evolutionary naturalism. According to Michael Denton, evolution is 'A Theory in Crisis':

---

8 T. F. Torrance, *Transformation & Convergence in the Frame of Knowledge* (Wm. B. Eerdmans: Grand Rapids, MI, 1984), 205, 206.
9. Thomas S. Kuhn, *The Structure of Scientific Revolutions* (Chicago: University of Chicago Press, 1970), 121.

... there can be no doubt that after a century of intensive effort biologists have failed to validate it in any significant sense. The fact remains that nature has not been reduced to the continuum that the Darwinian model demands, nor has the credibility of chance as the creative agency of life been secured.[10]

Our secularized culture may yet experience the replacement of the old, vastly popular evolutionary hypothesis by the creationist model (or paradigm), although Michael Denton, who holds evolutionism to be massively implausible, is not optimistic concerning its supplanting.[11] At very least one can note that the whole edifice of evolutionary theory is increasingly seen as a faith or dogma, rather than objective, empirical science, and its foundations are appearing shaky. The closed mechanistic framework in which it has existed is being surpassed and rejected in many areas of scientific endeavor, leaving a new approach more open to the reality of divine creation, or at least 'intelligent design'.[12]

Certainly this is not to imply that the majority of scientists have consciously left the philosophical underpinnings of the various forms of Dualism, Deism and Materialism. The tenacity with which these questionable philosophical assumptions hang on among some scientists is vividly illustrated in Professor Richard Dawkins of Oxford University. In a recent reprint of his enthusiastic defense of Darwinism, he states in the introduction to the 1996 edition: 'Evolution – The Greatest Show on Earth – The Only Game in Town!' (quoting an American Tee Shirt).[13] John Angus Campbell notes that 'huge edifices of ideas – such as positivism – never really die. Thinking people gradually abandon them and even ridicule them among themselves, but keep the persuasively useful parts to scare away the uninformed.'[14]

Dawkins, however, who delights in 'taking on' the Creationists, has been 'taken on' himself by Biochemistry Professor Michael Behe. Behe devotes several portions of his new book to demonstrating the scientific untenability, and the philosophical (not empirical) basis of Dawkins' evolutionism.[15]

---

10. Denton, *op.cit.*, 357.

11. *Ibid.*, 356, 357.

12. Michael Behe's *Darwin's Black Box: The Biochemical Challenge to Evolution* (The Free Press: New York, 1996) is illustrative of the powerful testimony that contemporary research in biochemistry is bearing against evolution and in favor of 'intelligent design'.

13. Richard Dawkins, *The Blind Watchmaker* (W. W. Norton & Co.: New York & London, 1996 [1986]), xi.

14. John A. Campbell, 'The Comic Frame and the Rhetoric of Science: Epistemology and Ethics in Darwin's *Origin*,' *Rhetoric Society Quarterly*, 24, 27-50 (quoted in Michael Behe, *op. cit.*, 284). Behe adds: 'This certainly applies to the way the scientific community handles questions on the origin of life.'

Nevertheless, though its fuller implications are resisted by many more than Dawkins, still as Torrance points out, '...a conceptual reform is now taking place ... with the fundamental shift in our understanding of the universe that has come with the advent of relativity theory and its unification of ontology and intelligibility in scientific knowledge.'[16] He adds:

> We now need a similar conceptual reform in our outlook upon the universe as a whole, after the myopia that overtook our vision during centuries of deism and secularism, and the loss of meaning that ... they brought about, that is, a habit of looking at the universe in such a way as to cut off its signitive or referential relations beyond itself. What we need is such a shift in the focus of our vision that, instead of looking at the universe in the flat, as it were, we look at it in a multidimensional way in which [it is] ... found to have meaning through an immanent intelligibility that ranges far beyond the universe to an ultimate ground in the transcendent and uncreated Rationality of God.[17]

The more science has learned about the depth of complexity, harmony and intelligibility of the universe, the more this remarkable natural realm has cried out for a supernatural origin. Professor Torrance, theologian and historian of science, poses the inescapable question:

> Why is there a universe and not nothing? What is the reason for this state of affairs, the existence of a universe that is accessible to rational inquiry? Yet the universe does not carry in itself any explanation for this state of affairs, and even the rationality embedded within it is not self-explanatory. This is certainly understandable, for contingent being cannot explain itself, otherwise it would not be contingent. Nevertheless, it does have something to 'say' to us, simply by being what it is, contingent *and* intelligible in its contingency ... it points beyond itself with a mute cry for sufficient reason ... the fact that the

---

15. Essentially, Behe shows that Dawkins quietly assumes (without the slightest scientific proof) the previous functioning existence of multicelled organisms of 'horrendous complexity' (Behe, op. cit., 46). That is to say, 'An *irreducibly complex* system cannot be produced directly (that is, by continuously improving the initial function, which continues to work by the same mechanism) by slight, successive modifications of a precursor system, because any precursor to an irreducibly complex system that is missing a part is by definition nonfunctional. An irreducibly complex biological system, if there is such a thing, would be a powerful challenge to Darwinian evolution. Since natural selection can only choose systems that are already working, then if a biological system cannot be produced gradually it would have to arise as an integrated unit, in one fell swoop, for natural selection to have anything to act on' (*Ibid.*, 39). Dawkins then assumes the very thing he sets out to prove, which is precisely what he accuses the Creationists of doing in following 'the holy book' (Dawkins, *op. cit.*, vi).
16. T. F. Torrance, *Reality and Scientific Theology* (Scottish Academic Press: Edinburgh, 1985), 43, 44.
17. *Ibid.*, 44.

universe is intrinsically rational means that it is capable of, or open to, rational explanation – from beyond itself.[18]

Thus, empirical science (as opposed to 'naturalistic' science which axiomatically cuts off any reference to the Transcendent) indicates the dependency of the finite universe upon an outside Source. It can take us that far, if no further.

> By its nature, science is concerned with discovering and formulating the differential laws of nature governing the processes of the universe, but it is incapable of establishing the initial conditions out of which the universe took its absolute rise and which ought surely to enter as rational equations into a full understanding of its singularity and intelligibility.[19]

Ultimately, empirical science at its very best can take us only a certain distance in the search for the final cause of created reality. By its very contingent intelligibility it teaches the profound lesson that things which are limited and dependent call out for a source that is unlimited and non-dependent on anything outside itself. It is to that source we must look for a fuller apprehension of the origin of creaturely reality.

Now in the nature of the case, we are dealing here with a unique situation: the bringing into being of the space/time universe by a transcendent Source, who – according to the Scriptures – spoke worlds into existence out of nothing by the word of His power. Science can suggest that a powerful intellect outside the natural realm is required to make sense of what is here. But to know precisely Who it is and how He brought it into being necessarily takes us beyond natural observation and repeatable experimentation. Our sole source of knowledge of such a unique, unrepeatable event as creation and such an absolute and infinite Being as the Creator leaves us limited mortals completely dependent upon Him for our information.

In other words, faith is required in this Creator and in the words He has spoken as the proper mode of understanding that which lies outside merely human knowledge. It is essential to realize that faith, far from being emotional wish-fulfillment or irrational sacrifice of the normal intellect, is actually the only appropriate mode of rational knowledge when God and His mighty works are in view. As Torrance has written:

> ...knowledge of God is the basic act of the human mind and ... faith in its intellectual aspect is the adaptation of the reason in its response to the compelling claims of God as he makes himself known to us in his Word.[20]

---

18. T. F. Torrance, *op. cit.*, 52.
19. T. F. Torrance, *The Ground and Grammar of Theology* (University Press of Virginia: Charlottesville, 1980), 102.
20. T. F, Torrance, *Reality and Scientific Theology*, xi.

But does not reference to faith in God and His Word immediately take us outside the realm of natural science and relegate us to a severely restricted sort of religious discourse, quite disconnected from, or even antithetical to genuine scientific knowledge? Certainly that is how 'naturalistic' science and positivism judge the case.

Yet we must probe more deeply, for some of our greatest scientists, such as Albert Einstein and Michael Polanyi, have stated that faith (or belief) is essential to any kind of advance in physical science. '[Michael Polanyi] made a particular point of restoring to rigorous scientific activity the personal coefficient of knowledge and of showing that the human reason never operates outside a framework of basic beliefs.'[21] Polanyi went on to assert that 'No human intelligence ... can operate outside such a context of faith, for it is within that context that there arises within us, under compulsion from the reality of the world we experience, a regulative set of convictions or a framework of beliefs which prompts and guides our inquiries and controls our assessment of the evidence.'[22] And Albert Einstein spoke of 'faith' or 'belief' (as employed in the natural scientific context) as having 'extra-logical' status, but being nonetheless rational.[23]

A number of years before Einstein and Polanyi were thinking through these matters, Abraham Kuyper of the Free University of Amsterdam foresaw as a theologian some of the very issues these scientists would later raise. He saw that '... the indispensableness of faith goes much farther, and it may safely be said that with the so-called exact sciences there is no investigation, nor any conclusion conceivable except insofar as the observation in the investigation and the reasoning in the conclusion are grounded in faith'.[24]

So then, both theology and science must operate in their own peculiar ways on the basis of faith. How faith particularly works, of course, must depend upon the nature of the object which it seeks to know. Torrance has shown that 'belief in God calls for a mode of response in accordance with his nature as the transcendent Ground of all created being and intelligibility ... [so that] ... we have to reckon with a personal factor on both sides of the knowing relationship ...'[25] However, 'In natural science in which we interact with realities which are not themselves centers of rational consciousness, except insofar

21. T.F. Torrance, *Christian Theology & Scientific Culture* (New York: Oxford University Press, 1981), 62.
22. *Ibid.*, 64.
23. *Ibid.*, 69.
24. Abraham Kuyper, *Principles of Sacred Theology* (Wm. B. Eerdmans: Grand Rapids, MI, 1954), 131. See also pp. 133, 144, 145.
25. Torrance, *op. cit.*, 70, 71.

as human beings are included among them, the personal coefficient must function rather differently.'[26]

All of this is to say that the admission of faith as necessary to understanding something of the event of creation is in no sense antithetical to the way true science operates in its own field. But we must say more about faith and origins. In recent history, the greatest objection against employing any form of faith in God and His Word has arisen from secular evolutionists. Any sort of reference to God, supernatural causation and faith, they argue, takes one outside the boundaries of genuine science into the land of imagination and mythology. Only naturalistic evolution can honestly claim to be science. All else is faith, ignorance or superstition.

Sincere as such claims may be, they fail to realize that naturalistic evolution itself is a supreme act of faith: a religion, if you will. Phillip E. Johnson, Professor of Law at the University of California at Berkeley, whose speciality is the evaluation of evidences, has written a monograph demonstrating this faith-basis of evolution: *Evolution as Dogma: the Establishment of Naturalism*. He says: 'What the science educators propose to teach us as "evolution," and label as fact, is based not upon any incontrovertible empirical evidence, but upon a highly controversial philosophical presupposition.'[27]

In *Darwin on Trial*, Johnson discusses the astonishing lecture of Dr Colin Patterson, senior paleontologist of the British Natural History Museum, given at the American Museum of Natural History in 1981. 'His lecture compared creationism (not creation-science) with evolution, and characterized both as scientifically vacuous concepts which are held primarily on the basis of faith .... According to Patterson, Darwin's theory of natural selection is under fire and scientists are no longer sure of its general validity. Evolutionists increasingly talk like creationists in that they point to a fact but cannot provide an explanation of the means.'[28]

Lynn Margulis, Professor of Biology at the University of Massachusetts, has stated the position even more bluntly. She shows that molecular biology has as yet been unable to demonstrate the formation of a single new species by mutations, and concludes that neo-Darwinism is 'a minor twentieth-century religious sect within the sprawling religious persuasion of Anglo-Saxon biology'.[29]

26. *Ibid.*, 70.
27. Phillip E. Johnson, *Evolution as Dogma: the Establishment of Naturalism* (Foundation for Thought and Ethics, Houghton Publishing Co.: Dallas, Tx, 1990), 1, 2.
28. Phillip E. Johnson, *Darwin on Trial* (InterVarsity Press: Downers Grove, Ill., 2nd ed. 1993), 9, 10.
29. C. Mann (1991), 'Lynn Margulis: Science's Unruly Earth Mother,' *Science*, 252, 378-381.

Instead of the controversy over origins being between faith and science, in actuality it is between two different kinds of faith: the first, historic Christian faith in God, in His Word and in His intelligible creation (which gave rise to modern science); the second, faith in naturalism or materialist evolutionary monism. The fact that both are 'faiths' does not mean that they are equally valid, nor that either is beyond examination of its assumptions and rules of procedure.[30]

Either one begins with faith in an eternal God or with faith in eternal matter. There is nothing in between. Every religion, whether New Age or Christianity, Judaism, Islam, or Materialist Secularism has to start on one of two foundations. The first assumes an eternal God behind everything that makes sense of everything else. Those who deny Him inevitably manufacture an alternative. In modern terms, perhaps it will be expressed as electro-magnetism, gravity and nuclear structure as lying at the root of everything. In ancient times this alternative to God would have been something like eternal matter, of which God was merely a 'weak' co-existing 'Mechanic' (to use the words of fourth-century Church Father, Athanasius).[31] And this eternally existing material along with its limited and dependent 'mechanic' were thought to be somehow under the impersonal control of Greek 'fate' or the 'wheel of fortune'.[32]

Classical Greek tragedy, particularly some of the tragedies of the playwright, Euripides, provides a good illustration of this alternative

30. We refer you to the *Bibliographical and Technical Notes* at the end of Chapter I for further consideration of this crucial difference.
31. Athanasius, *De Incarnatione*, 2, 3 and 4: 'But others, including Plato, who is in such repute among the Greeks, argue that God has made the world out of matter previously existing and without beginning. For God could have made nothing had not the material existed already; just as the wood must exist ready at hand for the carpenter, to enable him to work at all. But in so saying they know not that they are investing God with weakness. For if He is not Himself the cause of the material, but makes things only of previously existing material, He proves to be weak, because unable to produce anything He makes without the material; just as it is without doubt a weakness of the carpenter not to be able to make anything required without his timber. For, *ex hypothesi*, had not the material existed, God would not have made anything. And how could He in that case be called Maker and Artificer, if He owes His ability to make to some other source – namely, to the material? So that if this be so, God will be on their theory a Mechanic only, and not a Creator out of nothing; if, that is, He works at existing material, but is not Himself the cause of the material. For He could not in any sense be called Creator unless He is Creator of the material of which the things have been made.'
32. Oxford University Classicist, Denis C. Feeney's recent masterpiece on the classical pagan view of the gods (in their epic poetry) shows how for the ancient Greeks and Romans, '... these gods are of the cosmos, not outside it. The gods (certainly not the Greek gods, and much less the Roman ones) did not create the world, but were born from its nature, so that Jupiter is an aspect of the way the world is' (Feeney, *The Gods in Epic: Poets and Critics of the Classical Tradition*, Clarendon Press: Oxford, 1993, 152). Feeney's chapter on Vergil's *Aeneid* (4) is a fascinating study of the impenetrable conflicts between the concepts of limited gods, human will, and what he terms 'the inviolability of Fate' (157).

to a Creator God. Ultimately, Greek tragedy rests on a materialist view of the Universe, the eternity of matter, behind which is a kind of dark impersonal fate or chance which controls our lives but does not have a human face. When Euripides' character, Medea, realized that one cannot make sense of life and people, she murdered some of her children. In this and other Greek tragedies, people scream out in pain and curse the darkness of the Universe, because life does not make sense. They are acting logically: if matter and impersonal chance are all there is, nothing makes sense. That is the origin of the tension in such tragedy: characters seeking to make sense of their world which the writer knows is unintelligible.

The modern naturalistic alternative to a Creator God, while very different in detail and sophistication from that of ancient Greek tragedy, leads after all to the same depressing results. Michael Denton in his incisive critique of evolutionary theory has shown the centrality of evolutionary faith to modern culture:

> The entire scientific ethos and philosophy of modern western man is based to a large extent upon the central claim of Darwinian theory that humanity was not born by the creative intentions of a deity, but by a completely mindless trial and error selection of random molecular patterns. The cultural importance of evolution theory is therefore immeasurable, forming as it does the centerpiece, the crowning achievement, of the naturalistic view of the world, the final triumph of the secular thesis which since the end of the middle ages has displaced the old naive cosmology of Genesis from the western mind.[33]

What are the results in the modern soul of the replacement of the Creator God by faceless time, chance and energy? William Provine of Cornell University has stated it clearly:

> The implications of modern science, however, are clearly inconsistent with most religious traditions .... No inherent moral or ethical laws exist, nor are there absolute guiding principles for human society. The universe cares nothing for us and we have no ultimate meaning in life.[34]

Leslie Paul's remarks concur:

> No one knows what time, though it will be soon enough by astronomical clocks, the lonely planet will cool, all life will die, all mind will cease, and it will all be as if it had never happened. That, to be honest, is the goal to which evolution is travelling, that is the benevolent end of the

33. Michael Denton, *op. cit.*, 357, 358.
34. William Provine, 'Scientists, Face it! Science and Religion are Incompatible,' *The Scientist*, September 5, 1988, 10. Quoted in Appendix by John Ankerberg & John Weldon to J.P. Moreland, ed., *The Creation Hypothesis: Scientific Evidence for an Intelligent Designer* (InterVarsity Press: Downers Grove, Ill., 1994), 289..

furious living and furious dying .... All life is no more than a match struck in the dark and blown out again. The final result ... is to deprive it completely of meaning.[35]

Tragedy and despair – in both ancient and modern forms – are based on a view that there is not a creation nor a Creator but that at the back of everything are impersonal forces, so that the Universe is faceless: it is ultimately dark out there. Such emptiness makes a tremendous difference in how to view everyday life as well as how to handle the mysteries of existence. But if a loving, infinite Person, who does have a face, (which we have seen in Jesus), is behind it all, then the struggles of life can bear a profoundly different meaning! The Holy Scriptures reveal the One Who stands behind all created reality.

The Bible does not start with an apology nor with an argument, it simply starts with God. Genesis 1:1 says: 'In the beginning God created the heavens and the earth.' In the New Testament the prologue to John's Gospel says: 'In the beginning was the Word and the Word was with God and the Word was God. All things were made through Him; without Him was not anything made that was made' (John 1:1-3). Hebrews 11:3 says: 'By faith we understand that the worlds were framed by the Word of God, so that things which appeared were not made of things that are seen.' The Bible starts off with a Person.

Evolutionism begins with impersonal material and energy, and is never able to answer the question of how it got there nor what it means once it is there. Indeed, as the famous Dutch theologian and statesman, Abraham Kuyper, once pointed out, naturalistic philosophy excludes the possibility of ever learning the truth about origins by neglecting essential facts about the condition of man (the learner): his fallenness, and his need for regeneration and for divine revelation.[36]

In contrast, the Bible tells us how energy and matter got here and in so doing, shows what it all means. It came through the creative speaking of a personal God, the one true God Who exists in three persons, Father, Son and Holy Spirit, Who is light, in Whom is no darkness at all. He is love, He is holiness, He is goodness. Out of His light and love and holy goodness He created this vast complex universe that we inhabit. And He is the One, the only One, who is able to give us the basic outline of what happened when He brought it into being.

---

35. Leslie Paul, *The Annihilation of Man* (New York: Harcourt Brace, 1945), 154. Quoted in Appendix to J.P. Moreland, *op.cit.*, 289

36. 'All prosecution of science which starts out from naturalistic premises denies the subjective fact of palingenesis, as well as the objective fact of a revelation, which immediately corresponds to this.' See Abraham Kuyper, *Principles of Sacred Theology* (Grand Rapids: Baker, 1980), 224.

God provides us such information in the first three chapters of Genesis, for since only God was there, we have to get our information about it from Him. Nothing could be more logical or more intelligent than to accept the information from the One who made it, from the One who was the eye-witness, from the One who is truth itself. It is to these early chapters of God's Word that we now turn.

TECHNICAL AND BIBLIOGRAPHICAL NOTES FOR CHAPTER ONE

1. The Changing Relationship of Theology and Science

A. Theology and the Rise of Science

A number of works have traced the rise of modern science out of the Biblical world-view. Among them are:

R. Hooykaas, *Religion and the Rise of Modern Science* (Wm. B. Eerdmans: Grand Rapids, 1974), 162pp. He traces the rise of science from Classical times through the Middle Ages, Renaissance, and particularly Reformation and Puritan Period, showing that '"classical modern science" arose only in the western part of Europe in the sixteenth and seventeenth centuries', and that 'Science is more a consequence than a cause of a certain religious view' (p.161). His study is of especial significance on the relationship of British Puritanism to early modern science, especially through the development of the Royal Society, a haven of many of the greatest seventeenth century scientists. Although for political reasons in post-Restoration England the Royal Society found it wisest to downplay its former religious affiliations, Hooykaas shows it to have been heavily Puritan.

The 1974-76 Gifford Lectures at Edinburgh University by the Distinguished Professor of the History of Science at Seton Hall University, the Benedictine priest, Stanley L. Jaki, *The Road of Science and the Ways of God* (Edinburgh, 1978) shows how and why science arose from within a Christian world-view. Jaki includes some judicious critique of Thomas Kuhn's *The Structure of Scientific Revolutions*. Elsewhere he particularly demonstrates the crucial importance of the biblical doctrine of creation to the development of Western science in *Science and Creation: From Eternal Cycles to an Oscillating Universe* (New York: Science History Publications, 1974).

An older work, but still valuable in demonstrating the rise of science out of Christian assumptions, is the famous process philosopher Alfred North Whitehead's *Science and the Modern World* (New York: The Free Press, 1953). He shows the essential presuppositions for Western Science of order, intelligibility, cause and effect (rooted in a created beginning) to have been elements made available to the West through the historic Christian faith.

Another useful volume is by E. H. Hutten, *The Origins of Science. An Inquiry into the Foundations of Western Thought* (Allen and Unwin: London, 1962).

Harold P. Nebelsick in *Circles of God: Renaissance, Reformation and the Rise of Science* (Scottish Academic Press: Edinburgh, 1984) discusses the significance of Christian theology for the development of natural science with special reference to the question of intelligible harmony within the universe as a major motivation for astronomical progress.

T. F. Torrance's award-winning *Space, Time and Incarnation* (Oxford University Press: London, 1969) specifically addresses the impact of Greek Patristic thought concerning the incarnation of Christ upon classical pagan views of space, and discusses the ramifications of this 'paradigm shift' for the wider development of physics. He charts the profound influence of Biblical and Patristic teaching that in Christ's incarnation the infinite God has taken flesh within the space/time structures of our world, so that it is open to divine presence and intervention, rather than being a mechanical organism, closed off from Him. This openness to a higher level of reality in order to make sense of the lower level is examined in light of the theorems of Kurt Gödel. In particular, he shows how modern forms of mechanistic positivism were effectively undercut by Gödel's observation that a system cannot be both closed and consistent at the same time. If it is to be consistent, then it must be open to a higher level of reality that cannot be explained from within the system. The relevance of this theorem to either logical positivism or scientific naturalism should be obvious, for the closed mechanistic view of the world as a complete and consistent system within itself has come under increasing pressure scientifically during the twentieth century. Hence we must consider contemporary changes in scientific epistemology.

B. Changes in Scientific Frameworks during the Twentieth Century

We have already discussed Thomas S. Kuhn's seminal *The Structure of Scientific Revolutions*, which seems to owe something to Michael Polanyi's *Science, Faith and Society* (Phoenix Edition: 1946).

Several chapters in various books by T. F. Torrance chronicle the significant shift in scientific thinking during the twentieth century from a post-Newtonian deistic (and later atheistic) view of the universe as a closed materialist mechanism to a world of open structures after the arrival of relativity theory and quantum physics: 'The Making of the "Modern" Mind from Descartes and Newton to Kant,' Chapter 1 of *Transformation & Convergence in the Frame of Knowledge*, and three other chapters in the same volume: 'The Place of Michael Polanyi in the Modern Philosophy of Science' (chapter 3); 'Christian Theology in the Context of Scientific Change' (chapter 4); 'Newton, Einstein and Scientific Theology' (chapter 8). Elsewhere in Torrance, see: 'The Stratification of Truth', chapter 5 in *Reality and Scientific Theology*, and two chapters in *The Ground and Grammar of Theology*: 'Emerging from the Cultural Split' (ch. 2) and 'Theological Science' (ch. 5). Chapter 1 of *Christian Theology and Scientific Culture* also deals with this theme under the title: 'Christianity in Scientific Change'.

Central to this change of framework from the world as closed, causal nexus to open structures has been the work of Albert Einstein. Two of his works most accessible to laymen are: *Out of My Later Years* (Secaucus, N.J.: Citadel, 1936) and *The World As I See It* (John Lane: London, 1935). Much more complex, but important to appreciating these changing assumptions from within physical science is A. Einstein and L. Infield, *The Evolution of Physics from Early Concepts to Relativity and Quanta* (Clarion Edition: New York, 1938).

Two volumes by others about Einstein are useful in explaining his accomplishments: W. Berkson, *Fields of Force. The Development of a World View from Faraday to Einstein* (Routledge and Kegan Paul: London, 1974), and L. Infield, *Albert Einstein. His Work and Influence on Our World* (Charles Scribner's Sons: New York, 1950).

Michael Polanyi has contributed massively to this change in scientific assumptions from closed materialist mechanism to an open universe. Two of his most important books are: *Personal Knowledge* (Routledge and Kegan Paul: London, 1958) and *Knowing and Being* (Routledge and Kegan Paul: London, 1969). T. F. Torrance has edited *Belief in Science and in Christian Life: The Relevance of Michael Polanyi's Thought for Christian Faith and Life* (The Handsel Press: Edinburgh, 1980). See also Richard Gelwick, *The Way of Discovery. An Introduction to the Thought of Michael Polanyi* (New York: Oxford University Press, 1977).

Another volume of general interest on this shift within twentieth century science is David B. Harned, *Images for Self-Recognition* (New York: 1977). Harned discusses the significance of the surpassing of dualism in scientific thought.

2. Empirical Versus Naturalistic Science and the Failure of Demarcationism

Although often overlooked in discussions of modern science, there is a crucial difference between the assumptions of naturalistic science and empirical science. Naturalist science, working on the basis of the positivistic view of the world as a closed, materialist nexus, which denies any reference to the Transcendent (an assumption long since surpassed in the New Physics, as we have seen above), is not the same as empirical science (termed 'operational science' as contrasted with 'origin science' in the Epilogue of Thaxton, Bradley and Olsen, *The Mystery of Life's Origin: Reassessing Current Theories*).

Much (though not all) of the 'battle' between theology and science since the seventeenth century has been between the contrasting assumptions of theism and those of naturalistic science. The famous nineteenth-century polemic by A. D. White, *A History of the Warfare of Science with Theology in Christendom* (London: 1896) is an illustration of the reduction of all science to naturalism.

Part of this 'battle' has also resulted from misunderstanding the actual teaching of classical theologians as regards science. In an otherwise valuable volume, F. W. Farrar (*History of Interpretation*, London, 1886, xviii) invents a quotation to show that Calvin supposedly opposed Copernicus. R. Hooykaas has corrected the record on this (*op.cit.*, 154), as well as showing the incorrectness of a 'quotation' alleging that the famous Puritan theologian, John Owen, attacked the teachings of Sir Isaac Newton (*ibid.*).

Our major concern here, however, is with the reduction of all science to naturalistic science. Two chapters in *The Creation Hypothesis: Scientific Evidence for an Intelligent Designer* (J. P. Moreland, editor, InterVarsity Press: Downers Grove, Ill., 1994) set forth the profound axiomatic differences between naturalistic and empirical science: Chapter 1, 'Theistic Science & Methodological Naturalism' by J. P. Moreland, and Chapter 2, 'The Methodological Equivalence of Design & Descent' by Stephen C. Meyer. Moreland critiques 'the assertion that science must presuppose methodological naturalism' (34) and also that 'Theistic science is religion and not science' (43).

> It is important to remember that these claims are not first-order claims *of* science about some scientific phenomenon. Rather, they are second-order philosophical claims *about* science. They are metaclaims that take a vantage point outside science and have science itself as their subject of reference. Thus the field of philosophy, especially philosophy of science will be the proper domain from which to assess these claims... (43).

Meyer quotes the assertion of Basil Willey ('Darwin's Place in the History of Thought' in *Darwinism and the Study of Society*, ed. M. Banton, Chicago: Quadrangle Books, 1961): 'Science must be provisionally atheistic, or cease to be itself' (Moreland, *op.cit.*, 69). Meyer shows that these sorts of claims constitute an *a priori* 'begging of the question', rather than being a necessary or integral part of true, empirical science. He correctly relates naturalist science to the school of logical positivism, which leading physicists (as we see in the writings of Polanyi in Section I of this Appendix) have rejected for much of this century. He writes:

...positivism's verificationist criterion of meaning did not achieve its own standard. That is, the assumptions of positivism turn out to be neither empirically verifiable nor logically undeniable. Furthermore, positivism's verificationist ideal misrepresented much actual scientific practice. Many scientific theories refer to unverifiable and unobservable entities such as forces, fields, molecules, quarks and universal laws. ... Clearly, positivism's verifiability criterion would not achieve the demarcation desired. (74)

In particular, Moreland and Meyer deal with 'demarcationism' in naturalist science; an attempt to preclude any evidence from consideration (such as creation by an intelligent designer) which would challenge the assumptions of naturalism, even if such evidence is empirically based. Meyer responds to the demarcationist procedure that 'To be scientific a theory must be naturalistic' (81).

To assert that such theories [as intelligent design rather than evolution] are not scientific because they are not naturalistic simply assumes the point at issue. Of course intelligent design is not wholly naturalistic, but why does that make it unscientific? What noncircular reason can be given for this assertion? What independent criterion of method demonstrates the inferior scientific status of a nonnaturalistic explanation? (82).

On the contrary, as Laudan has written in his 'Demise of the Demarcation Problem' (in *But Is It Science?* ed. M. Ruse, Buffalo, N.Y.: Prometheus Books, 1988): 'one cannot define science in such a way as to confer automatic epistemic authority on favored theories simply because they happen to manifest features alleged to characterize all "true science". When evaluating the warrant or truth claims of theories, we cannot substitute abstractions about the nature of science for empirical evaluation' (paraphrased in Moreland, *op.cit.*, 76).

Meyer and others have noted that this naturalist (or positivist) procedure constituted 'one of the principal criteria of science adopted by Judge William Overton after hearing the testimony of philosopher of science Michael Ruse in the Arkansas creation-science trial of 1981' (*ibid.*, 77). Law Professor Phillip Johnson discusses extensively the non-objective and obscurantist nature of demarcationism in *Darwin On Trial*. Referring to the details of Judge Overton's decision, he writes:

...empiricism is *not* the primary value at stake. The more important priority is to maintain the naturalistic world-view and with it the prestige of 'science' as the source of all important knowledge. Without Darwinism, scientific naturalism would have no creation story...

To prevent such a catastrophe, defenders of naturalism must enforce rules of procedure for science that preclude opposing points of view....

As long as scientific naturalists make the rules, critics who demand positive evidence for Darwinism need not be taken seriously. (118)

Michael Behe discusses the scientific impropriety of 'Ruse's rule' as used by Judge Overton[37] as well as Richard Dickerson's rule that science must explain 'the behavior of the physical and material universe in terms of purely physical and material causes, without invoking the supernatural'.[38] As Behe points out, 'Dickerson does not say scientific evidence has shown that the supernatural has never affected nature .... Rather, he argues that in principle, science should not invoke it. The clear implication is that it should not be invoked *whether it is true or not.*'[39]

A small volume dealing at length with the demarcationist legal decision against 'creation-science' in Arkansas is Norman L. Geisler's *The Creator in the Courtroom. "Scopes II". The Controversial Arkansas Creation-Evolution Trial* (Mott Media: Milford, MI, 1982). It was written after the Creationists lost the case by the rendering of Judge Overton's decision, as discussed above. Of particular value in this book is the courtroom testimony of Dr Geisler (113-118) and Professor N. Chandra Wickramasinghe of Wales, co-author with Sir Fred Hoyle, who turned against Darwinian evolution (without accepting Biblical creation), of *Evolution From Space* (J.M. Dent: London, 1981). The testimony of Wickramasinghe (a Buddhist) is found on pp. 148-153 of Geisler's book.

Chapter 9 of Johnson's *Darwin On Trial* ('The Rules of Science') gives a lucid survey of the rules of naturalistic demarcationism, and evaluates them as unacceptable in any normal court of law or within empirical scientific procedure itself. Elsewhere Johnson rightly notes that 'The time when scientific naturalism could not be challenged is already finished' (Moreland, *op.cit.*, 8).

3. Evolution As Dogma

Phillip Johnson's *Evolution As Dogma: The Establishment of Naturalism* has been previously mentioned. In it he makes the important methodological point that '... faith in naturalism is no more "Scientific" (i.e. empirically based) than any other kind of faith' (5). He adds:

Philosophical naturalism is so deeply ingrained in the thinking of many educated people today, including theologians, that they find it difficult even to imagine any other way of looking at things.... Since there is nothing outside of nature, and since *something* must have produced all

---

37. Behe, *op. cit.*, 287, 288.
38. *Ibid.*, 238.
39. *Ibid.*, 239

the kinds of organisms that exist, a satisfactory naturalistic mechanism must be waiting to be discovered ....

The absence of proof 'when measured on an absolute scale' is unimportant to a thoroughgoing naturalist, who feels that science is doing well enough if it has a plausible explanation that maintains the naturalistic worldview. The same absence of proof is highly significant to any person who thinks it possible that there are more things in heaven and earth than are dreamt of in naturalistic philosophy. (8).

Johnson speaks of the naturalistic worldview (or faith or dogma) as being 'as problematical as any other set of metaphysical assumptions when it is placed on the table for examination rather than being taken for granted as "the way we think today"' (13). Johnson devotes Chapter 10 of his *Darwin on Trial* to 'Darwinist Religion' and Chapter 5 to 'The Fact of Evolution'. In both of these he demonstrates the dogmatic, non-empirical character of naturalistic Darwinism. He remarks that '... Darwinism fails as an empirical theory' (66) and that 'Recasting the theory as fact serves no other purpose than to protect it from falsification' (68).

Far from wishing to impugn the sincerity of scientific naturalists, Johnson observes that '... they are as a rule so steeped in naturalistic assumptions that they are blind to the arbitrary elements in their own thinking' (118). But that of course does not remove the fact that much of their program is based on faith (or dogma) rather than empirical reality. Michael Denton in *Evolution: A Theory in Crisis* makes a similar point (76, 77). G. A. Kerkut, a biochemist, who was critical of conventional evolutionary theory, but did not accept creation, similarly stated: 'It seems at times as if many of our modern writers on evolution have had their views by some sort of revelation ...' (*Implications of Evolution*, Oxford: Pergamon Press, 1960, 150).

One of the strongest evidences that the leading dogma of scientific naturalism is based on faith and not empirical research is the impossibility of falsifying it. Sir Karl Popper's *Conjectures and Refutations: The Growth of Scientific Knowledge* (Harper, 1963) showed the centrality of the possibility of falsification to truly empirical hypotheses, and its impossibility to faith conjectures. Chapter 12 of Johnson's *Darwin On Trial* ('Science and Pseudoscience') discusses the significance of Popper's distinction between the empirical scientific work of Einstein and the 'pseudoscientific' methodology of Marx and Freud. 'Popper saw that a theory that appears to explain everything actually explains nothing' (Johnson, *op.cit.*, 148). And Darwinism, being unfalsifiable, fits into the latter category.

Dr Magnus Verbrugge, who applies some of the epistemological insights of the Dutch Calvinist philosopher, Herman Dooyeweerd (his father-in-law), to theories of chemical evolution, mentions the insistence of J. Monod that religion be kept out of science. Ironically, he shows Monod himself introducing 'religion' into science, by quoting some speculations of Monod on the place of DNA in evolution (Verbrugge, *Alive: An Enquiry into the Origin and Meaning of Life,* Ross House Books: Vallecito, CA, 1984, 117). Verbrugge says:

> This is beautiful language.... But it is not scientific language. It expresses a religious commitment.... He declares chance to be the non-dependent agency on which all else depends for its existence. So he makes this abstract concept into something divine, endowed with the power to create.... *(ibid.).*

The undeniable fact that naturalistic science replaces faith in the God of Scripture with faith in something else (be it time, chance, evolution or whatever) should come as no surprise to those who have some familiarity with the teachings of Holy Scripture. For as St. Paul teaches in Romans chapters 1 and 2, and as John Calvin paraphrases it, the mind of man is an inveterate idol factory (John Calvin, *Institutes of the Christian Religion,* Book I. chapter V. 12).

QUESTIONS FOR STUDY

1. Why is the question of origins crucial to understanding who we are? How has the humanistic viewpoint of man as an evolved creature affected the way in which people are treated politically?

2. For what two reasons is an understanding of the doctrine of Creation important to us?

3. In the late 1890s, James Denney noted that a problem occurred with the separation of religious and scientific ideas. Why must the church seriously address scientific ideas and particularly Creation?

4. What is 'Deism'? What are some of the results of holding to this idea?

5. What is a 'paradigm'? What is a 'paradigm shift'?

6. Why has evolution been called 'a theory in crisis'?

7. In what sense could Darwinism be called 'a religious sect'?

8. Why is evolutionary faith so important to materialistic Humanism?

9. If the universe is accessible to rational enquiry, can empirical science give us a final cause for reality?

10. What are the true concerns of science, and what are its limits?

11. Can natural observation and repeated experimentation reveal the source of the universe? Why or why not? What is needed?

12. Why is faith essential to any kind of advance in physical science?

13. According to Abraham Kuyper, how does naturalistic philosophy exclude the possibility of ever learning ultimate truth?

14. What is the essence of the controversy between the two views of origins?

15. Explain why tragedy and despair are rooted in an evolutionary view of origins.

Chapter Two

Interpretation and Outline of the First Three Chapters of Genesis

G OD in His Word has given us information concerning creation that we could have received in no other way than by divine revelation, for no one was there to observe it, and it cannot be repeated as an experiment in a laboratory. So important is this information that He begins His Word with this subject. Genesis 1:1 states: 'In the beginning God created the heavens and the earth.'

In order to understand this first verse of the Bible, it is necessary to look at the larger context out of which it comes. This wider look involves considering how to interpret the book of Genesis, and more particularly the first eleven chapters of it. To accomplish this goal two related matters must be addressed: what type of literature does Genesis comprise, and what is its basic outline?

First, what kind of literature is found in these first eleven chapters of the earliest book of the Bible? Particularly since the introduction into Western thought of the assumptions of vast ages of the cosmos and of evolutionary theory, many Biblical interpreters have attempted to avoid the obvious conflict between a straightforward reading of the text and opposing naturalist theories of origins. They have done so by suggesting that Genesis 1-11, and especially the first three chapters, are poetic writings, rather than chronological history. This position is surprisingly common among people who generally hold to a high view of Scriptural authority, and the historical details of its development are discussed in *Technical and Bibliographical Notes* at the end of this chapter.

The late Edward J. Young of Westminster Seminary in Philadelphia, an authority of massive erudition in Hebrew and cognate languages, has responded to evangelical claims that Genesis 1-3 is poetry rather than serious history. He addresses the question: 'Is Genesis Poetry or Myth?' as follows:

> To escape from the plain factual statements of Genesis some Evangelicals are saying that the early chapters of Genesis are poetry or myth, by which they mean that they are not to be taken as straightforward accounts, and that the acceptance of such a view removes the difficulties.... To adopt such a view, they say, removes all troubles with modern science... Genesis is not poetry. There are poetical accounts of creation in the Bible – Psalm 104, and certain chapters in Job – and they differ completely from the first chapter of Genesis. Hebrew poetry had certain characteristics, and they are not found in the first chapter of Genesis. So the claim that Genesis One is poetry is no solution to the question. The man who says, 'I believe that Genesis purports to be a historical account, but I do not believe that account', is a far better interpreter of the Bible than the man who says, 'I believe that Genesis is profoundly true, but it is poetry.'[1]

In a word, Genesis 1 is not written according to the canons of Hebrew poetry with various types of parallelism. As Professor John Currid states: '... there is no indication of figurative language in Genesis 1. If the narrative is to be considered imagery, one would expect to encounter many of the essentials of figurative language (e.g., schema, metaphor, and other tropes), but there are none.'[2] Rather, the first eleven chapters of it are written as historical narrative much the same way that I and II Chronicles are written. That is, they are theological interpretations of actual states of affairs that have occurred in the space/time cosmos.

There are, of course, important differences between, let us say, the Chronicler's account of King Hezekiah's reign and the Mosaic account of the creation. The former takes place within the space/time realm, while the latter displays the bringing into being of this entire realm. Creation has a primeval uniqueness about it (as Final Consummation has its own kind of conclusive uniqueness); a uniqueness not possessed

1. Edward J. Young, *In the Beginning: Genesis 1-3 and the Authority of Scripture* (Banner of Truth Trust: Edinburgh, 1976), 18, 19.
2. John Currid, 'A Cosmology of History From Creation to Consummation', in *Building A Christian World View, II*, ed. Hoffecker (Presbyterian & Reformed Publ. Co.: Philadelphia, PA, 1987), 44, 45.

by the account of any particular king's earthly reign. Nevertheless, this uniqueness of creation and consummation does not place the Scriptural accounts of them into a literary category outside the recording of factual, chronological events, as Saint Augustine shows in his sensible discussion of the 'literal' (as opposed to allegorical), and yet unique nature of Genesis Chapter One.[3]

Simply stated, the writer of Genesis meant to say what the historic Christian Church (until the mid-nineteenth century) believed he said. That is, he intended to speak factually of what happened at the beginning, with no less historical reality than the Chronicler speaks of Hezekiah or Luke speaks of the Virgin Birth of Christ.

A further confirmation of the non-poetic, historical nature of the Genesis account of creation is found in the way the New Testament uses these early chapters. Certainly for those who take the New Testament seriously, and are committed to the person and work of the Lord Jesus Christ as truth itself, the New Testament approach to Genesis will be of highest consequence. No amount of exegetical straining can find the slightest poetic view of Genesis 1-11 in the books of the New Testament. One can disagree with the New Testament's literal, historical usage of Genesis 1-11, but one cannot honestly find in its pages anything less than a straightforward reading of these chapters as literal, relevant facts.

Henry M. Morris has usefully summarized the New Testament's usage of the Old:

> The New Testament is, if anything, even more dependent on Genesis than the Old. There are at least 165 passages in Genesis that are either directly quoted or clearly referred to in the New Testament. Many of them are alluded to more than once, so that there are at least two hundred quotations or allusions to Genesis in the New Testament.
>
> It is significant that the portion of Genesis which has been the object of the greatest attacks of skepticism and unbelief, the first eleven chapters, is the portion which had the greatest influence on the New Testament. Yet there exist over one hundred quotations or direct references to Genesis 1-11 in the New Testament. Furthermore, every one of these eleven chapters is alluded to somewhere in the New Testament, and every one of the New Testament authors refers somewhere in his writings to Genesis 1-11. On at least six different occasions, Jesus Christ Himself quoted from or referred to something

---

3. Augustine, *The Literal Meaning of Genesis*, Vol. 2 (Translated and Annotated by John H. Taylor in *Ancient Christian Writers* No. 42, Quasten et al. editors, Newman Press: New York, 1982), Book Eight, Chapters 1 to 3. St. Augustine does not understand the six days of creation in the same way they are presented in this book. For more details of his approach, see *Bibliographical & Technical Notes* for Chapter Six.

or someone in one of these chapters, including specific reference to each of the first seven chapters.

Furthermore, in not one of these many instances where the Old or New Testament refers to Genesis is there the slightest evidence that the writers regarded the events or personages as mere myths or allegories. To the contrary, they viewed Genesis as absolutely historical, true, and authoritative.[4]

Similarly, Walter T. Brown lists some seventy one New Testament references to the early chapters of Genesis and concludes:

a. Every New Testament writer refers to the early chapters of Genesis (Genesis 1-11).

b. Jesus Christ referred to each of the first seven chapters of Genesis.

c. All New Testament books except Galatians, Philippians, I and II Thessalonians, II Timothy, Titus, Philemon, and II and III John have references to Genesis 1-11.

d. Every chapter of Genesis 1-11 except chapter 8 is referred to somewhere in the New Testament.

e. Every New Testament writer apparently accepted these early chapters of Genesis as being historically accurate.[5]

In summary, the type of literature found in Genesis 1-11 is historical narrative, though of a unique variety. Not only is it necessary to bear this in mind in order to interpret these chapters faithfully, but it is also necessary to consider the outline or basic structure of the larger unit in which this material is found. Literary structure and larger context are always important to a clear understanding of shorter passages.

The outline of the book of Genesis falls into two parts. The first part is the creation itself (1:1 through 2:3), and the second part could be called 'the generations' or 'the family tree' (2:4-50:26). Since our concern is largely with the first two chapters of Genesis, their structure must be examined more closely in order to interpret the parts properly in light of the whole.

Genesis 1:1 gives a general and inclusive account of creation: '... God created the heavens and the earth.' The writer of Genesis could not have made a broader statement than that. 'Heavens and the earth' is a way of saying 'everything that exists', whether galaxies, nebulae

4. Henry M. Morris, *The Genesis Record* (Baker Book House: Grand Rapids, Mich., 1976), 21, 22.
5. Walter T. Brown, *'In The Beginning...'* (Center For Scientific Creation: Phoenix, AZ, 1989), 117.

or solar systems; all things from the farthest reaches of outer space to the smallest grain of sand or bacterial microbe on planet earth; absolutely everything was created by God. As Wolfgang Capito reminds us, the Nicene Creed summarizes the entire range of the creative activity in stating that, 'He is the creator of all things, visible and invisible.'[6] 'All things' include the various ranks of angels, and every form of life from whales and elephants to viruses. 'All things' include every form of energy and matter; the speed of light, nuclear structure, electromagnetism and gravity, and all the laws by which nature operates. 'All things' come from what God was doing in Genesis 1:1. Behind the creation of 'all things' stands the Living God, who has always existed as Father, but has not always been Creator (as Saint Athanasius, the great fourth century champion of the Nicene Faith frequently states[7]).

Then Genesis 1:2-31 gives a more detailed account of how God created 'all things' ('the heavens and the earth'). The verses immediately following, 2:1-3, summarize God's all inclusive creative activity. The very next verse, Genesis 2:4, is important for the structure of Genesis; it stands in the Hebrew text like a great signpost on a major highway, pointing the way forward into the rest of the book. Its words 'These are the generations' (in Hebrew *toledoth*) offer a clue that this is where the second part of Genesis begins, with a great narrowing down of emphasis from the whole creation to one selected area, namely, the story of mankind.

It is important not to miss the significance of these words indicating such a major shift in the direction the book is taking. It is important to realize that this phrase of Genesis 2:4, 'These are the generations', start the next section of the book (i.e., are 'a superscription' or 'title'), rather than finish the earlier section (i.e., as 'a subscription' or 'summary'). This shift is crucial to a lucid understanding of the first three chapters of Genesis, as we shall see.

---

6. Capito, *op. cit.*, 40: 'Quod quidam in symbolo quotidie, quisque pro se profitemur, Credo in Deum patrem omnipotentem creatorem coeli et terrae. Et Nycena synodus id explicans addit, Visibilium omnium atque invisibilium.'

7. e.g. See Athanasius, *Contra Arianos:* 'Therefore it is more pious and more accurate to signify God from the Son and call Him Father, than to name Him from His works only and call Him unoriginate. For the latter title, as I have said, does nothing more than signify all the works, individually and collectively, which have come to be at the will of God through the Word; but the title Father has its significance and its bearing only from the Son. And, whereas the Word surpasses things originated, by so much more doth calling God Father surpass the calling Him unoriginate' (I. 10. 34). Also, '...God's creating is second to His begetting; for Son implies something proper to Him and truly from that blessed and everlasting Essence; but what is from His will, comes into consistence from without, and is framed through His proper Offspring who is from It' (II. 14. 2).

Professor E. J. Young states:

> The phrase, 'These are the generations of the heavens and the earth', is a superscription and not a subscription. In other words, it does not bring to a close what has just gone before. It is rather an introduction to what follows .... The phrase 'These are the generations of the heavens and the earth' tells us that we are not going to read further about creation, but about something that came from heaven and earth, and in particular, man, whose body comes from the created earth....[8]

After providing grammatical reasons why Hebrew usage requires 'These are the generations' to be a superscription,[9] Young goes on to explain why reading Genesis 2:4 as a boundary marker that points forwards and not backwards makes so much difference to interpreting correctly these early chapters:

> It does not say that this is a second account of creation. Not at all! Instead, it tells us that it is going to talk about what has come from heaven and earth. Let us realize then that this phrase, 'These are the generations of the heavens and the earth', must be a superscription, that it must introduce what follows, and it is entirely incorrect to say that it is a subscription. It therefore follows that all attempts to show that there are contradictions of the first chapter in the second chapter fall by the board.[10]

Far from being a merely academic and technical question, there are important consequences if the interpreter confuses 'superscription' (or 'title') and 'subscription' (or 'summary'). Failing to realize that Genesis 2:4 points forwards instead of backwards is the reason that some Bible translations (such as the Moffatt Translation and The Anchor Bible) imply that the verses after Genesis 2:4 actually constitute a second account of creation, in which the order of events does not agree with those given in the first account.[11] In addition to reading the direction of 'the signpost' wrongly, other factors, such as different names of God and slightly different vocabulary between the first two chapters of Genesis were taken by nineteenth century 'higher critics' to indicate two (or possibly three or four) different and contradictory creation accounts from various primitive sources.[12]

Once we see which way the Genesis 2:4 signpost points us, we can clearly comprehend that there is only one account of creation (found

---

8. Young, *op. cit.*, 61, 63.

9. *Ibid.*, 62.

10. *Ibid.*, 64, 65.

11. The text of Matthew 19:4 would seem to indicate that Christ saw a unity in what some have claimed were two creation accounts.

12. See *Technical and Bibliographical Notes* at the end of this chapter for a response to 'the documentary hypothesis' which invented the problem of two contradictory accounts of creation.

in Genesis Chapter 1), not two accounts. Genesis 2 does not deal with the entirety of creation, nor is it concerned with the particular order of events as is Chapter 1. Instead of constituting a contradictory repetition of Chapter 1, the material in Genesis 2:4-3:24 accomplishes something else in order to open the gates for the grand story of redemption; the central theme of the whole Bible.

One can illustrate what it accomplishes by comparing these chapters to a newspaper or to a canvas painting. Genesis 1 can be compared to the headlines of the newspaper and the bold print immediately under them, giving the main outline of what happened. Genesis 2 is more like the detailed small print that follows, filling out selected parts of the story, of greatest interest to the readers. Or, if Genesis 1 and 2 were compared to a canvas painting, Genesis 1 gives a view of the whole canvas, while Genesis 2 shines a spotlight on one specific portion of the painting, focusing attention on one major subject: the human race.

Far from repeating (and internally contradicting) Genesis 1, Genesis 2:4-3:24 may be thought of as the bridge leading from the general creation of all things to the specific concern of the rest of the sixty-six books of the Bible: the redemption of mankind, chief image-bearer of the Creator of the entire cosmos. Hence it should not be surprising to find a somewhat different order of events in chapter 2 from those of chapter 1. The explanation is simple, once one understands the structure and purpose of these two earliest chapters. Chapter 1, the 'headlines' or 'whole picture' is meant to provide chronological sequence, whereas chapter 2 is there to develop one aspect of the picture or story. The concern of chapter 2 is not chronological order, but emphasis on a chosen theme, preparing the way for all the rest of divine revelation.

This brief look at type of literature and structure of Genesis should prepare us to understand more clearly the first verse of the Bible with its stupendous teaching of 'creation out of nothing' by a God who was always there. We turn to this theme in the next chapter.

TECHNICAL AND BIBLIOGRAPHICAL NOTES FOR CHAPTER TWO

1. Problematic Liberal and Evangelical Interpretations of Genesis 1-3

It is not always realized how rapidly much of the Christian Church accommodated its teaching on origins to nineteenth-century theories of evolution and the vast ages required for it to take place. Dr Nigel Cameron has devoted an illuminating chapter of *Evolution and the Authority of the Bible* to this intellectual change within the nineteenth-century church.[13] He demonstrates that the popular conception of massive resistance to evolutionary teaching among nineteenth-century Christian intellectual leadership is not the case. On the contrary, Cameron states:

> In other areas, evangelical Christians have taken their stand on the teaching of the Bible and refused to allow consensus opinions of the secular and liberal Christian world to determine their own. Yet here there has been a remarkable readiness to fall in line, irrespective of the teaching of Scripture.[14]

Cameron then shows that: 'As the new scientific thinking, first in geology and then in biology, began to take hold in the nineteenth century, biblical commentators hastened to accommodate their interpretation of Scripture to the latest orthodoxy in science.'[15] After studying a large number of nineteenth-century Christian commentaries on Genesis, Cameron concluded:

> Evidently every single commentator, with the exception of [Thomas] Scott, argues against the traditional idea of the flood. They believe it is necessary to harmonize the interpretation of Scripture with what the consensus of educated men believe...:[16]

Phillip Johnson rightly points out that it was not the clergymen who opposed Darwin, but rather fossil experts.[17] He writes:

> ...Darwinism so fitted the spirit of its age that the theory attracted a surprising amount of support from religious leaders. Many of Darwin's early supporters were either clergymen or devout laymen, including his most prominent American advocate, the Congregationalist Harvard Professor Asa Gray. Supporters of 'evolution' included not just persons we would think of as religious liberals, but conservative Evangelicals such as Princeton Theological Seminary Professor Benjamin Warfield.[18]

Leading nineteenth-century theological writers were generally agreed in rejecting the traditional straight-forward reading of Genesis 1-11 in terms of recent creation and universal Flood, but they differed in their interpretation of the biblical text. Cameron summarizes the differing approaches to the Genesis account fairly in contrasting how liberals and conservatives harmonized the ancient text with modern Darwinism:

---

13. Nigel M. De S. Cameron, *Evolution and the Authority of the Bible* (Exeter: The Paternoster Press, 1983), Chapter 6: 'Genesis and the Commentators: an historical perspective
14. *Ibid.*, 17, 18.
15. *Ibid.*, 72.
16. *Ibid.*, 80, 81.
17. Phillip Johnson, *Darwin on Trial*, 45.
18. *Ibid.*, 205.

...the liberals by rejecting the scriptural testimony to an universal flood; the conservatives by re-interpreting Scripture in a more congenial fashion. As Whitelaw openly admits, this is a deliberate matter of policy on their part. So while conservative writers, committed by their doctrine of Scripture to maintaining the truth of whatever Scripture says, impose a non-literal reading on the text, liberal writers, not obliged to agree with the Bible, readily admit that Scripture teaches something (a world-wide flood) which did not happen.[19]

In other words, conservative writers, in trying to make the Scripture acceptable to current scientific thought, have not only misinterpreted it in a way which abandons the actual meaning of the text, but have succeeded only in coming to a mediating position supported neither by Scripture nor by science .... Liberal writers like [S.R.] Driver, who felt no compulsion to defend the truth of the accounts, were franker and much more faithful in their exegesis.... The middle ground, which evangelicals then as now desired to occupy, is untenable.[20]

Examples of the more exegetically honest approach are found in Professor Marcus Dods of New College, Edinburgh in the nineteenth century and in Professor James Barr of Oxford University in the late twentieth. Dods wrote:

All attempts to force its [i.e. Genesis 1 and 2] statements into...accord are futile and mischievous... (and) to be condemned because they do violence to Scripture, foster a style of interpretation by which the text is forced to say whatever the interpreter desires, and prevent us from recognizing the real nature of these sacred writings.[21]

Cameron comments on Dods' honesty: 'The candid interpreter, says Dods, cannot avoid being literal; "if, for example, the word 'day' in these chapters does not mean a period of twenty-four hours, the interpretation of Scripture is hopeless" [Dods, 4].'[22]

More recently, Oxford Professor James Barr (author of *Fundamentalism*, a book rejecting traditional supernatural Christianity with its high view of Scripture) has written to much the same effect as Dods: "... so far as I know there is no professor of Hebrew or Old Testament at any world-class university who does not believe that the writer(s) of Genesis 1-11 intended to convey to their readers the ideas that: (a) creation took place in a series of six days which were the same as the days of 24 hours we now experience; (b) the figures contained in the Genesis genealogies provided by simple addition a chronology from the beginning of the world up to later stages in the Biblical story;

19. Cameron, *op.cit.*, 81.
20. *Ibid.*, 82, 83.
21. Marcus Dods, *Expositor's Bible* (T. & T. Clark: Edinburgh, 1888), 4.
22. Cameron, *op. cit.*, 76.

and (c) Noah's flood was understood to be world-wide and to have extinguished all human and land animal life except for those in the ark. Or to put it negatively, the apologetic arguments which suppose the 'days' of creation to be long eras of time, the figures of years not to be chronological, and the flood to be a merely local Mesopotamian flood, are not taken seriously by any professor, as far as I know.'[23]

To summarize, liberal scholars of both 19th and 20th centuries admit that the text of Genesis is clearly meant to be taken in a literal, historical sense, although they deny its claims to speak accurately to our space/time cosmos. A large percentage of conservative evangelical scholars refuse to interpret the Genesis text in its plain historical or literal sense in order to accommodate it to the premises of the reigning world view concerning origins. It is the contention of the present volume that neither approach does full justice to the truth claims of Scripture nor makes sense of the actual cosmos. This diverse interpretative agenda must be openly addressed in any serious attempt to do justice to the teaching of the Word of God on creation.

This chapter does not discuss specifically the liberal interpretative agenda, which holds that the Scriptural teaching taken in its literal sense is historically inaccurate, as for instance the proposal of Marcus Dods: 'If anyone is in search of accurate information regarding the age of this earth, or its relation to the sun, moon and stars, or regarding the order in which plants and animals appeared upon it, he is referred to recent text books.'[24] Instead, our entire volume constitutes a general response to the position that objective science necessarily rejects a serious interaction with Biblical teaching on origins. While differing with the liberals concerning the historical and scientific accuracy of Genesis, one must respect them for their more candid exegesis of the ancient text.

Of more direct concern to this chapter, however, is the pervasive influence of the interpretative principle held by so many evangelical scholars that one must take a fundamentally different hermeneutical approach to the first eleven chapters of Genesis from the rest of Scripture (in order to accommodate significant aspects of the naturalist world view). As noted above, many evangelical commentators abandoned the plain, chronological exegesis of Genesis 1-11, and argued that it was proper to do so from within the nature of the text itself, since

---

23. James Barr, A personal communication to David C. C. Watson, 23 April 1984, quoted in Creation Research Quarterly, 1984. See Professor Barr's much fuller discussion of evangelical ploys with the Genesis accounts in his *Fundamentalism* (The Westminster Press: Philadelphia, 1978), chapter 3, 'The Bible – First Stage', Section 1 – 'Being Literal', pp.40-55.
24. Dods, *op. cit.*, 1.

this section of Genesis was poetic, rather than chronological history. Cameron addresses their position in chapter 6 of *Evolution and the Authority of the Bible*, as does David N. Livingstone in *Darwin's Forgotten Defenders: The Encounter Between Evangelical Theology and Evolutionary Thought* (1987).

We saw earlier in this chapter that E. J. Young carefully evaluates this claim that Genesis 1-11 is poetic, and finds it totally lacking in scholarly merit in his *In the Beginning: Genesis 1-3 and the Authority of Scripture*, especially in chapters 1 and 2. His earlier exegetical studies of this subject should also be consulted: *Studies in Genesis One* (Presbyterian & Reformed Publ. Co.: Phillipsburg, N.J., 1964) and *Genesis 3* (Banner of Truth Trust: London, 1966).

2. 'The Documentary Hypothesis' and Conflicting Creation Accounts

For the last century and a half a large percentage of commentators and theologians have interpreted Genesis 1-3 (and the rest of the Scriptures) through the framework of the Documentary Hypothesis, one of the central theories of German Higher Criticism that became popular throughout the educated world. Rejecting the inspiration and truth claims of Scripture, these liberal scholars tried to explain the Bible in terms of evolutionary development from various, disparate primitive sources (or documents – whence 'documentary' hypothesis). Later editors supposedly worked over and collated these ancient documents or sources into what became the books of the Bible, leaving many internal inconsistencies and contradictions.

The first five books of the Bible or the Pentateuch, traditionally understood to have come from the hand of Moses, was – without compelling historical, linguistic or textual evidence – said to have been composed from at least four different sources, which were much later woven together, and by 'pious' pretence passed off as the work of earlier authors. The first three chapters of Genesis, for instance, were claimed to have been composed largely from three particular documentary sources. One came from the school of the Yahwist (because he or they employed the name 'Yahweh' or 'Jehovah' for God) and another from the Elohist school (which used the divine name 'Elohim'). And, we are told, elements from 'the Priestly' and 'Deuteronomic' Schools were also involved. According to this theory which arose from the nineteenth century humanist imagination, the Yahwist gave one account of creation (largely found in chapter two of Genesis), while the Elohist (in conjunction with the Priestly) gave another creation account (inconsistent with the other one), largely found in Chapter One.

Nearly fifty years ago the Princeton scholar, Oswald T. Allis, effectively answered such 'higher critical' claims (such as variant or contradictory sources and multiple authorship of Genesis) in a book that has not yet been refuted: *The Five Books of Moses* (Philadelphia: Presbyterian & Reformed Publ. Co., 1947). His careful historical and linguistic research shows the Documentary Hypothesis not to be based on any compelling evidence from within the biblical text nor within known history, but rather based on the evolutionary theory of Darwin transposed into historiography. Even from within the ranks of scholars who accept many of the evolutionary assumptions of 'Higher Criticism', there have been serious challenges to this Documentary Hypothesis, such as the 1987 work of R. N. Whybray, *The Making of the Pentateuch: A Methodological Study*. While not advocating Mosaic authorship, Whybray demolishes the documentary approach, and among other criticisms, particularly notes the refusal of Higher Critical advocates of JEDP to take into account the cultural differences between ancient Israel and modern Europe.[25]

Later works such as the standard conservative Old Testament Introduction of E. J. Young[26] as well as the *Commentary on Genesis* and *The Documentary Hypothesis* by the Jewish scholar, Umberto Cassuto of Jerusalem University confirm Allis' main argument for the unity of the Pentateuch, and his contention that the documentary hypothesis is a figment of the 'Enlightenment' European mind.[27] Part One of R. K. Harrison's *Introduction to the Old Testament* carefully critiques the documentary theory in light of international scholarship through the 1960s.[28] Kenneth A. Kitchen of Liverpool University dealt helpfully with some aspects of Mosaic authorship in light of significant modern historical and linguistic research in ancient Near Eastern data.[29]

Some of the most careful scholarship from both Christian and Jewish sources, therefore, confirms the traditional belief in the single authorship of Genesis, and shows that the related theory of two contradictory creation accounts has no grounds in reality, but is (1) an imposition upon an ancient text of inappropriate evolutionary ways

---

25. R. N. Whybray, *The Making of the Pentateuch: A Methodological Study* (JSOT Press, 1987).
26. Edward J. Young, *Introduction to the Old Testament*.
27. Umberto Cassuto, *The Documentary Hypothesis and Composition of the Pentateuch* (English Translation, Jerusalem, 1961).
28. R. K. Harrison, *Introduction to the Old Testament* (Wm. B. Eerdmans Publ. Co.: Grand Rapids, MI, 1969), 1-82.
29. Kenneth A. Kitchen, *Ancient Orient and Old Testament* (London: The Tyndale Press, 1966). He contrasts the 'idealistic theories of the Old Testament scholars' (such as the JEDP theory) with the 'relatively objectively based disciplines of the Orientalists', who deal with original, empirical material (such as hieratic ostraca and cunieform tablets), rather than philosophical pre-conceptions (pp.23, 24).

of thought, and (2) as we saw above, a misreading of a superscription as though it were a subscription.

The ground should now be clear to consider what the Genesis creation account teaches concerning the uniquely divine action, 'In the beginning God created...' This is the concern of Chapter Three.

QUESTIONS FOR STUDY

1. It is often argued that Genesis 1-3 is poetry and not history. Are there poetic accounts of creation found in the Bible? If so, where?

2. What are the implications of dealing with Genesis 1-3 as if they were poetry?

3. Give evidence that confirms that Genesis is an historic account rather than poetic. What is it that sets Genesis 1-3 apart from other historic writings?

4. What is the subject matter of each *major* part of the book of Genesis?

5. In what way is the New Testament dependent on Genesis 1-11?

6. What is the *basic* outline of Genesis?

7. Has God always been a Creator? Has he always been a Father?

8. What is the significance of Genesis 1:1? What does it encompass?

9. What is the significance of Genesis 2:4? Why is it important to read it as pointing forward?

10. As compared with Genesis 1, what is the primary concern of Genesis 2?

11. How does a correct understanding of Genesis 2:4 solve the problem of apparent internal conflict between the first two chapters?

Chapter Three

An Absolute Beginning

THE very first words of the Bible: 'In the beginning God created the heavens and the earth...' teach the absolute beginning of all things (space, time, energy, matter). The concept of the absolute creation of all things out of nothing by an eternally pre-existent intelligence is not an easy one for the human mind to grasp. Our finite experience has many analogies of relative creation (changing something that already exists), but no analogy of absolute creation (making something out of nothing). It is important, however, to gain some appreciation of this vital distinction between absolute and relative creation in order to come to terms with the actual teaching of Genesis 1:1.

To do so we must first look at the implications of the grammatical structure of 'In the beginning God created...', and then at the meaning of the Hebrew usage of the particular verb form 'God created'. The Authorized Version of the Bible ('King James Version') correctly renders the sense of this original Hebrew phrase as an independent statement, grammatically separate from verse two. This teaches, as plainly as could be done, that at a particular point in eternity, the immortal God brought everything into existence out of nothing. Thus the material space/time realm has an absolute beginning. It did not exist before God spoke it into existence. The implications of this are immense and we shall explore some of them presently.

However, some modern translations of Genesis render verse one as a temporal clause – 'When God began to create' – as though it were dependent for its meaning on verse three (And God said: 'Let there be light...'). But this rendition implies that 'When God began creating...' there was something already in existence for him to work on (hence 'relative' creation, rather than 'absolute' creation). The *Technical and Bibliographical Notes* for this chapter discusses this mistranslation in some detail. It shows that Hebrew usage requires an independent statement in Genesis 1:1, clearly implying the speaking into being of all things out of nothing by an infinitely powerful and timeless Deity.

According to the plain meaning of Genesis 1:1 in the original Hebrew, the infinite, personal God at a particular, chosen point in eternity, *created* all reality outside Himself out of nothing that existed previously. The specific Hebrew verb that is used by the writer of Genesis (*bara'* in the Qal stem), is a much more limited word than the one we employ in English for 'create'. While historical, grammatical details are listed in the *Technical and Bibliographical Notes*, we may summarize the position here.

'God *created*...' (*bara'* when used in the Qal stem of Hebrew) is employed in the Scriptures only with reference to the divine agency. This Hebrew verb form has a uniqueness about it; an absoluteness. It means that the infinite, personal Triune God of the Bible made something out of nothing (in Latin, *ex nihilo*), that is, without pre-existing material.[1]

As St. Augustine wrote in his *Confessions*: 'For you created them from nothing, not from your own substance or from some matter not created by yourself or already in existence, but from matter which you created at one and the same time as the things that you made from it, since there was no interval of time before you gave form to this formless matter.'[2] To convey this truth negatively, Wolfgang Capito states that to assume, contrary to the Scriptures, pre-existing matter, is to transfer the eternal attributes of God Himself to finite material.[3]

---

1. A ninth century Christian writer, Fredegisius, who was Abbot of Saint Martin of Tours (804-834), owing to Platonist influence, held in his *Epistola de nihilo et tenebris* that 'nothingness' was necessarily 'something'. He held this 'something' to be a type of undifferentiated matter out of which God shaped the world. The Church rejected this Platonic speculation as contrary to the meaning of Scripture (as in Bishop Agobrad of Lyon's *Liber contra objectiones Fredegisi abbatis*). See for Fredegisius, Migne, *Patrologia Latina* 105, 751-756, and for Agobard, *Ibid.*, 104, 159-171.
2. Saint Augustine, *Confessions, A New Translation* by R. S. Pine-Coffin (The Penguin Classics, 1961), XIII. 33.

In other words, God spoke worlds into existence 'by the Word of His power'. 'In the beginning' there was absolutely nothing except the one, true God, Father, Son and Holy Ghost, existing in an ineffable fullness of life, light, peace and joy; possessing within His triune self all that was needed for plenitude of love and meaning, and lacking nothing for significant relationship and purpose in being. John 1:1-18 expands this Trinitarian picture of God's eternal life, as does John 17 and Ephesians chapters 1-3.

Twelfth century Christian scholar, Richard of Saint Victor (in his classic *De Trinitate*) captures the gist of the New Testament amplification of Genesis 1:1 in his teaching that the infinite God the Father so loved God the equally infinite Son (related in bonds of love by the co-equal God the Spirit) that He brought into being *ex nihilo* a finite, material world to be peopled with creatures in the likeness of His Son in order that as the Son's bride, they could share in the beatitude of the divine life in a way appropriate to finite creatures in God's personal image. To provide a beautiful bride for his Son, the eternal Father created an entire universe, and in it a world which previously had no existence whatsoever as the nursery and home in which the bride would be reared. Such a stupendous gift from the Father to the Son required an absolute creation out of nothing.

As finite humans we are familiar enough with the concept of 'creation out of something' (that is, with pre-existing material). Developing something that is already there is, in the Biblical sense, 'secondary' creation or 'relative' creation. And the Bible has specific words which carry this meaning, such as a potter taking clay and forming it into a jar upon his wheel, or a carpenter using wood and tools to construct a chest, or perhaps a painter employing oils, brush and canvas to 'create' a portrait. At times a verb (different from bara') which implies relative creative activity is employed with reference to God, as in Genesis 2:7: 'And the LORD God formed man of the dust of the ground...' This 'creative' activity is 'relative' or 'secondary' creation. It improves material already at hand. That is the only kind of creative experience that humans can know.

What Genesis 1:1 teaches is infinitely different from our limited experience. 'In the beginning' there was nothing; God spoke, and then there was something – indeed, everything. Such springing into reality through the utterance of the divine Word is not an action with

---

3. 'Quod aliquid sit ante principium creatum, id omnium pugnat rationi. Quomodo enim creatura tum fuerit, ubi nondum fuit ullius creaturae initium. Et non creatum esse, id est esse sine initio, quodquidem in unum Deum competit. Solus enim Deus sempiternus est. Et sempiternum et sine initio esse sunt idem. Quis iam non videt impietatem ex tali novatione atque contorsione scripturarum elucentem?' In Capito, *op. cit.*, 31, 32.

which humans can readily identify, for only an infinite Power could accomplish it, as Capito wisely stated.[4] While man can never fully comprehend this infinitely divine action, there are a few passages in Scripture which cast light upon its supernatural nature.

Hebrews 11:3 comments on the creative action of Genesis 1:1: 'Through faith we understand that the worlds were framed by the Word of God so that things which are seen were not made of things which do appear.' This verse conveys the real meaning of creation *ex nihilo* (or 'without pre-existing material'). It is a way of saying that the visible reality we perceive: the room we are presently in, the larger building, the trees, the soil, our bodies, the stars do not originally come from other things that we can see (or even theorize), such as simpler life forms: protozoa, amoeba or sheer dust, as though they were a rearrangement of earlier types of matter. Instead, things that we see were made out of things that do not appear; that is to say, out of nothing.

In biblical terms, the Triune God spoke and a cosmos sprang into existence, whereas there was absolutely nothing of a created, finite nature before this divine speaking. Psalm 33:6 and 9 refer to this utterly unique event: 'By the word of the LORD were the heavens made: and all the host of them by the breath of his mouth .... For he spake, and it was done; he commanded, and it stood fast.'

A New Testament passage from the apostle Paul's writings also casts light upon this unique event of absolute creation. Romans 4:17 speaks of the patriarch Abraham's faith in an extremely difficult situation. The context of this verse is not the original creation, but a miraculous event which could be brought about only by someone as powerful as the divine Creator. When Abraham was around one hundred years old and Sarah, his wife, ninety, God reconfirmed his promise that He would renew their reproductive capacities so that they could have a son from their own bodies.

The second part of Romans 4:17 then gives a certain analogy to the original creative action of God: '... God, who quickeneth the dead, and calleth those things which be not as though they were.' In other words, there is nothing ('those things which be not'); God speaks, and there is something. In Genesis 1 and 2, out of nothing but a divine word, an entire universe springs forth. In Romans 4, out of one whose body was as good as 'dead' (for reproductive purposes), and out of 'the deadness' of his elderly wife's womb (v. 19), the creative command brings forth a son. There is a similarity between Genesis 1:1 and Romans 4:17, for in both cases, 'He calleth those things which

---

4. 'Et nulla res finita infiniti effectus causa est', Capito, *op. cit.*, 28.

be not as though they were'. Only a divine Creator can do this, and hence it is a unique action which stretches our minds beyond human experience.

Granted then that divine creation of 'those things which be not' bears a uniqueness outside human knowledge, one would not expect to find direct 'proof' of creation from within known scientific laws. That is not to say, however, that those laws which are operative within the natural realm could not bear an indirect testimony to absolute creation. Generally speaking, the First and Second Laws of Thermodynamics are considered to be among the most widely accepted, proven bases of physics. And they do seem to render an indirect witness to the necessity of divine creation.

While the reader is referred to the *Technical and Bibliographical Notes* for details, we may broadly summarize the direction in which these laws point here. The first Law of Thermodynamics is called 'the law of conservation of energy'. It states that energy can neither be created nor destroyed. Energy can change from one form into another, but its total amount remains the same.[5] 'Energy' includes all created reality, for in terms of Einstein's famous equation: $E = mc^2$ [Energy is equivalent to matter times the speed of light squared], matter is just another form of energy. Hence physical matter is included within the range of the laws of Thermodynamics.

This first law indicates that since energy (including matter) is not now being created nor destroyed, there must have been a point outside physical time when creative energies were in operation, which no longer obtain within our natural realm. Another way to phrase it is this: '... energy (matter) cannot be naturally created from nothing.'[6] Something, or rather, someone, outside the natural space/ time process is required to explain how a world in which material reality is not being created could have come into being.

The Second Law of Thermodynamics, or the law of entropy, further confirms the verdict of the First Law: that energy, matter cannot be accounted for within present physical processes. It provides an illustration of what one of Gödel's Theorems indicates, that a system cannot be both closed and consistent at the same time. To be consistent, it must be open to a higher level of reality.[7] The law of entropy states that in every interchange of energy in the cosmos, there is a tendency for a certain amount of that energy to pass into non-reversible heat energy, which is no longer available for productive

5. See R. L. Wysong, *The Creation-Evolution Controversy* (Inquiry Press: Midland, Mich., 1978), 239.
6. *Ibid.*, 241
7. See *Technical and Bibliographical Notes* of Chapter One, p.9.

work. The law of entropy also indicates that given enough time and enough interchanges of energy, so much non-reversible heat energy will be built up, that the universe will suffer a heat death.

Sir James Jeans shows how the law of entropy testifies to the necessity of a beginning:

> The more orthodox scientific view is that the entropy of the universe must forever increase to its final maximum value. It has not yet reached this: we should not be thinking about it if it had. It is still increasing rapidly, and so must have had a beginning; there must have been what we may describe as a 'creation' at a time not infinitely remote.[8]

That is to say, according to the law of entropy, all physical reality is 'running down'. Entropy is increasing, which leads to disorder and finally to a uniform distribution of all heat energy, the results of which would be death. But the creation (with its high order and productive life) had to have occurred under non-entropic conditions; under conditions that are no longer operative. As Gordon J. Van Wylen points out in his *Thermodynamics*:

> A final point to be made is that the second law of thermodynamics and the principle of increase in entropy have great philosophical implications. The question that arises is how did the universe get into the state of reduced entropy in the first place, since all natural processes known to us tend to increase entropy? ... The author has found that the second law tends to increase his conviction that there is a Creator who has the answer for the future destiny of man and the universe.[9]

In summary, the two laws of Thermodynamics indicate the necessity of some power outside present, known processes to have originally brought it all into existence. Something outside and above the vast complex of space, time, energy, material is required to have initiated it; something not relative to it, but free from it (which is the root meaning of the Latin word *absolute*: 'loosed' or 'free'– *solutus*, 'from'– *ab*). That is, the laws of Thermodynamics can tell us that an absolute creation is necessary.

The *irreducibly complex* structure of functional biological systems such as cells also cry out for an absolute beginning by an 'intelligent Designer'. Biochemical Professor Michael Behe has written an entire book to demonstrate this crucial point, which he believes is scientifically sufficient to make macroevolution impossible and to require something like absolute creation (which he terms 'intelligent design'). He states that 'At the tiniest levels of biology – the chemical life of the cell – we have discovered a complex world that

---

8. James Jeans, *The Mysterious Universe* (Macmillan Publishing Co.: New York, 1932), 181.
9. Gordon J. Van Wylen, *Thermodynamics* (New York: John Wiley & Sons, 1959), 169. Quoted in Walter T. Brown, Jr., *op.cit.*, 47.

radically changes the grounds on which Darwinian debates must be contested.'[10] 'In summary,' he adds, 'as biochemists have begun to examine apparently simple structures like cilia and flagella, they have discovered staggering complexity, with dozens or even hundreds of precisely tailored parts.... As the number of required parts increases, the difficulty of gradually putting the system together skyrockets, and the likelihood of indirect scenarios plummets. Darwin looks more and more forlorn. New research on the roles of the auxiliary proteins cannot simplify the irreducibly complex system. The intransigence of the problem cannot be alleviated; it will only get worse. Darwinian theory has given no explanation for the cilium or flagellum. The overwhelming complexity... push us to think it may never give an explanation.'[11]

The incredibly complex structures of living systems not only rule out gradual evolution by mutation and natural selection, they also require absolute creation; that is, being made 'full grown' or fully functional. Behe shows why: 'The conclusion of intelligent design for physically interacting systems rests on the observation of highly specified, irreducible complexity – the ordering of separate, well-fitted components to achieve a function that is beyond any of the components themselves.'[12] Hence, it is clear that '...if something was not put together gradually, then it must have been put together quickly or even suddenly.'[13]

Behe raises this question, which only sudden creation, rather than gradual evolution, can answer: 'When is it reasonable to conclude, in the absence of firsthand knowledge or eyewitness accounts, that something has been designed? For discrete physical systems – if there is not a gradual route to their production – design is evident when a number of separate, interacting components are ordered in such a way as to accomplish a function beyond the individual components. The greater the specificity of the interacting components required to produce the function, the greater is our confidence in the conclusion of design.'[14]

Important as the combined witness of the laws of thermodynamics and the irreducible complexity of living systems is to absolute creation, still they cannot tell us what or who it was, nor how he did it. Behe's observation is, to say the least, an understatement: 'Although the fact

---

10. Behe, *op. cit.*, 31.
11. *Ibid.*, 73.
12. *Ibid.*, 223.
13. *Ibid.*, 187.
14. *Ibid.*, 194.

of design is easily seen in the biochemistry of the cell, identifying the designer by scientific methods might be extremely difficult.'[15]

For that information we must look to the ancient Hebrew verb bara' (in its Qal stem). It conveys the concept of absolute creation when it tells us who initiated all things and how he did it in the words of Genesis 1:1: 'In the beginning, God created...' We are now prepared to consider the first motions of this absolute creative activity. They occurred on Day One of creation (Genesis 1:1-5). Chapter Four is devoted to this primal theme.

TECHNICAL AND BIBLIOGRAPHICAL NOTES FOR CHAPTER THREE

1. Grammatical Structure of Genesis 1:1

We have discussed the importance of the grammatical structure of Genesis 1:1 in relationship to verses 2 and 3 for properly translating the phrase 'In the beginning God created...' as an independent phrase. Some translations have interpreted this verse as a dependent clause (in some cases actually emending the word *bara'* to the infinitive construct form *b'roh*) leading to the rendering of it as 'When God began to create...' As we have seen above, this rendition implies that 'In the beginning of the creating', there was already material upon which He could work (presented in verses 2 and 3, according to this view).

But there is no textual evidence for any such emendation in the Hebrew text, nor does normal grammatical usage support the translation of verse 1 as a dependent (temporal) clause or 'construct'. According to ordinary Hebrew grammar, this phrase of verse 1 has to be rendered as an independent (or 'absolute') phrase, since the finite verb (bara') is not preceded by the construct form, nor does the context demand a construct meaning. Grammatically and contextually, the best translation is the traditional 'absolute' or 'independent' one: 'In the beginning, God created.'

Professor E. J. Young suggests that a major reason for this newer translation as dependent (or temporal) of a clause that is grammatically and contextually clearly independent is the influence of the Babylonian creation story:

> ... it [the Babylonian creation story – i.e. Enuma Elish] begins with two long temporal dependent sentences and concludes on the ninth line with an independent statement. Hence, say the modern, as the

---

15. *Ibid.*, 251.

Babylonian creation account begins in that way, Genesis chapter one, being a similar cosmogony from the ancient world, must begin in the same way .... The Hebrew does not begin that way, but it begins: 'In the beginning God created the heavens and the earth.'[16]

Much helpful information on the grammatical and theological ramifications of this question can be found in other writings of E. J. Young: 'The Relation of the First Verse of Genesis One to Verses Two and Three,' in *Westminster Theological Journal*, XXI (May 1959), 138-139, and also his *Studies in Genesis* 1 (Presbyterian & Reformed Publ. Co.: Phillipsburg, N. J., 1964).

2. Significance of the Hebrew Verb *Bara'*

We have noted that the Hebrew verb *bara'* in the Qal stem is used only of God in the Scriptures, and implies absolute creation (without pre-existing material). This concept is utterly different from other ancient pagan creation stories, such as the Babylonian *Enuma Elish* or the Greek poem on origins by Hesiod, *Theogony*. Both of these ancient cosmogonies picture a god working on some sort of already existing primeval 'stuff'. They are variations of 'relative' creation; not absolute. As A. Heidel writes in his *Babylonian Genesis*: 'The opening chapters of Genesis as well as the Old Testament in general refer to only one Creator and Maintainer of all things, one God who created and transcends all cosmic matter. In the entire Old Testament, there is not a trace of theogony, such as we find, for example, in *Enuma Elish* and in Hesiod.'[17]

While *bara'* in the Qal stem indicates absolute creation, there are other verbs in the Old Testament for creating, but these imply 'relative' creation. Three major Hebrew verbs for relative creation must be noted: *bara'* (when in stems other than Qal), *asa'* and *ya'ad*.

Bara' seems to come from the root 'to cut off' or 'separate'. In Joshua 17:15, 18 it is used for cutting down trees. Perhaps from the concept of cutting and splitting came the sense of forming. The Septuagint translation of the Hebrew Old Testament into Greek renders this as *ktizein*. Thus, *bara'* (when not in the Qal stem) is used in contexts of secondary (or relative) creation. Several passages employ it to indicate the shaping of something that already exists: Genesis 1:21, 25; 5:1; Isaiah 45:7, 12; 54:16; Amos 4:13; 1 Corinthians 11:9; Revelation 10:6. This form of the verb is also used to describe something that comes about under the providential control of God: Psalm 104:30; Isaiah 45:7, 8; 65:18; 1 Timothy 4:4.

---

16. E. J. Young, *op. cit.*, 23, 24.
17. A. Heidel, *The Babylonian Genesis* (Chicago: University of Chicago Press, 1942), 97.

The verb *asa'* is translated in the Septuagint by *poiein*, and means to form something that is already there (with three biblical exceptions in which, according to the context and sense of the passage, it bears the meaning of absolute or primary creation: Genesis 2:4; Proverbs 16:4 and Acts 17:24). Elsewhere, this term is used to indicate secondary creation: Genesis 1:7, 16, 26; 2:22; Psalm 89:47. In Psalm 74:17, *asa'* refers to providential bringing forth.

The third verb, *ya'ad* is rendered *plassein* in the Septuagint, and with one exception (which refers to absolute creation in Psalm 90:2) also implies relative creation (Gen. 2:7,19; Ps. 104:26; Amos 4:13; Zech. 12:1). The idea of providential bringing forth is found occasionally, when this verb is employed in Deuteronomy 32:18; Isaiah 43:1, 7, 21; 45:7.

All three of these verbs (implying relative creation) are used in Isaiah 45:7: 'I form the light, and create darkness; I make peace, and create evil; I am Jehovah, that doeth all things.' The generating of light and darkness are aspects of relative creation, while the making of peace and evil are aspects of divine providence. They are all in a different grammatical and theological category from the absolute creative activity indicated by *bara'* in the Qal stem.

3. The Witness of the Laws of Thermodynamics and of the Irreducible Complexity of Living Systems to Absolute Creation

By means of the grammatical structure of Genesis 1:1, and through the careful usage of particular Hebrew verb forms, we have seen that the Bible clearly teaches the concept of absolute creation. But there is also, at least indirectly, a witness borne to this concept of creation out of nothing by the first and second Laws of Thermodynamics as well as by the irreducible complexity of living systems. We have briefly alluded to their significance for primary creation. Here it may be helpful to provide a few major references to this question, and to address recent attempts to avoid the implications of Thermodynamics by evolutionary theorists (which is, of course, directly connected to the difficulty of explaining the irreducible complexity of natural systems or structures).

The standard text of Van Wylen, *Thermodynamics*, has already been mentioned. There are three important chapters on thermodynamics and creation in Thaxton, Bradley and Olsen: 'Thermodynamics of Living Systems' (6); 'Thermodynamics and the Origin of Life' (7), and 'Specifying How Work is to be Done' (9).[18] R. L. Wysong's *The Creation – Evolution Controversy* includes a very useful chapter for

---

18. Charles B. Thaxton, Walter L. Bradley and Roger L. Olsen, *The Mystery of Life's Origin: Reassessing Current Theories* (Philosophical Library: New York, 1984).1988).

laymen on thermodynamics (16). Readers of French should refer to the two brief, but excellent papers by Professor Frederick Skiff of the University of Maryland in *Positions Créationnistes* in 1987 and 1988 on 'L'hypothèse évolutioniste face aux lois de la thermodynamique: notes sur l'application des arguments tirés de la thermodynamique à la question opposant la création à la generation spontanée'.[19]

Any discussion of thermodynamics and creation would be incomplete without reference to contemporary evolutionist attempts to evade the force of thermodynamic law (especially the law of entropy) against the concept of macroevolution. A representative illustration of this attempt is found in the work of J. S. Wicken, *Evolution, Thermodynamics and Information*.[20]

The major problem for evolutionary theory is that thermodynamic law specifies continuous increase in entropy, which entails greater randomness, disorganization and decay in the whole energy matter spectrum. But evolution posits precisely the opposite: greater organization, gain of information and development of structures. This cannot be true on a cosmic scale if the laws of thermodynamics are correct (which evolutionary scholars do not deny). Their greatest difficulty in holding to cosmic improvement has been described by Sir Arthur Eddington as 'time's arrow' (i.e. the law of entropy). That is, the arrow of time (universal decay) flies in the wrong direction for evolution to have taken place.

T. H. Blum has dealt with this massive problem in *Time's Arrow and Evolution* (Princeton: Princeton University, 1968). He offers a solution in terms of 'open system' thermodynamics (that is, a closed system will run down rather than develop or 'evolve' unless open to an outside source of energy and/or information). 'Closed systems' are succinctly discussed in Thaxton, Bradley and Olsen,[21] and 'open systems' are also surveyed in the same volume.[22]

In spite of valiant efforts to turn aside 'time's arrow' by means of open systems, in the first place, the finite universe by definition is not 'open' in the sense that infinite amounts of energy or matter may be constantly available for productive development of structures in an energy/matter realm that has decay written into every interchange of energy that occurs within it.[23] Secondly, even though our planet

---

19. Frederick Skiff in *Positions Créationnistes* (Association Création, Bible et Science: Case Postale 4, CH 1001 Lausanne, Switzerland), No. 3 (November 1987), and No. 5 (November 1988).
20. J. S. Wicken, *Evolution, Thermodynamics and Information* (New York: Oxford University Press. 1987).
21. Thaxton *et al.*, *op.cit.*, 117-122.
22. *Ibid.*, 123-126.

is temporarily an 'open' system insofar as the sun pours light into it (sometimes called 'the sun-earth system'), infusion of heat energy alone is not sufficient to reverse the arrow of entropy without the presence of something else of utmost importance.

That utterly essential element which must be present in addition to energy for life itself (including any development of it) to occur is information or design. As Bradley and Thaxton have written: '...the origin of life problem is fundamentally a problem of information.'[24] They go on to ask: 'If energy flow through the system cannot "create" the requisite information implicit in the remarkable specificity required for biopolymers, and if inherent self-ordering tendencies in matter are too weak to account for the observed molecular complexity, what is left?...'[25]

Dr Carl Fliermans has noted that even information itself is insufficient to explain a successfully functioning system.[26] Something more is required, and that is a way of recognizing information and retrieving it for the purposes of the system. 'Information recognition' must be in place from the beginning for the system to function. This is inconsistent with the evolutionary scenario, which ignores both information and information retrieval.

Two illustrations of how energy minus information (or design) will not explain how order, life and development can occur within even an open system should be sufficient to refute the evolutionist's dodge of time's entropic arrow. Blum's example of the sunlight causing healthy growth (or even evolutionary development) of plants does not take into account the necessity of design; that is, 'information' built into the cellular structure of the plant, which allows the process of photosynthesis to convert heat energy into the building of cells. Without this inbuilt design of photosynthesis, the heat of the sun would be destructive.

The presumed 'evolution' of chemical elements in the primeval oceanic 'biotic soup' into single, and then multiple celled organisms, propelled by the sun's powerful rays, also sidesteps the crucial factor of information. Without some inbuilt informational mechanism to translate heat energy into a system-building function, the effect of heat on chemicals in the supposed primeval sea would have been to destroy them.

---

23. However, as we argued in Chapter One, it is open in senses other than physical thermodynamics; in particular to the transcendent control of its Creator. But here we are using 'open' and 'closed' in the technical sense of thermodynamic law.
24. See their chapter, 'Information & the Origin of Life' in J. P. Moreland, *op. cit.*, 190.
25. *Ibid.*, 192.
26. Dr Carl B. Fliermans in a personal communication to the author, 18 December 1996.

Some purposeful design (or 'information' on how 'successfully to proceed') must have been imparted to matter, or direct heat would have caused it to deteriorate, rather than develop. Even the famous evolutionary cosmologist, Carl Sagan admits: 'It is not known whether open-system thermodynamic processes in the absence of replication are capable of leading to the sorts of complexity that characterize biological systems.'[27]

Wysong summarizes the evidence of thermodynamic law against the unsuccessful evolutionist evasion of 'time's arrow' of calling in 'open system' thermodynamics:

> Why is it that life – one billionth part of the weight of the earth – appears to complexify while the rest of the physical world runs down? .... One of the reasons for the seeming biological anachronism is that life increases order not only because of outside energy input (an open system), but also because of design, a preexisting metabolic motor, complexity, DNA ....
>
> Neither open system thermodynamics nor the organization in life independently account for systematic biological ordering. They are both necessary. The uniqueness of life, however, is not due to open system thermodynamics, but rather to life's inherent structural mechanism that allows the channelling of energy into useful processes. Life simply 'postpones' the second law with respect to biological processes much the same way as the law of gravity is 'postponed' by a rocket ship.[28]

As Thaxton, Bradley and Olsen have shown, 'A source of energy alone is not sufficient, however, to explain the origin or maintenance of living systems. The additional crucial factor is a means of converting this energy into the necessary useful work to build and maintain complex living systems from the simple biomonomers that constitute their molecular building blocks.'[29]

Part of the failure of some scientists to recognize this necessity is rooted, as Dr Frederick Skiff notes, in a confusion over the meaning of 'information'. He states: 'Actually there is plenty of confusion over the term "information" because as it is used technically it has to do with describing complexity. The word in its technical sense does not have anything to do with meaning. Thus, people like Wicken can imply that "information" can arise spontaneously. This is because he and others have failed to make a further important distinction (beyond the categories of order, disorder and complexity) which has to do with linguistic complexity. Linguistic complexity is a distinguishing

27. Carl Sagan, 'The Definition of Life', in *Encyclopedia Britannica*, 13, (1973), 1083A; quoted in Wysong, *op.cit.*, 244.
28. Wysong, *op.cit.*, 244, 245.
29. Thaxton *et al.*, *op.cit.*, 124.

feature of biology, being most prominent in DNA .... In technical terms, there is a very important distinction between "information" and "design".'[30]

Whether it be photosynthesis in plants, or DNA in cell replication, some kind of intelligent design has to have been built into the physical elements and their fields to enable them to make productive use of whatever sort of energy may be available (rather than being destroyed by such energy which otherwise operates in terms of inexorable entropic law).

Or to state it another way, merely adding together various natural elements in the presence of energy sources can never produce the *irreducibly complex* structures which make up our world. Chapter 9 ('Intelligent Design') of Behe's *Darwin's Black Box* shows that no matter how many combinations one assumes of two or more separate cells or systems (as in evolutionary symbiotic theory), 'Because symbiosis starts with complex, already functioning systems, it cannot account for the fundamental biochemical systems...'[31] The same is true of 'other examples of irreducibly complex systems' such as 'aspects of DNA replication, electron transport, telomere synthesis, photosynthesis, transcription regulation and more.'[32] Gradualism cannot begin to explain such stupendous complexity and elegance; inbuilt information (or purposive design) is required.

The general failure of evolutionary science to recognize the implications of information (or design) as essential to functioning systems has long since 'trickled down' to the popular culture of the Western world. For instance, the best-selling American novelist, Michael Crichton, who popularizes certain aspects of 'chaos theory' as well as traditional evolution, tries to avoid facing the implications of external design (or information), which he realizes is essential to natural systems. He does so simply by asserting that 'self-ordering' is, by definition, the nature of complex systems. Logically, this is like denying God's existence, but then transferring the attributes of God to nature. Rather than facing the question of how and why natural systems work in orderly fashion, he simply states that they do so, since that is how they are.[33] This is not far from what the famous French evolutionary theologian, Teilhard de Chardin did earlier this century. As Marcel de Corte has pointed out, 'Teilhard breathes into

30. Frederick Skiff in a personal communication to the author on 20 October 1996.
31. Behe, *op.cit.*, 189.
32. *Ibid.*, 160.
33. In *The Lost World* (Alfred A. Knopf: New York, 1995), a novel which follows up his *Jurassic Park* (seen by millions in its film adaptation), Crichton states: 'The ability to adapt is characteristic of complex systems – and may be one reason why evolution seems to lead toward more complex organisms' (p. 4), and 'Self-organization elaborates in complexity as the system advances toward the chaotic edge' (p. 65).

his concepts a sort of personality, he transforms them into active principles, he gives them personhood.'[34] Making this sort of 'faith' (nonscientific) jump is undoubtedly one way to avoid the major question.

Although it is an unwelcome question in many quarters, enquiring minds still raise it: who wrote the program by which these systems operate? This design or information so essential to the functioning of natural systems did not come from the heat of the sun, nor from the chemicals upon which it operates its otherwise destructive forces. Where did it come from? Who programmed design into living systems whether 'open' or 'closed'? This is the question that has been universally avoided by evolutionary theory as it seeks shelter from 'time's arrow', as well as from the implications of the irreducibly complex structures of physical reality.

The clue to this unwelcome question is given in an article by Charles H. Bennett in *Scientific American*, 'Demons, Engines and the Second Law'.[35] Walter T. Brown comments on Bennett's conclusions as follows:

> Based on modern advances in the field of information theory, the only way known for the entropy of an isolated system to decrease is through the use of intelligence .... Since the universe is far from its maximum entropy level, a vast intelligence is the only known means by which the universe could have been brought into being.[36]

Or, as Michael Behe states it: 'The result of these cumulative efforts to investigate the cell – to investigate life at the molecular level – is a loud, clear, piercing cry of "*design*!" The result is so unambiguous and so significant that it must be ranked as one of the greatest achievements in the history of science.'[37]

We must turn to the teaching of Genesis 1:1-5 to learn Who that 'vast intelligence' is, and how He proceeded to impart both information and continuing energy to the matter He brought into being out of nothing on the first day of creation. These matters are discussed in Chapter Four.

---

34. '... il leur insuffle de la sorte une personnalite, il les transforme en principes actifs, il les hypostasie.' See Marcel de Corte, *L'intelligence en péril de mort* (Club de la culture française: Paris, 1969), 171-185. The same sort of unjustified 'leap in logic' (transferring personality traits to impersonal matter) is crucial to the theory of abiogenesis (see *Technical and Bibliographical Notes* for Chapter 9).
35. Charles H. Bennett, 'Demons, Engines and the Second Law,' in *Scientific American*, November 1987, 108-116.
36. Brown, *op. cit.*, 29.
37. Behe, *op. cit.*, 232, 233.

QUESTIONS FOR STUDY

1. What is the difference between 'absolute' and 'relative' creation?

2. Why is it important that Genesis 1:1 is a statement independent of verse 2?

3. In what ways is the word 'created' (*bara*) unique?

4. What does Capito say is wrong with believing God used pre-existing matter?

5. Give some New Testament illustrations of absolute creation.

6. What are the First and Second Laws of Thermodynamics, and how do they imply a divine Creator?

7. What does Michael Behe mean by 'irreducibly complex structures' and how do they imply divine creation?

Chapter Four

Day One of Creation: Creation 'Out of Nothing' and the Beginning of the Formative Process

THE first day of creation is not only the beginning of space and matter, it is also the beginning of time. From all eternity only the living God had existed; Father, Son and Holy Spirit, an everflowing fountain of life, light and love (to use terms from both Genesis and Revelation). This infinite and personal triune God needed nothing outside of Himself (including the creation). Since He possessed a total sufficiency of inter-relational blessedness, satisfaction and fulfillment within His own life, He lacked nothing.

God's lack of anything outside Himself to be who He always was surpasses the power of our limited minds to comprehend, since everything that we experience around us had to have a beginning, and thus needs something outside itself to be brought into existence. But the triune God is beyond the need of origins. His very name in Exodus 3:14 indicates this: 'I am that I am'. He needs nothing outside Himself to explain Himself. All things depend on Him, and not vice versa.

As Novatian of Rome, third-century Christian writer, said: 'God is beyond origin,'[1] and Gregory Nazianzen, famous Cappadocian bishop, wrote in the fourth century: 'In the beginning He was; uncaused; for what is the Cause of God?'[2] The thirteenth-century theologian, John Duns Scotus, worked out much of his proof of the necessary existence of God in light of this insight from Genesis 1:1 and Exodus 3:14 in 'Proof C' of *De Primo Principio*. There he states in his 'fourth conclusion' that a being that is 'simply first' and able to exert efficient causality actually exists, for only an actually existent nature is capable of exercising this degree of causality. As proof, Scotus points out that 'Anything to whose nature it is repugnant to receive existence from anything else, exists of itself if it is able to exist at all. To receive existence from something else is repugnant to the very notion of a being which is first in the order of efficiency.'[3]

In our own century, Karl Barth has summarized the position well: 'Because He is God, as such He already has and is His own being. Therefore this being does not need any origination and constitution. He cannot "need' His own being because He affirms it in being who He is... what needs origination and constitution in order to be, what can need existence, is not God Himself, or His reality, but the reality which is distinct from Himself.'[4]

Yet out of the rich and serene blessedness of His life, at a certain point in eternity He spoke a world into existence, and so created space, matter and time. His Word tells us that in six days God prepared this space, matter, time realm to be a fit habitation for a race He would create during the last (sixth) day in His own image and to share in His own inner-Trinitarian fellowship. The cumulative work of these six days demonstrates how God employed both of his creatures (matter and time) to prepare the stage for the crown of his creative activity: humankind.

Remembering that time, as well as space and matter is a creature and servant of the God who made it, will provide the proper perspective for interpreting the work of Day One through Day Six. Thus, time is not absolute (nor is space and matter). From our human perception time is the experience of continuity as measured by the motion of the various celestial bodies (earth, sun, moon and stars: days, months and

---

1. Novatian, *De Trinitate*, XXXI. 190 ('extra originem est').
2. Gregory Nazianzen, *The Fourth Theological Oration*, xix.
3. John Duns Scotus, *A Treatise on God As First Principle: A Latin text of the De Primo Principio*, translated into English with a commentary (Wolter, Allan B., Translator, 2nd Ed.), Chicago: Franciscan Herald Press, 1982, 52.
4. Karl Barth, *Church Dogmatics*, Volume II, *The Doctrine of God*, First Half-Volume (Edinburgh: T. & T. Clark, 1964), 306.

years). Before the material realm was brought into being there was no time; only God's eternity had existence. As Saint Augustine explains:

> With the motion of creatures, time began to run its course. It is idle to look for time before creation, as if time can be found before time. If there were no motion of either a spiritual or corporal creature, by which the future moving through the present would succeed the past, there would be no time at all. A creature could not move if it did not exist. We should, therefore, say that time began with creation rather than that creation began with time. But both are from God. For from Him and through Him and in Him are all things.[5]

The book of Revelation teaches us that eventually 'time will be no more' (Rev. 10:6). Yet the joyful life and relationships of God and his redeemed creation will exist in an equally real, but different sort of way.[6]

Time had a beginning and will have an end. It is a servant, not a master. With this in mind, it should not be thought preposterous that God, as it were, 'harnesses' time (as well as matter and space) to provide an orderly pattern of historical existence for the crown of His handiwork, mankind, His own image-bearer. As the second century Church writer, Justin Martyr, reminds us, 'God, the Creator of all things is superior to the things that are to be changed.'[7] Or again, with St. Augustine, 'For God made the creatures that were to be in the future in such a way that without Himself being subject to time He made them subject to time.'[8]

Only from this viewpoint can we make sense of the fact that an infinitely powerful God chose to organize all that He had created out of nothing into a habitable universe in the space of six days rather than in a nanosecond of time or a hundred billion years. In other words, to understand Genesis 1-3 (and to make sense of life itself), we must

---

5. Augustine, *The Literal Meaning of Genesis*, Vol. I: *Ancient Christian Writers*, No. 41, Quasten et al. editors, John H. Taylor, translator (Newman Press: New York, 1982), Book 5, chapter 5 (153, 154).
6. What it will mean to live outside the time we know here on earth in the different arrangement of the eternal realm, where apparently past and future are equally available or 'spread out' in the present is to say the least a mystery in our pilgrim state. Continuity and orderly relationship will be as real as now in our limited time series, but somehow the fallenness and decay of post-Adamic time will be 'healed'. T. F. Torrance's *Space, Time and Resurrection*, (The Handsel Press: Edinburgh, 1976) shows that this 'healing' and surpassing of our decaying time started in Christ's bodily resurrection and will be completed on the Last Day of human history. And, difficult as it is to grasp, eternity seems to be not just a healing of time, but a surpassing of it. John's Gospel speaks of the communication of Christ's resurrection to believers (both here and hereafter) as 'eternal life', loosing them from the ravages of decaying time, and bringing them into another realm, the fullness of which can only be experienced after death and final resurrection. (See, for instance, John, chapters 3, 5, 11, 14).
7. Justin Martyr, *First Apology*, ch. xx.
8. Augustine, *op. cit.*, Book 4, chapter 35 (145).

seek, with the help of divine revelation, to interpret time through God, rather than God through time. That is, God 'delimits' time; time does not delimit either the being or the actions of God. He uses time, as He uses matter and space, without in any sense being inconvenienced or hampered by it in accomplishing His chosen purposes.

The proper question to ask, therefore, is not 'why did an infinite power and intelligence take six days rather than a split second to create all things out of nothing?', nor yet 'would it not have been easier and thus more likely for Him to have used a process requiring billions of years to form all that is?' Instead, in order to grasp the true situation, one must let Him relate how He did it, as regards space, matter and time. Taking this approach, we shall be in the good company of St. Augustine and St. Anselm, who sought to follow Isaiah's wise counsel: 'If ye will not believe, surely ye shall not be established' (Isa. 7:9). In the matter of time and days of creative work, the perspective of faith is not to speculate on how God could have done it, but to stand on what He tells us concerning His procedure both temporally and materially.

From this vantage point we consider the foundational activities of the Creator on Day One:

> In the beginning God created the heavens and the earth. And the earth was without form and void; and darkness was upon the face of the deep. And the Spirit of God moved upon the face of the waters. And God said, Let there be light: and there was light. And God saw the light, that it was good: and God divided the light from the darkness. And God called the light Day, and the darkness he called Night. And the evening and the morning were the first day (Gen. 1:1-5).

The first day of creation saw three unique, miraculous actions of God. They are: the absolute creation of all things (space, matter and time) out of nothing; the beginning of a shaping process to prepare the world to be inhabited by plants, animals and men, and the commanding forth of light (as part of that process to make the earth habitable).

Absolute Creation on Day One

In the last chapter, we looked at the first unique divine action of Day One: the absolute creation of all things out of nothing. We need to note here that this first verse of Genesis 1 is a complete grammatical thought structure on its own, serving as ' ... a broad, general, declaration of the fact of the creation of the heaven and the earth. [Its] terms ... include all things.'[9] According to Hebraist John Currid:

---

9. E. J. Young, *Studies in Genesis One* (Presbyterian and Reformed Publishing Co.: Philadelphia, Penn., 1964), 9.

The Hebrews had no single word to describe the universe. When they wanted to express the concept of all reality they spoke in terms of 'the heavens and the earth' (*hassamayim we'et ha'ares*). So, when Melchizedek blessed Abram in the name of the Sovereign God of the universe, he said, 'Blessed be Abram of El Elyon, possessor of heaven and earth' (Gen. 14:19). The expression 'the heavens and the earth' is a figure of speech called a merism, in which two opposites are all-inclusive. Thus, when Melchizedek commented that God owned heaven and earth, he meant not only the places of heaven and earth, but also everything in them and on them. As well, when the Genesis writer stated that God created the heavens and the earth, he meant that God fashioned the entire universe.[10]

So Genesis 1:1 stands by itself and gives us the broadest possible picture of God creating the whole cosmos. Then verses 2-31 'likewise constitute a narrative complete in itself.'[11] The fact that these verses stand by themselves grammatically (and hence are not dependent on v. 1) is important to a clear understanding of absolute creation of all things out of nothing. The independence and unity of these verses is integral to a correct interpretation of the work of the six days, because it demonstrates that when God created all things (in v. 1), he had no pre-existing material to work with.

But if on the contrary, we take these verses to be a grammatical appendage to the verb *bara'* of verse one, then 'the meaning would be that when God began the activity expressed by *bara'* the three-fold condition described in verse two was already present.... The work expressed by *bara'*, whatever else it might be, could not be that of absolute creation.'[12] Normal usage of Hebrew grammar[13] as well as the immediate context of Genesis 1[14] both indicate the independence of verses 2-31 from the verb 'created' in verse l, and instead demonstrate

---

10. John D. Currid, 'An Examination of the Egyptian Background of the Genesis Cosmogony', p.31.
11. *Ibid.*, 11.
12. *Ibid.*, 8.
13. In Hebrew, to have a narrative clause that stands by itself as a complete grammatical structure, there must be not only circumstantial clauses, describing particular conditions, but also a finite verb, which tells us just when these conditions were in operation. Now Genesis 1:2 consists of three circumstantial clauses, describing the condition of the primeval earth when God's shaping process began. Verse 2 lacks its own finite verb. Hence, these circumstantial clauses must be connected to a nearby finite verb in order to obtain their full meaning.
14. The context indicates that they should not be connected to the immediately preceding finite verb of verse one (*bara'*), but to the finite verb in verse three, immediately afterwards: 'And God said.' Since verses 2-31 constitute a complete narrative, it is more likely that the controlling finite verb for verse 2 comes from its own context (in this case, verse 3), than from a verb in a preceding, grammatically distinct narrative. (See *Bibliographical & Technical Notes* at the end of this chapter for more details on this point.) Therefore, verse 2 is dependent on verse 3, and its meaning may be paraphrased in the words of E. J. Young as: 'At the time when God said, "Let there be light", a threefold condition was in existence' (which is described by the three circumstantial clauses of verse 2). [Young, *op. cit.*, 9.]

the dependence of the circumstances described in verse 2 on the verb 'and God said' in verse 3.

To summarize the interpretative point at issue, the three-fold condition of the primeval world of 'without form and void', 'darkness on the deep', and 'the Spirit of God moving' occurred only *after* the absolute creation of all things from nothing. They describe the situation when God began shaping what he had made by speaking light into it. They do *not* refer to the situation when God originally created, for nothing at all was in existence that could be 'formless', 'void', 'dark' or 'moved upon'. So, instead of pointing backwards, verse two points forwards, and leads us into a new narrative section of the ancient text. We now begin consideration of what this section tells us concerning the work of the first day, immediately after the absolute creation of all reality.

Beginning of the Process to Make the Earth Habitable

Verses 2-31 of Genesis chapter one relate a process involving six days of formative (and at times creative) shaping of the material, spatial mass from an unstructured form into a beautiful home for the human race. The famous German commentator, Gerhard Von Rad, has referred to this process as the turning of a chaos into a cosmos.[15] A pale illustration of the contrast between verse 2 (chaos) and verse 31 (cosmos) might be the difference between first entering into a confusing workshop stuffed with tools and raw materials (v. 2) and then going into an immaculately beautiful Georgian mansion, with all the furniture and decorations elegantly appointed in their perfect place (v. 31).

Genesis 1:2 clearly indicates that the original, created elements of verse 1 were not yet differentiated, separated and organized. Verse 2 tells us by means of three circumstantial clauses what it was like before God begins the shaping process which will result in a beautiful cosmos. That is, according to the text, the earth was 'desolation and waste'; 'darkness was upon the face of the deep'; and 'the Spirit of God was brooding over the waters'.

The original condition of the newly created earth was 'desolation' (*tohu*) and 'waste' (*bohu*). The Hebrew noun *tohu* (desolation) is used in Isaiah 45:18, where we are told that the earth was not created with the purpose of being *tohu*. As Aalders comments, tohu can literally mean 'emptiness':

> The word appears in other places in the Old Testament also. Sometimes it is translated 'vanity' or 'vain things' (1 Sam. 12:21; Isa. 40:17, 23; 59:4). In other passages it is used of 'chaos' or a 'trackless waste' (Job 12:24; Ps. 107:40). Obviously the basic idea of the word is a state of

---

15. Gerhard Von Rad, *Commentary on Genesis*, 49-51.

wildness because there is nothing there. Thus it depicts the loneliness and forsakenness of the barren desert.'[16]

'Desolation' or 'emptiness' is joined to a word of similar meaning, *bohu*, translated 'void' in the Authorized Version. *Bohu* is used in only two other Old Testament texts: Isaiah 34:11 and Jeremiah 4:23. In particular, Jeremiah is referring to the original 'chaotic' condition of the earth (and employs this as a threat of judgement on the land of Israel). Aalders' suggested translation of *bohu* as 'formlessness' seems to fit the context. 'The meaning it conveys is that the earth still had not been given the ordered form it now has.'[17] Or as E. J. Young says, *tohu* and *bohu* '... describe the earth as not habitable.'[18]

The second circumstantial clause of verse 2 speaks of 'darkness over the deep.' This describes two things, as Aalders notes: '(1) That there was no light on the earth; (2) That the earth was not constituted as a firm body. This is confirmed by the next statement ... "The Spirit of God was hovering over the waters." It would be logical to assume that the term "waters" refers to the same substance as "the deep." This, then, confirms the idea that we must not think of the earth in its original state as being in a firm or solid condition.'[19]

While one cannot be certain, perhaps the scene of the early earth in verse 2 was, to borrow an image from Wolfgang Capito, something like 'an abyss filled with a confusion of undifferentiated water and mud' in complete darkness, which would 'unhinge any human mind that attempted to penetrate it'.[20] Dr Henry M. Morris has proposed this description:

> The picture presented is one of all the basic material elements sustained in a pervasive watery matrix throughout the darkness of space. The same picture is suggested in 2 Peter 3:5: '... The earth standing out of the water and in the water'.[21]

Commenting on the related creational passage in Proverbs 8:27, '... he set a compass upon the face of the depth (or 'deep')', Morris writes:

> The fact that this 'compass' had to be 'set' on the face of the deep shows that the face of the deep originally had no such sphericity – it was formless, exactly as intimated in Genesis 1:2. Elements of matter and molecules of water were present, but not yet energized. The force

16. G. Ch. Aalders, *Genesis, Volume I*, translated by William Heynen (Zondervan: Grand Rapids, MI., 1981), 53, 54.
17. *Ibid.*, 54.
18. Young, *op.cit.*, 13.
19. Aalders, *op.cit.*, 54.
20. 'Abyssus enim lutum est aquis admixtum. Proinde coelum ac terra quiddam fluxum et perturbatum erant, quod quidem humanae mentis aciem prope effugerit', Capito, op. cit., 36.
21. Henry M. Morris, *The Genesis Record* (Baker Book House: Grand Rapids, Mich., 1976), 50.

of gravity was not yet functioning to draw such particles together into a coherent mass with a definite form. Neither were the electromagnetic forces yet in operation and everything was in darkness.[22]

The third circumstantial clause describing the original condition of the earth in Genesis 1:2 adds a divine element to the spatial, material elements of the previous two clauses: 'And the Spirit of God was moving upon the face of the waters.'[23] The participle translated 'moving' seems to mean 'hovering' or 'brooding'.[24]

This 'brooding' of the Spirit of God over the waters is a major detail in the Creation account, not a minor one. It demonstrates vividly the biblical worldview of a God whose hand and direct presence are never lifted from the elements and working of the material order. This third circumstantial clause of verse 2 is the direct antithesis of any sort of philosophical Deism or theological Dualism, both of which assume a vast gap between the living God and the space time cosmos. Deism pictures a remote Deity unable or unwilling to intervene immediately in the natural realm. That assumption explains much of the traditional and contemporary resistance to the biblical teaching of creation, as well as to the reality of miracles, Christ's incarnation and intercessory prayer. It must be remembered that this deistic gap between God and the real world is merely a philosophical assumption; an axiom of naturalistic religion, as it were, not a scientific fact.

We may infer from this clause that the divine presence by 'brooding' or 'hovering' over the waters was in direct charge of the whole process. His 'brooding' appears to be a way of conveying the concept of an immediate interaction with the natural elements to begin shaping them from an uninhabitable earth into an ordered cosmos. Wolfgang Capito pictures this transcendent interaction with earthly elements as 'divine virtue from the Spirit of the Lord warmly brooding over the inchoate, confused particles, until his active presence reduces them to the most beautiful and perfect order at the conclusion of the six days' work'.[25]

---

22. *Ibid.*, 51. Although Morris's point on primeval darkness and formlessness is well grounded, there is a scientific problem here with the assertion that molecules existed without being energized. Dr Frederick Skiff has noted that 'electric force is essential to the structure of molecules' (personal communication, *ibid.*).

23. The translation 'Spirit of God' rather than 'mighty wind' is discussed in *Technical & Bibliographical Notes*.

24. As it does in the Pi'el stem of the Hebrew verb in Deuteronomy 32:11, picturing God's guidance of His people like an eagle brooding over its nest.

25. 'Et spiritus Dei ferebatur super aquas, id est, super universum illud inchoatum, quod erat coelum et terra. Nam rude illud rerum omnium auspicium, divina virtus, spiritusque Domini fovebat super incubans, donec sex dierum operibus absolutum, omnem ornatum suum consequeretur.' Capito, *op. cit.*, 36, 37.

The commentator, H. C. Leupold, interprets 'hovering' as 'an intensified and vitalized type of vibration'. He goes on to say: 'We should not be averse to holding that the foundation for all physical laws operative in the world now was laid by this preparatory activity. Other passages relative to the Spirit as 'the formative cause of all life' are to be found: Job 26:13; 27:3; Psalms 33:6; 104:30; 143:10; Isaiah 34:16; 61:1; 63:11.'[26] Or to state it somewhat differently, 'The germs of all that is created were placed into dead matter by Him. His was the preparatory work for leading over from the inorganic to the organic.'[27]

In more scientific terminology, Henry M. Morris pictures this moving, vibrating activity of the Spirit of God as the imparting of energy to organize and shape the primeval matter:

> It is significant that the transmission of energy in the operations of the cosmos is in the form of waves – light waves, heat waves, sound waves, and so forth. In fact (except for the nuclear forces which are involved in the structure of matter itself), there are only two fundamental types of forces that operate on matter – the gravitational forces and the forces of the electromagnetic spectrum. All are associated with 'fields' of activity and with transmission by wave motion.
>
> Waves are typically rapid back and forth movements and they are normally produced by the vibratory motion of a wave generator of some kind. Energy cannot create itself. It is most appropriate that the first impartation of energy to the universe is described as the 'vibrating' movement of the Spirit of God Himself.[28]

The Sending Forth of Light

A third divine action occurred on the first day of creation: 'And God said, Let there be light: and there was light' (Gen. 1:3). Elsewhere in Scripture we learn that God Himself is uncreated light (e.g. John 8:12; 1 John 1:5; Rev. 21:23; 22:5). But now the One who is light and 'dwells in light inapproachable' (1 Tim. 6:16) commands forth created light into the darkness of the yet unformed earth.

The speaking into existence of the created light is the first of a series of three separations accomplished by the Creator which were essential to make the chaos into a cosmos. On Day One, light separates day and night; on Day Two the 'firmament' separates the upper waters from the earth, constituting an atmosphere or 'breathing space', and on Day Three, the waters below the heavens are collected into seas, and thus separated from the dry land. These three separations show the

---

26. H. C. Leupold, *Exposition of Genesis*, Volume I (Baker Book House: Grand Rapids, Mich., 1965), 50.
27. *Ibid.*
28. Morris, *op.cit.*, 52.

mighty hand of God shaping and organizing the dark, watery mass in the direction of a beautiful garden; a fit and lovely dwelling place for plants, animals and humankind.

Henry Morris would seem to be right in suggesting that with the coming of the light on the first day, '... there was established a cyclical succession of days and nights – periods of light and periods of darkness.'[29] He adds:

> Such a cyclical light-dark arrangement clearly means that the earth was now rotating on its axis and that there was a source of light on one side of the earth corresponding to the sun, even though the sun was not yet made' (Genesis 1:16).[30] [Since] '...the presence of visible light waves necessarily involves the entire electromagnetic spectrum ... setting the electromagnetic forces into operation completed the energizing of the physical cosmos...[31]

The question of how there was light on earth before the sun was created (on Day Four – Gen. 1:14) brings us back to the biblical view of reality, which never separates in deistic fashion God from the elements he created and controls. We are simply not told what the source of light was before the sun was placed in the sky. All the text says is that God spoke and the light was there.

John Calvin's admonition should be taken to heart if we wish to grasp reality as it is, untrammeled by man-centered assumptions which would bring God down to our finite level:

> Therefore the Lord by the very order of the creation, bears witness that he holds in his hand the light, which he is able to impart to us without the sun and moon.[32]

Should this be thought difficult for one who is light?

It is significant that the first time God speaks in Scripture, light appears. According to Psalm 119:130, 'The entrance of thy Word giveth light'. It was so in the old, original creation, and the apostle Paul tells us that something similar happens in 'the new creation', when a person whose life is darkened and condemned by sin, becomes 'light in the Lord' (Eph. 5:8). In 2 Corinthians 4:6, he quotes directly from Genesis 1:3: 'For God, who commanded the light to shine out of darkness, hath shined in our hearts, to give the light of the knowledge of the glory of God in the face of Jesus Christ.' Such an enlightening of the human personality as it is enabled to see who the Son of God really is, constitutes nothing less than 'a new creation' (2 Cor. 5:17).

---

29. *Ibid.*, 55.
30. *Ibid.*
31. *Ibid.*, 56.
32. John Calvin, *Commentaries on the First Book of Moses Called Genesis*, 76.

The analogy between the two creations is fascinating. Only someone so great as the mighty Creator God could speak light into the darkness of the primeval earth in the first creation. Only He – the Almighty Word, the uncreated Light – is able to speak light into the dark human soul of the smallest child or greatest king, and thus bring it into a new birth (see John chapter three and Jeremiah chapter thirty-one), making the chaos of sin into the cosmos of a new creation in Christ. And in both cases, the instrument of transforming enlightenment is his spoken word, which never 'returns to him void' (Isa. 55:11). His 'fiat' command (as the Latin translation of the Bible phrases 'let there be') always finds fulfillment. Whenever God commands light into the dark, formless elements of earth or into the spiritually blind energies of self-defeating human psychology, light appears in both scenes and beauty replaces disorder.

The Goodness of Creation

Unlike many kinds of pagan philosophy, which view physical reality as unclean or bad, Genesis teaches that God delights in material reality. Genesis 1:4 employs an 'anthropomorphic' expression (stating a divine action in 'earthly' or 'human' terms beneath God's infinite dignity in order to help us understand a profound truth): 'And God saw the light, that it was good...' This means that God made material reality (including visible light) and was pleased with it. Aalders grasps the sense of 'God saw that it was good' (which is used several times in the creation account of the various aspects of what God made: vv. 10, 12, 18, 21, 25, 31): 'It is used to convey to us the fact that in each part of God's creative work there was a perfection which completely fulfilled God's will.'[33] Similarly, the fourth-century Cappadocian Church Father, Basil the Great, commented: 'What [God] esteems beautiful is that which presents in its perfection all the fitness of art, and that which tends to the usefulness of its end. He, then, who proposed to Himself a manifest design in His works, approved each one of them, as fulfilling its end in accordance with His creative purpose.'[34]

Church fathers such as Novatian were right in stating that the creation is good because the Creator is good, '...the works of a good Creator can only be good.'[35] Or as St. Augustine later wrote, 'Therefore, because He is all-powerful and good, He made everything exceedingly good...'[36] That is to say, God Himself is the original standard of goodness and

33. Aalders, *op.cit.*, 57.
34. Basil, *The Hexameron*, III. 10.
35. Novatian, *De Trinitate*, IV. 21.
36. Augustine, *op. cit.*, Book Four, chapter 16 (122).

beauty, not something outside Himself. Novatian effectively captures this point in his third century *De Trinitate*:

> What could you possibly say then that would be worthy of Him? He is more sublime than all sublimity, higher than all heights, deeper than all depth, clearer than all light, brighter than all brilliance, more splendid than all splendour, stronger than all strength, mightier than all might, more beautiful than all beauty, truer than all truth, more enduring than all endurance, greater than all majesty, more powerful than all power, richer than all riches, wiser than all wisdom, kinder than all kindness, better than all goodness, juster than all justice, more merciful than all mercy. Every kind of virtue must of necessity be less than He, who is the God and source of all virtue.[37]

The incomparable goodness of God, Who created all things, means that visible light (v. 4), dry land and seas (v. 10), various kinds of animal life (v. 25), as well as the physical bodies which somehow express the inner personalities of men and women are good. The physical and bodily, therefore, is no less good than the 'spiritual'. Owing to the continuing influence of pagan Neoplatonic philosophy through the Middle Ages down to today, the Church has often missed the Scriptural (and divine) appreciation and pleasure in physical reality, such as natural beauty and marital sexuality. God 'saw' that these things were good. We shall see in Genesis Chapter Two, that the 'terminal' human problem does not occur because we have a physical body instead of being 'pure spirits' (as many ancient Greeks and modern Hindus would hold). Rather, all problems and ills, preliminary and terminal, are rooted in rebellion against the totally good Creator. After all, the first rebellion took place because of a choice that man made in his mind or spirit. Genesis does not portray the body (or the body and spirit relationship) or the wider realm of nature as the source of our problems.

Like Genesis, and unlike Neoplatonism or 'New Age' thought, ancient or modern, the Psalmist had read the goodness of creation in accordance with Genesis (see, for example, Psalms eight, nineteen, sixty-five, one hundred and four, one hundred and forty-eight). When the modern church joins the Psalmist in his appreciation of God's physical creation, the world may see a new outburst of creative beauty in art, music and poetry. And that is just what the divine Creator was doing on Day One of the original creation: beginning to shape a formless chaos into a beautiful cosmos.

The English poet, John Dryden, expressed imaginatively something of the divine process of turning original chaos into the beauty of

---

37. Novatian, *op. cit.*, II. 16.

cosmos in his 1687 *A Song for St. Cecilia's Day* (later set to music by
Handel):

> When nature underneath a heap
> Of jarring atoms lay,
> And could not heave her head,
> The tuneful voice was heard from high:
> 'Arise! ye more than dead.'
> Then cold and hot, and moist and dry,
> In order to their stations leap,
> And music's pow'r obey.
>
> From harmony, from heav'nly harmony,
> This universal frame began.
> From harmony to harmony,
> Through all the compass of the notes it ran,
> The diapason closing full in man.
>
> As from the pow'r of sacred lays
> The spheres began to move,
> And sung the great Creator's praise
> To all the bless'd above;
> So when the last and dreadful hour
> This crumbling pageant shall devour;
> The trumpet shall be heard on high,
> The dead shall live, the living die,
> And music shall untune the sky.

Day Two of creation continues this shaping of barrenness into beauty,
but before looking into its activity, we must consider two other
matters thought by many to be related to the first day: the creation of
angels and the supposed 'gap' between verses one and two of Genesis
Chapter One.

TECHNICAL AND BIBLIOGRAPHICAL
NOTES FOR CHAPTER FOUR

The Grammatical Dependence of Verse 2 on the Verb of Verse 3

We discussed earlier the significance of whether the three circumstantial
clauses of verse 2 are controlled by the finite verb 'created' in verse of
chapter 1, or by the finite verb 'God *said*' in verse 3.[38] Some general
reasons, grammatical and contextual, were offered for placing the
clauses of verse 2 with 'And God said' of verse 3. This matter is

---

38. See pages 68-71.

carefully discussed by E. J. Young on pages 11 and 12 of *Studies in Genesis One*.

One quotation from Young's discussion of the grammatical grounds for this connection should summarize well our position:

> The first act in forming the present universe was God's speaking. The verb *w'yomer* is introduced by waw consecutive, but it should now be clear that *w'yomer* is not the second verb in a series introduced by *bara'* of verse one. Verse one is a narrative complete in itself. Verses 2-31 likewise constitute a narrative complete in itself. In this narrative the first verb is *w'yomer*. No previous verb in the perfect appears.
>
> In a narrative in the past time we often find the first verb in the perfect and each succeeding verb in the imperfect with *waw* consecutive. The first verb, however, i.e., the verb in the perfect, need not be expressed. Such is the case in the narrative comprised by verses 2-31. The first action mentioned in this narrative is that of the *w'yomer* of verse three.[39]

Thus both context and Hebrew grammar support the translation of verse 1 as the absolute creation of all things, and verse 2 as descriptive of what this newly created order was like when God spoke the command: 'Let there be light.'

'The Spirit of God' rather than 'Mighty Wind' in Verse 2

Some translations and commentaries have reduced the infinite 'Spirit of God' of Genesis 1:2 to a finite 'mighty wind'. Claus Westermann translates it as 'God's wind'.[40] His translation has 'wind' in small case letters, indicating it is not understood as referring to a personal being. Similarly, Von Rad translates it 'fearful storm' (*Gottessturm*).[41]

E. J. Young replies to such reductions of Spirit of God to wind on pages 36 and 37 of *Studies in Genesis One*, and also in an excursus on pages 38-42. Young lists three main reasons why 'Spirit' may not reasonably be reduced to wind. First, Moses could have used the common expression for wind, which is found in Jonah 1:4 and Job 1:19, but rather, uses the word for Spirit. Secondly, 'the participle ["hovering"] does not describe the blowing of a wind.'[42] Thirdly, 'mention of a mighty wind at this point would be out of place.'[43] That is, the first two clauses of verse 2 show how the earth was uninhabitable. 'If the third clause simply states that a mighty wind was blowing ... it does not contribute to showing that the earth was uninhabitable ...

39. Young, *op.cit.*, 11.
40. Claus Westermann, *Genesis: A Practical Commentary*, translated by David E. Green (William B. Eerdmans Publ. Co.: Grand Rapids, Mich., 1987), 4.
41. Von Rad, *op.cit.*, 49, 50.
42. Young, *op.cit.*, 36.
43. *Ibid.*, 37.

On the other hand, the traditional interpretation reveals that despite the fact that the earth was not then habitable, all was under the control of God's Spirit.'[44]

The direct, active personal presence of the infinite God in the created order is perhaps *the* crucial point for a Biblical understanding of creation. The remaining chapters of this volume explore the wonders wrought by the coming into being of the intelligible universe. Such wonders could have been produced only by the personally present and directly active Spirit of God.

---

44. *Ibid.*

QUESTIONS FOR STUDY

1. Was God lonely before He created the world and man?

2. How is God beyond origin?

3. Why is time a creature as well as material and space?

4. Why does it seem to have taken God six days to create the world, rather than a split second or millions of years?

5. What three things had their beginning on the first day of creation?

6. What is meant by the figure of speech called a 'merism'? How is it used in Genesis 1?

7. Discuss how the movement from Genesis 1:2 to 1:31 can be called the turning of a chaos into a cosmos.

8. How is Genesis 1:1 separated from verses 2-31 and why is it important that verse 2 looks forward rather than back to verse 1?

9. From the three circumstantial clauses of verse 2, describe the chaos that immediately follows the creation of heaven and earth.

10. Deism and the 'brooding of the Spirit over the deep' stand in direct antithesis to one another. Why? Show how Deism affects contemporary thinking.

11. What may be the origin of energy in the universe?

12. What are the three separations the Creator used in turning the chaos into cosmos?

13. How does John Calvin address the question of whether there was light before the sun's creation?

14. Compare the creation of the world, and the new creation of an individual in Christ.

15. Contrast the pagan view of material reality with the biblical view.

Chapter Five

Creation of Angels and 'The Gap Theory'

SOME interpreters have connected two other matters to the first day of creation: the creation of angels during the first day, and a supposed gap between the creation of all things in verse one, and the formative activity, beginning in verse two. While neither of these items is mentioned in the Genesis text, it is appropriate to deal with them here before going on to the work of the other days of creation week.

The Creation of Angels

Neither Genesis, nor any other text in Scripture states when the angelic beings were actually created. What is definite is that angels are creatures, and thus do have a beginning. They are immortal, but only the Triune God is eternal, without beginning or ending. Reserve is necessary on such a speculative subject that has not been revealed to us by God in his Word.

Some have thought that since angels are '...all ministering spirits, sent forth to minister for them who shall be heirs of salvation' (Heb. 1:14), they may not have been created until the sixth day, when mankind, the primary focus of their activities, was created. But that is not a compelling argument, for we find them worshipping God in the heavenly scenes depicted in the book of Revelation (e.g. Rev. 5:11). So worship of God is central to their lives as well as care of mankind.

That worship depicted in Revelation, is, of course, connected with the redemption of the whole created order in the consummation. But if they are seen worshipping God at the consummation of history, they may well have been worshipping Him at its very beginning, even before man was on the scene. Hebrews 1:6 and 7 also refer to angelic worship, but the primary purpose of those quotations from the Old Testament[1] is to show the superiority of Christ to angels, not to deal with their origin. Since the primary focus of these passages is worship, they do not indicate that the angels could only have come into existence with or after mankind.

Perhaps the angels were brought into being on the very first day of creation. In Job 38:4-7 we are told that the angels were present when the foundations of the earth were laid, and were rejoicing over it all. Psalm 104:2-5 speaks of the shining of God's light during the original creative process, and mentions the angels just before reference to 'laying the foundations of the earth'. Thus they appear after the creation of all things and before the earth is made a solid body (possibly referring to either the energizing work of the Holy Spirit on Day One, and/or the separation of the waters from the land on Day Three). These passages from Job and Psalms are certainly poetic, and are presumably not meant to be interpreted in the same precise, chronological sense required by Genesis 1 and 2. Poetic though its literary form is, it must mean something, and bear reference to a true state of affairs. Such passages may take us as far as we can go safely in consideration of the question: when were the angels first created?

It has been suggested that since the angels are at times related to the stars (e.g. Jud. 5:20; Dan. 8:10; Jude 13; Rev. 1:20), they may have been created on the same day as the luminaries – the fourth. That is possible, but the passages above from Job 38 and Psalm 104 appear to indicate their presence at least by the third day.

The question itself is not important for a proper understanding of creation. What is significant, however, is to bear in mind that they are finite, created spirits; part of the larger creation by the infinite God out of nothing. In the words of the Nicene Creed, He alone is Creator 'of all things visible and invisible'.

The 'Gap Theory'

While the question of the time of the creation of angels is a speculative question arising from within the scriptural framework, the 'gap

---

1. Hebrews 1:6 is quoting the Septuagint of Deuteronomy 32:43 (with a possible reference to Psalm 97:7), and Hebrews 1:7 quotes Psalm 104:4.

theory' is a reading into the scriptural account of something from quite outside the text. It refers to a supposed 'gap' of millions of years between Genesis 1:1 and 1:2.

This theory is an example of what can be properly termed 'an exegesis of desperation'. The idea apparently goes back to the outstanding evangelical theologian and church statesman of Scotland, Dr Thomas Chalmers. In the early nineteenth century, under pressure from the intellectual community which claimed irrefutable proof for vast ages of the world as well as the existence of fossils much older than the biblical Adam, Dr Chalmers proposed inserting a gap of millions of years between the first two verses of Genesis to accommodate these aeons of earth history with their fossils into the traditional biblical story of beginnings. The theory held that verse one recorded the original creation, which was ruined by God's judgement on the cosmos owing to Satan's fall from holy, angelic status. This judgement wiped out the first earth, leaving a thick layer of sedimentation containing pre-historic fossils. Hence, the argument for vast earth ages claimed by nineteenth-century uniformitarian geologists could be safely accepted without threatening the integrity of the Genesis account in the succeeding verses.

Supposedly, verse 2 gives a picture of a judged, ruined cosmos ('without form and void'), while verse 3 conveys a re-creation or restitution of it, this time to be populated by humankind rather than angels. This theory would set the beginning of creation week in verse 3, rather than verse 1, contrary to what both Jews and Christians had always understood.

This 'gap' or 'restitution' theory was popular in many conservative circles during the last half of the nineteenth and first half of the twentieth centuries. It found its way into widely published study Bibles, commentaries and sermons. Its influence has rapidly waned during the last forty years, largely because of its poor scholarship, which we shall examine directly. One must be sympathetic to Dr Chalmers and those evangelicals who have followed him in this largely exploded approach, by appreciating their sincere desire to make the best of a bad situation. Nevertheless, it is not a fair and straightforward reading of Scripture, nor does it successfully reconcile the biblical picture of origins with 'scientific' naturalism. The 'gap' theory should serve as a model of what Christians should *not* do in their legitimate desire to speak Biblical truth into a world held in the tight grip of humanistic premises.

The major problem is that it reads into Scripture what is not there in any careful, scholarly examination of the relevant texts. As the German pastor and Old Testament scholar, Karlheinz Rabast, pointed out in 1951, '...it is unlikely that Scripture would pass over such a great catastrophe in silence when it mentions in this context less important matters.'[2] On the contrary, both Old and New Testaments make heavy reference to the significance of the flood of Noah in destroying the earth, without any mention of this supposed pre-Adamic catastrophe. There is no biblical reference anywhere to any other world-wide catastrophe than that in Noah's day.

Furthermore, the few biblical references offered by the gap theorists to buttress their position fail to render them support. Their major text, Isaiah 45:18, when looked at carefully, certainly does not do so: 'For thus saith the Lord that created the heavens... he created it not in vain, he formed it to be inhabited...' Their argument is that since God did not create the earth to be 'void and uninhabited' (similar terms to those of Gen. 1:2), therefore, after the earth's first creation, it was made a desolate place owing to divine judgement on Lucifer's rebellion.

But what Isaiah 45:18 means accords perfectly with the traditional interpretation of Genesis 1:2: the elements of the early earth which had been created out of nothing in Genesis 1:1 were only temporarily *'tohu'* and *'bohu'*. For the divine purpose to form the earth into a habitable dwelling place would be accomplished during the work of the next five days. The sixteenth century Reformer and commentator, Capito, appositely compared the temporary *'tohu'/'bohu'* status of the inchoate created elements to a baby in the womb during the early period of gestation.[3] It is not a picture of fallenness (as the Gap Theory suggests), but rather one conveying lack of full development.

Other minor texts pressed into 'gap' service also fail to support the theory. Genesis 1:28, for instance, in the Authorized Version reads: 'Be fruitful and multiply, and replenish the earth...' They argue that 'replenish' implies a prior destruction and emptying of the pre-Adamic world. However, the Hebrew verb translated 'replenish' in the 1611 Version simply means 'fill', and is translated this way in nearly all contemporary versions.

Even more theologically significant is the clear Biblical teaching running throughout Old and New Testaments (as in Genesis chapter three and Romans chapter five) that death and disintegration of the entire cosmos came through Adam's sin, for Adam was the covenant head and representative of the whole creation, not Lucifer. Although Lucifer fell before Adam, his fall did not bring death into the rest of the created order, because Adam, not Lucifer, was the representative figure (or 'covenant head') of the whole creation, thus taking it down with him into judgement.

---

2. K. Rabast, *Die Genesis*, 1951, pp.15-19, paraphrased in E. J. Young, *op.cit.*, 15, 16.
3. Capito, *op. cit.*, 38, 39.

Moreover, God pronounces 'good' seven times in Genesis chapter one as He surveys the created order. If the early earth bore the scars of a previous wreckage through a layer of judgemental sediment laced with dead fossils, how could he have pronounced it all 'very good' (as in the summary statement in Gen. 1:31)?

The gap or restitution theory contains other inconsistencies. The first chapter of Genesis as well as Exodus 20:11 ('For in six days the Lord made the heavens and the earth, the sea and all that in them is...') indicate that absolutely all things were created during this week of primeval work. But the gap theorists (or restitutionists) would hold – contrary to this clear teaching – that all things (except man) were made long before the six days of creation.[4]

Also the restitution theory would require the sun to have shone in order to make earthly life possible, millions of years before the fourth day of creation when the sun and moon were placed into the heavens for the first time. If, as we suggested earlier, the angels (which would include Lucifer who became known as Satan after his fall) might not have been created until the second or third day of creation week, how could a non-existent being have induced a primeval judgement before his appearance on the scene?

Such questions would be irrelevant to a naturalist who rejects the authority of the Scriptures, but they are of major and detrimental consequence to the gap theorists, who do maintain sincere allegiance to the Word of God. Evolutionary naturalists would not be impressed by the attempted compromise of the gap thinkers, for it leaves too many traces of supernatural purpose in it, and a desolated earth with preserved fossils from before the 'second creation' would not fit the naturalist picture of either 'big bang' or 'steady state' chaos which preceded the evolutionary ascent of the primates.

Perhaps the greatest value in surveying this largely abandoned theory lies in its didactic quality. It teaches us first, the futility of reading into Scripture what is not there in order to force a hasty compromise with anti-theistic thought. Secondly, as we shall see in later chapters of this volume, it teaches us to put the same kind of sceptical, foundational questions to the dogmas of humanistic authorities that they have long put to the authority of Scripture. Unfortunately, many well-intentioned evangelicals were too ready to adjust the teachings of Scripture to authority-claims of naturalistic science without taking the time and effort to examine radically the presuppositions, evidences and procedures of those highly vaunted authorities.

---

4. They, of course, posit a sort of re-creation or restitution of the various orders of life during the supposed 'week of renewal' which is said to begin in Genesis 1: 2.

In the light of changing paradigms with fuller data supporting creation, more material is available to enable a critical examination of evolutionary doctrines of development and chronology than in the nineteenth century, when the gap theory was originated. Research since the 1960s which is favorable to creation requires such an examination. This forms the basis of chapters seven and eight, which put both presuppositional and evidential questions to one of the strongest bulwarks of the naturalistic story of origins: the age of the earth. To do so, we must first examine the Biblical meaning of 'day' in Chapter Six.[5]

TECHNICAL AND BIBLIOGRAPHICAL NOTES FOR CHAPTER FIVE

How Do We Interpret the Fossil Record?

One of the major problems the gap theory was invented to solve was the discovery of a remarkable number of fossils in various earth structures, which seemed to require a human history much older than the time allotted by the Genesis genealogies to Adam and his descendants. The gap theorists therefore wished to maintain the integrity of the 'recentness' of the Biblical genealogies and at the same time explain the existence of apparently ancient fossil remains. They did this by positing the existence of a pre-Adamic race (whose remains were represented in the fossils). Then they suggested that this pre-Adamic race was destroyed in a judgement (that fell between verses 1 and 2 of Genesis chapter 1).

We have already discussed why there is no gap between these two verses in the actual Hebrew text. What remains to be addressed here is this question: does the existence of a massive number of fossil forms indicate either the high antiquity of the human race and/or evolutionary development of those fossil forms? Since Chapters 7 and 8 of this book are largely devoted to the age of the universe, we will postpone that subject and deal here with what the fossil record actually teaches us concerning the basic stability of human and animal forms over the millennia.

Most of us have been taught in school that the fossil record is a strong evidence for evolutionary development, allegedly demonstrating slow, upward evolution from simple to more complex species. In

---

5. In addition to E. J. Young's work refuting the 'gap theory', a careful critique is offered is A. J. Monty White's *What About Origins?* (Dunestone Press, 1978). The most thorough survey of this theory is by Weston W. Fields, *Unformed and Unfilled: The Gap Theory* (Baker Book House: Grand Rapids, Mich., 1976).

actual fact, the fossil record is one of the greatest empirical evidences *against* evolution, for its findings contradict the very premises of evolutionary theory, and instead speak of sudden appearance of species and lack of intermediate, or gradual links. In other words, these fossil facts are concordant with the Genesis record of immediate creation and stability of the kinds.

Without giving any extensive discussion of this important evidence here, we will provide some essential bibliographical references for interested readers.

1. The Fossil Record in General

Fossil evidence demonstrates historic and lasting discontinuity between the various species, which is precisely what would be predicted by the Genesis account, and runs contrary to the most central predictions of evolutionary theory. Chapter 8, 'The Fossil Record', of Michael Denton's *Evolution: A Theory in Crisis* surveys the evidence. He writes:

> The virtual complete absence of intermediate and ancestral forms from the fossil record is today recognized widely by many leading paleontologists as one of its most striking characteristics .... The fossils have not only failed to yield the host of transitional forms demanded by evolution theory, but ... nearly all extinct species and groups revealed by paleontology are quite distinct and isolated as they burst into the record ....[6]

He adds:

> There is no doubt that as it stands today the fossil record provides a tremendous challenge to the notion of organic evolution, because to close the very considerable gaps which at present separate the known groups would necessarily have required great numbers of transitional forms...[7]
>
> Considering that the total number of known fossil species is nearly one hundred thousand, the fact that the only relatively convincing morphological sequences are a handful of cases like the horse, which do not involve a great deal of change, and which in many cases like the elephant may not even represent phylogenetic sequences at all, serves to emphasize the remarkable lack of any direct evidence for major evolutionary transformations in the fossil record.[8]

Chapter 4, 'The Fossil Problem', of Johnson's *Darwin on Trial*, chronicles Darwin's awareness of the absence of fossil links between the discontinuous groups as a severe problem for his theory. He argued in the late 1850s that future discoveries would locate these 'missing

---

6. Denton, *op. cit.*, 165, 166.
7. *Ibid.*, 172.
8. *Ibid.*, 185.

links' and thus vindicate his theory.[9] The truth is, however, that '...the fossil problem for Darwinism is getting worse all the time.'[10]

In 1979, Dr David Raup, Dean of the Field Museum of Natural History in Chicago, which possesses one of greatest fossil collections in the world, candidly wrote:

> Well, we are now about 120 years after Darwin and the knowledge of the fossil record has been greatly expanded. We now have a quarter of a million fossil species but the situation still hasn't changed much. The record of evolution is still surprisingly jerky, and, ironically, we have even fewer examples of evolutionary transition than we had in Darwin's time. By this I mean that some of the classic cases of Darwinian change in the fossil record, such as the evolution of the horse in North America, have had to be discarded or modified as a result of more detailed information – what appeared to be a nice simple progression when relatively few data were available now appears to be much more complex and much less gradualistic. So Darwin's problem has not been alleviated in the last 120 years and we still have a record which does show change but one that can hardly be looked upon as the most reasonable consequence of natural selection.[11]

Stephen J. Gould comments on the weight of fossil finding against evolutionary theory: 'New species almost always appeared suddenly in the fossil record with no intermediate links to ancestors in older rocks of the same region.'[12] In the same article, he revealed that:

> The extreme rarity of transitional forms in the fossil record persists as the trade secret of paleontology. The evolutionary trees that adorn our textbooks have data only at the tips and nodes of their branches; the rest is inference, however reasonable, not the evidence of fossils.... Most species exhibit no directional change during their tenure on earth.... In any local area, a species does not arise gradually by the steady transformation of its ancestors; it appears all at once and 'fully formed'.[13]

Similarly, David B. Kitts of the School of Geology and Geophysics, University of Oklahoma, commented: 'Despite the bright promise that paleontology provides a means of "seeing" evolution, it has provided some nasty difficulties for evolutionists, the most notorious of which is the presence of "gaps" in the fossil record. Evolution

9. Johnson, *op. cit.*, 46, 47.
10. *Ibid.*, 57.
11. David M. Raup, 'Conflicts Between Darwin and Paleontology', *Field Museum of Natural History Bulletin*, Vol. 50, No. 1, January 1979, 25.
12. Stephen J. Gould, 'Evolution's Erratic Pace', *Natural History*, May, 1977, 12.
13. *Ibid.*, 14.

requires intermediate forms between species and paleontology does not provide them.'[14]

Scott M. Huse summarizes the findings of the empirical fossil evidence:

a. The imagined jump from dead matter to living protozoans is a transition of truly fanciful dimension, one of pure conjecture.

b. There is a gigantic gap between one-celled micro-organisms and the high complexity and variety of the metazoan invertebrates.

c. The evolutionary transition between invertebrates and vertebrates is completely missing...

d. The evolutionary advance from fishes to amphibians is totally nonexistent...

e. There are no connecting links between amphibians and the altogether different reptiles...

f. There are no transitional forms between reptiles and mammals.

g. There are no connecting evolutionary links between reptiles and birds. *Archaeopteryx* was once highly acclaimed as such a link but has since been acknowledged by paleontologists to have been a true bird.

h. There are no intermediate or transitional forms leading up to man from an apelike ancestor. Fossil hominoids and hominids cited by evolutionists to demonstrate evolution are actually fossils either of apes or men, or neither. There is no valid scientific evidence to suggest that they are fossils of animals intermediate between apes and men.[15]

Some who are committed to evolutionary theory, even when the facts do not demonstrate it, have suggested a concept to preserve evolution from the force of such facts. Particularly they have done this by means of a hypothesis advanced in 1977 by Gould and Eldridge, called 'punctuated equilibrium' or 'saltationism' (i.e. evolution is still true, but must have proceeded by means of sudden 'jumps'). Phillip Johnson realistically responds:

> The trouble with saltationism, however, is that when closely examined it turns out to be only a meaningless middle ground somewhere between evolution and special creation. As Richard Dawkins puts it, you can call the Biblical creation of man from the dust of the earth a saltation. In terms of fossil evidence, saltation just means that a new form appeared out of nowhere and we haven't the faintest idea how.

---

14. David B. Kitts, 'Paleontology and Evolutionary Theory,' *Evolution*, Vol. 28, September 1974, 467, quoted in Walter T. Brown, *op. cit.*, 47.

15. Huse, *op. cit.*, 45.

As a scientific theory, 'saltationist evolution' is just what Darwin called it in the first place: rubbish.[16]

2. Human and 'Pre-Human' Fossils

Robert E. Kofahl, among many others, concludes that 'Most of the "fossil men" were merely animals having no connection to the human race.'[17] An example is given by Roger Lewin: 'The dethroning of Ramapithecus – from putative first human in 1961 to extinct relative of the orangutan in 1982 – is one of the most fascinating, and bitter, sagas in the search for human origins.'[18] Other examples abound.

> Human remains were discovered in 1856 in a cave in the Neander Valley, which was the source of the name Neanderthal.... [T]extbook drawings ... portrayed them with bestial features, bull necks, haunched over posture, and knees which could not be straightened. In 1956 respected evolutionary scientists reexamined the bones and concluded that they were of an individual who suffered from severe skeletal malformation resulting from rickets and arthritis .... They were true men, *Homo sapiens.*'[19]
>
> The Peking Man or *Sinanthropus* fossils reportedly found in 1928 and succeeding years were never permitted to leave China.... When carefully compared, these reports show that Peking Man was an animal, probably a large monkey or baboon, not a man.... There is much appearance of fraud in the history of the Peking fossils.'[20]

Probably the most famous recent fossil discovery said to be an ancestor of humankind is 'Lucy', a partial skeleton found by D. C. Johanson in Ethiopia in the early 1970s, supposedly part of the 'Australopithecine' group.[21] Huse responds to Johanson's claims of 'Lucy's' being an ancestor of humans:

> ...Johanson's conclusion is pure speculation. Anatomist Charles Oxnard, using a computer technique for analysis of skeletal relationships, has concluded that the australopithecines did not walk uprightly, at least not in the same manner as humans. In this connection, it should be mentioned that the chimpanzee spends a considerable amount of time walking upright. Thus, there is no valid scientific basis for a conclusion of bipedalism in Lucy. Lucy and her relatives are probably just varieties of apes.[22] Gary Parker discusses 'Lucy' and the 'australo-pithecines' in

---

16. Johnson, *op. cit.*, 61.
17. Kofahl, *op. cit.*, 72.
18. Roger Lewin, *Bones of Contention* (New York: Simon and Schuster, Inc., 1987), 86.
19. Kofahl, *op. cit.*, 74, 75.
20. *Ibid.*, 76.
21. Charles Oxnard, Professor of Anatomy and Human Biology of the University of Western Australia (who is not a creationist) based his *The Order of Man* (Yale University Press, 1984) upon a complex computer analysis of australopithecine fossils. His research indicates that these fossils are actually an extinct form of ape, having no connection to the human race.
22. Huse, *op. cit.*, 102..

some detail in Chapter 3, 'The Fossil Evidence' of *Creation: The Facts of Life.*[23]

In sum, the fossil evidence presents no credible 'pre-human' ancestors. Humanity, like the other 'kinds' suddenly appear in the rock strata (often much lower than supposedly earlier life forms, as evidenced in the Calaveras, California skulls as well as those of Castenedolo in Italy[24]). What the fossil record evidences is *not* a gradual, upward development of increasingly complex forms of life, but rather the sudden appearance of developed life forms.

The fossil record not only indicates sudden appearance of living structures, but also another significant fact of ancient history. Geological structures and fossil remains suggest a cataclysm resulting in the sudden death of millions of creatures and rapid burial under such great pressure that their forms have been preserved. There is evidence of the sudden death and burial of multitudes of animals throughout many parts of the world. Genesis 6 to 9 indicates that this massive catastrophe was the universal Flood. Although this volume deals only with the first two chapters of Genesis, and thus does not significantly address the later subject of the Flood[25], it should be noted that increasing amounts of research on this subject continue to be published, and will undoubtedly play a major role in displacing the ever-weakening uniformitarian geological thesis, which is the underpinning of evolution, with a catastrophe paradigm, which is viable both Biblically and scientifically, and thus fits with special creation and the rest of the Genesis record.[26]

---

23. Gary Parker, *Creation: The Facts of Life* (Master Book Publishers: San Diego, CA, 1984), 111-119.

24. See Brown, *op. cit.*, 52, and Wysong, *op. cit.*, 373.

25. Some attention is given to geological and fossil evidences for the universal flood in Chapter 8, pp. 162-167.

26. A few representative examples are found in: Morris and Whitcomb, *op. cit.*, especially the first six chapters; Henry M. Morris, *Biblical Cosmology And Modern Science*, chapters 2 and 7; Walter T. Brown, *op. cit.*, pp. 33-149; 174-186; Wysong, *op. cit.* chapter 20.

Questions For Study

1. Are angels created? If so, what does the Bible tell us about when?

2. Are they immortal or mortal?

3. What are the primary duties of angels?

4. Explain what is meant by the 'Gap Theory'.

5. Why did Christian scholars invent the 'Gap Theory'?

6. What Biblical reasons stand against it?

7. What is the value of discussing a predominantly abandoned theory?

Chapter Six

'Days' of Creation – Their Biblical Meaning

THE work of the first day of creation confronts us with the major difference between biblical Christianity and secular Naturalism: absolute creation out of nothing by an infinite, personal God, as opposed to the eternality of matter or energy. Probably the second major and unbridgeable gap between the biblical picture of reality and that of humanist philosophy is the question of time and, specifically, the age of the cosmos. Vast ages are necessary to make viable the secularist, impersonal alternative to divine creation: the theory of evolution. Owing to the intellectual shift by the early nineteenth century to the assumption of vast ages of the earth, first in geology, and then in biology, and soon in history and every other field, those who took the Scriptures seriously faced difficult questions in interpreting the days of creation week.

Hence from the early or mid-nineteenth century onwards, there have been a variety of interpretations of 'day' among even conservative Bible commentators. Before we examine these varied interpretations, however, we must first consider how the Genesis account, and the broader biblical record, use 'day'.

Biblical Usage of 'Day'

The Bible generally employs the word 'day' (*yom* in Hebrew) to signify either a twenty-four hour solar day, or the daylight portion of those hours. When modified by a number or ordinal (as 'Day One' or 'Day Two') its universal Scriptural usage means normal solar day.[1] Sometimes 'day' is used in Scripture to indicate a general period of time not precisely defined (as in Job 7:6, 'My days are vanity...'; or Psalm 90:9, 'Our days are passed away in thy wrath'.) But in such cases, 'day' still means a finite succession of normal days: not, by any stretch of the exegetical imagination, vast ages. 'Day' (*yom*) can also occasionally be used of a portion of the year, such as wheat harvest (Gen. 30:14), but here again, nothing other than a few weeks limited duration of normal solar days can be intended: not thousands or millions of years.

The frequent prophetic expression 'the Day of the Lord' is obviously a very special kind of day, and whatever its prophetic significance, appears to mean an ordinary day, which becomes extraordinary because of God's final intervention. In no sense can it be used to mean vast ages, nor does it contradict the general biblical usage of 'day' as normal solar day. As St. Hilary of Poitiers said about the day of judgement in the third century: 'one day is hidden that all others may be revealed.'

There are a few Scriptural texts which make it clear that 'day' is being employed in another sense than 'twenty-four hours'. 2 Peter 3:8 is the pre-eminent example of such usage: '...one day with the Lord is as a thousand years...' But here the very context indicates plainly that the normal, historico-literal significance is not intended. This kind of exceptional usage cannot legitimately be read back into a normal sequence of days (as though, for instance, because of 2 Peter 3:8, the seven creation days automatically lasted seven thousand years), unless the literary and grammatical context of the passage in question required such a shift in meaning. Textual evidence in Genesis 1 and 2 indicates no such shift, but rather seems to require a sequence of normal solar days.

Scientist Henry M. Morris seems correct in marshalling the evidence that 'day' in Genesis 1 and 2 signifies a normal solar day:

> Furthermore, 'God called the light Day, and the darkness he called Night.' As though in anticipation of future misunderstanding, God

---

1. The apparent exception to this universal usage, pointed out by Dr Hugh Ross in *Creation and Time* (NavPress: Colorado Springs, Col., 1994), 47 of Hosea 6:2, 'after two days He will revive us; on the third day He will raise us up' is not a clear exception. Since it is not absolutely certain what the prophecy means (does it refer to the restoration of Israel to the land? Does it refer to the resurrection of Christ, and thus, that of His people in Him?) we are in no position clearly to deny a sequence of three normal days. At very least, such a reference is far too weak to disestablish the universal Scriptural usage of ordinals connected with days meaning ordinary solar days.

carefully defined His terms! The very first time He used the word 'day' (Hebrew *yom*), He defined it as the 'light', to distinguish it from the 'darkness' called 'night'.

Having separated the day and night, God had completed His first day's work. 'The evening and the morning were the first day.' This same formula is used at the conclusion of each of the six days; so it is obvious that the duration of each of the days, including the first, was the same.... It is clear that, beginning with the first day and continuing thereafter, there was established a cyclical succession of days and nights – periods of light and periods of darkness.

Such a cyclical light-dark arrangement clearly means that the earth was now rotating on its axis and that there was a source of light on one side of the earth corresponding to the sun, even though the sun was not yet made (Gen. 1:16). It is equally clear that the length of such days could only have been that of a normal solar day.

In the first chapter of Genesis, the termination of each day's work is noted by the formula: 'And the evening and the morning were the first [or "second," etc.] day.' Thus each 'day' had distinct boundaries and was one in a series of days, both of which criteria are never present in the Old Testament writings unless literal days are intended. The writer of Genesis was trying to guard in every way possible against any of his readers deriving the notion of nonliteral days from his record.[2]

Further confirmation of Genesis 'days' as plain, solar days is provided by the reason annexed to the fourth commandment ('Remember the Sabbath day to keep it holy') in Exodus 20:11: 'For in six days the LORD made heaven and earth, the sea, and all that in them is, and rested the seventh day: wherefore the LORD blessed the sabbath day, and hallowed it.'[3] The crucial point here is that God's creative work, followed by rest,

---

2. Henry M. Morris, *The Genesis Record*, 55, 56.

3. Eminent evangelical Old Testament scholar, Dr Gleason Archer, has argued against the implications of this passage as evidence for twenty-four hour days as follows: 'By no means does this demonstrate that 24-hour intervals were involved in the first six "days", any more than the eight-day celebration of the Feast of Tabernacles proves that the wilderness wanderings under Moses occupied only eight days' (in 'A Response to the Trustworthiness of Scripture in Areas Relating to Natural Science,' *Hermeneutics, Inerrancy, and the Bible*, ed. Earl. D. Radmacher and Robert D. Preus (Grand Rapids, MI.: Academic Books, 1986), 329. With all due respect, one must respond: 'Why not?' His comparison between the time analogies involved in weekly Sabbath observance and yearly Tabernacles observance does not prove the point (that the weekly pattern for mankind to follow bears no direct time relationship to creation week). For the same Pentateuch that makes clear that eight days' dwelling in tabernacles would call to mind the forty years of wilderness wandering, also makes clear that the weekly six days of work followed by one day of rest exactly parallels the divine activity during creation week. It is an illogical procedure to empty the seven days of creation of their temporal meaning because the Feast of Tabernacles lasted eight days each year rather than forty years each year! This kind of argument against *yom* meaning twenty-four hour days by an otherwise excellent scholar would seem to indicate the exegetical weakness of the case against creation days as anything other than ordinary solar day. It is not far from the category of exegetical desperation.

forms the pattern of wholesome life for His image bearer, mankind. Apparently, mankind is so important to the infinite God that He arranged His creative activity specifically to set the structure for human life. That must be a major reason why God created over six days rather than in a split-second (or a hundred billion years).

Such a conclusion is far from preposterous once we take seriously the incarnation of the eternal Son of God as a true human in order to redeem humanity. If the infinite God condescended to take on our flesh in the person of his Son, His having organized the time series of creation week around the interests of the human race (the future bride of the Son of God) is – though wonderful to contemplate – not inconsistent with such covenant love and condescension. Indeed, the incarnation of the Agent of creation within the finite time series (without Himself ceasing to be infinite) seems a much more amazing miracle than the creation itself. In the light of a God who accommodates Himself to the very dust of the earth, there should be no reluctance to realizing His accommodation of His awesome and infinite power to a specific flow of time. Time and dust are God's finite creatures and servants; not His masters.

There have been three other main arguments from the text of Scripture for interpreting days other than normal solar days. Two of them may be mentioned briefly, and the third requires more detailed consideration. First, there is the true observation that since the sun was placed in the heavens only on the fourth day, the first three days could not be called 'normal solar days' strictly speaking. Therefore, it is inferred, the first three days may have lasted for many ages. If the context of Genesis 1 gave us no more information to draw on, this observation would be of serious moment. But the very fact that, as we have seen, '... each "day" had distinct boundaries and was one in a series of days, both of which criteria are never present in the Old Testament writings unless literal days are intended'[4], constitutes an answer from within the immediate Genesis context to the question. Exodus 20:11 further supports the straight-forward understanding of all seven days as normal days of the same length.

A second argument for lengthening twenty-four days of creation week to long periods of time is based on the absence in the Genesis text of the concluding phrase 'and the evening and the morning were the *seventh* day' from the Sabbath. Dr Hugh Ross, for example, states that the absence of this formula 'strongly suggests that this day has (or had) not yet ended'.[5] He then draws this conclusion: 'From these passages

---

4. Morris, *op.cit.*, 56.
5. Ross, *op. cit.*, 49.

[Ps. 95 and Heb. 4] we gather that the seventh day of Genesis 1 and 2 represents a minimum of several thousand years and a maximum that is open ended (but finite). It seems reasonable to conclude then, given the parallelism of the Genesis creation account, that the first six days may also have been long periods of time.'[6]

To say the least, this places a great deal of theological weight on a very narrow and thin exegetical bridge! Is it not more concordant with the patent sense of the context of Genesis 2 (and Exod. 20) to infer that because the Sabbath differed in quality (though not – from anything we can learn out of the text itself – in quantity), a slightly different concluding formula was appended to indicate a qualitative difference (six days involved work; one day involved rest)? The formula employed to show the termination of that first Sabbath: 'And on the seventh day God ended His work which He had made; and He rested on the seventh day from all His work which He had made' (Gen.2:2) seems by the normal rules of biblical interpretation to intend an end just as definite as that of 'and the evening and the morning were the first day'. This is the more compelling as we recall the purpose of God's having taken six days to work and one to rest: to provide an orderly, life-sustaining pattern for His image-bearers. But if the absence of this conclusory formula means the divine pattern of Sabbath rest for mankind continued for thousands of years, how could humans have fulfilled God's command to work six days each week (Exod. 20:9)?

Such arguments for making creation week several thousand (or million) years long do seem contrived and artificial when one looks closely at the immediate text of Genesis and the wider biblical context. Exegetes have to engage in a sort of modern casuistry to make Genesis 'day' mean anything other than ordinary solar day. After grappling with similar evangelical reconstructions of creation week, one has to appreciate the exegetical honesty of the liberal, nineteenth-century Scottish Professor Marcus Dods (previously quoted), when he wrote that 'if, for example, the word "day" in these chapters does not mean a period of twenty-four hours, the interpretation of Scripture is hopeless'.[7]

Fourth-century church father, St. Ambrose of Milan, faithfully summarized the biblical usage of day in his *Hexameron:*

> The beginning of the day rests on God's word: 'Be light made, and light was made.' The end of day is the evening. Now, the succeeding day follows after the termination of night. The thought of God is

---

6. *Ibid.*
7. Marcus Dods, *op.cit.*, 4.

clear. First He called light 'day' and next He called darkness 'night'. In notable fashion has Scripture spoken of a 'day', not the 'first day'. Because a second, then a third day, and finally the remaining days were to follow, a 'first day' could have been mentioned, following in this way the natural order. But Scripture established a law that twenty-four hours, including both day and night, should be given the name of day only, as if one were to say the length of one day is twenty-four hours in extent.'[8]

The Framework Hypothesis

A third approach to avoiding the force of the normal sense of day during creation week has been called 'The Framework Hypothesis'. This theory evades the chronological sequence of six twenty-four hour days (and one day of rest) by a novel method: introducing a disjunction between 'literal' chronological order and 'literary' framework within the text of Scripture. Professor Arie Noordzij of the University of Utrecht in 1924 first developed this 'framework theory'. He noted a parallelism between the first three days and the second three days of creation, and drew unusual consequences from it.

E. J. Young paraphrases Noordzij's theory:

> That the six days do not have to do with the course of a natural process may be seen, thinks Noordzij, from the manner in which the writer groups his material. We are given two trios which exhibit a pronounced parallelism, all of which has the purpose of bringing to the fore the preeminent glory of man, who actually reaches his destiny in the sabbath, for the sabbath is the point in which the creative work of God culminates and to which it attains.... What is significant is not the concept 'day', taken by itself, but rather the concept of 'six plus one'.
>
> Inasmuch as the writer speaks of evenings and mornings previous to the heavenly bodies of the fourth day, continues Noordzij, it is clear that he uses the terms 'days' and 'nights' as a framework (kader). Such a division of time is a projection not given to show us the account of creation in its natural historical course, but, as elsewhere in the Holy Scriptures, to exhibit the majesty of the creation in the light of the great saving purpose of God.... Why then, we may ask, are the six days mentioned? The answer, according to Noordzij, is that they are only mentioned to prepare us for the seventh day.[9]

This approach has been widely popularized during the last thirty or so years through the writings of Professor Meredith Kline of

---

8. St. Ambrose in *The Fathers of the Church: St. Ambrose, Hexameron, Paradise, Cain and Abel*, John J. Savage, trans. (New York: Fathers of the Church, Inc., 1961), vol. 42, 42–43.
9. A summary of Arie Noordzij, *God's Word en der Eeuwen Getuigenis* by E. J. Young, 'The Days of Genesis', in *Westminster Theological Journal*, Vol. XXV, No. 1 (Nov. 1962), 3-5.

Westminster West Seminary, well-known Reformed Old Testament scholar and author of significant research on Covenant Theology. In his 'Commentary on Genesis' he states:

> The prologue's literary character [i.e. Genesis 1:1–2:3], however, limits its use for constructing scientific models, for its language is that of simple observation and a poetic quality, reflected in the strophic structure, permeates its style. Exegesis indicates that the scheme of the creation week itself is a poetic figure and that the several pictures of creation history are set within the six work-day frames not chronologically but topically...[10]

This 'Framework Hypothesis' with its underlying disjunction between 'literal' chronological meaning and 'literary' significance has been expanded in greater length by Professor Henri Blocher of the Evangelical Faculty of Theology of Vaux sur Seine in his *Révélation des Origines*.[11] Blocher opposes the 'literal' interpretation which assumes the plain chronological historicity of the work of the six days of creation week by means of a 'literary' understanding. Accordingly, 'the form of the week which is attributed to the creation is an artistic arrangement, a sober anthropomorphism which need not be taken literally.'[12] Thus one avoids a conflict with modern assumptions of a massively ancient universe, leaving room for evolutionary development.

One of the frequent components of the whole 'Framework' approach to avoiding a chronological reading of the seven days of Genesis 1 and 2 is the suggestion by Dr Kline that Genesis 2:5 ('no plants were in the earth ... for the LORD God had not caused it to rain upon the earth') implies the operation of providential processes during the creation, which could not fit into six twenty-four days. Therefore, he concludes, Genesis means to teach not a chronological sequence of creation, but '...a figurative framework [in which] the data of creation history have been arranged according to other than strictly chronological considerations'.[13]

How, then, is this 'Framework Hypothesis', with the dichotomy underlying it, to be evaluated?[14] One would not lightly disagree with such distinguished evangelical Christian scholars were not

---

10. Meredith Kline, 'Commentary on Genesis' in *The New Bible Commentary Revised*, Edited by D. Guthrie *et al*. (Wm. B. Eerdmans Publishing Co.: Grand Rapids, Mich., 1971), 81, 82.
11. Henri Blocher, *Révélation des origines* (Presses Bibliques Universitaires: Lausanne, 1979 and 1988). English translation: *In the Beginning* (Inter-Varsity Press: Downers Grove, Ill., 1984).
12. Blocher, *op.cit.*, 43.
13. Meredith Kline, 'Because It Had Not Rained' in *The Westminster Theological Journal*, Vol. XIX, 154.
14. Precise details and evaluation of this 'evidence' for a non-chronological reading of the six creation days are provided in *Technical and Bibliographical Notes* at the end of this chapter.

the underlying issue of such surpassing importance to all biblical interpretation. Much more is at stake here than the admittedly complex question of how old the earth is. Even if one wished to opt for an ancient cosmos, the mode they have chosen to achieve it is too high a price to pay in terms of the truth claims of the entire biblical text. For, in the interests of this theory, they have introduced a potentially disastrous dichotomy between literary form and historical, chronological viability in interpreting biblical texts. It is naive to suppose that such a far-reaching hermeneutical dualism could be stopped at the end of the second chapter of Genesis, and would not be employed in other texts that run contrary to current naturalistic assumptions.

No one, to the best of my knowledge, has more incisively penetrated the heart of this matter than Jean-Marc Berthoud, Reformed scholar of Lausanne in Switzerland. In an interchange of letters with Professor Henri Blocher (which has since been published), Berthoud uncovers the primary assumption by which the framework theory functions.[15] He discusses Blocher's criticism of a 'literal' (or 'literalist') interpretation of the Bible, and his replacement of it by a 'literary' approach.[16]

In response to this dualism between literary form and historical reality, Berthoud replies: '... the literalist-literary opposition that one sees throughout your book is a scheme inadequate to biblical realities.... You begin with the unspoken presupposition that what you term *literary refinement and literal reading* are basically mutually exclusive.'[17] Berthoud rightly suggests that this axiomatic disjunction between literary form and literal meaning is a philosophical position, that does not come from the Bible itself.

> What difficulty would it be for [the Author of the Universe] to cause the most complex, refined literary form to coincide with the very way in which He Himself created all things in six days? Artistic form is in no sense opposed to an actual relation of facts, especially since the Author of the account is none less than the actual Creator of the facts which are described in that account.... Thus it is your constant opposition of a literary interpretation to a literal interpretation that I question. For the real question is not at all prose as opposed to poetry, literary interpretation as opposed to literal interpretation, but rather true interpretation as opposed to false interpretation. The real opposition is between true literary style and false literary style, true literal style and false literal style.[18]

15. In the periodical *Positions Créationnistes*, No. 12, May 1990, published by 'Comité de l'Association Création Bible et Science' (Case postale 4, CH 1001 Lausanne, Switzerland).
16. *Ibid.*, 5 ff.
17. *Ibid.*, 5, 6. (My translation of the original French in all citations).
18. *Ibid.*, 7, 8.

James B. Jordan has similarly addressed this unnecessary dichotomy:

> The 'framework hypothesis' ... [which] argues that the six days are not spans of time, but only a literary convention for presenting a six-fold creation. The fundamental problem with this view is that it needlessly opposes a theological interpretation to a literal one ... the theological dimension of creation in six days lies precisely in its being a temporal sequence ... God had no reason to make the world in six days, except as a pattern for His image, man, to follow. Where the Bible later uses a three-day or six-day, or seven-day pattern theologically, it is always in terms of the flow of time from a beginning to an end. The framework hypothesis Platonizes the time sequence into a mere set of ideas. In its attempt to be theological, the 'framework hypothesis' misses the whole theological point.[19]

Berthoud believes that the underlying philosophy of this disjunction between 'literary' and 'literal' (or with Jordan, 'theological' and 'literal') is a sort of revived nominalism, such as was practiced by the late Medieval scholar, William of Occam. Commenting on the type of exegesis of which Blocher's writing is an example, Berthoud states: 'What is taking place here is in fact nominalist exegesis.... For Occam, the form or the name [whence "nominalism"] has no real or true relation to the thing named or signified. Similarly here [in the "Framework Hypothesis"] literary form has no actual relation to the temporal reality of creation.'[20]

Occam's splitting apart of words or terms in the mind from external realities is a matter of no small import in the way one looks at the world and in the way one interprets literary texts (whether ancient or modern). Commenting on Occam's Second Distinction in the First Book of his *Commentaries on the Four Books of (Lombard's) Sentences* (Question VI, E), Paul Vignaux notes that according to this classical nominalist procedure, 'It is not the [actual] things that we know, but propositions about things.... The content of thought matters little; we are presented here with a purely formal point of view.... The sort of logic which is the starting point of nominalism makes from [one's mental concept] a mere word; the knowing process does not result in a true grasping of external content by the mind, but merely gives a word about a thing which remains exterior to it, and thus thought plays the role of a kind of algebra.'[21]

---

19. James B. Jordan, *Through New Eyes: Developing a Biblical View of the World* (Wolgemuth & Hyatt: Brentwood, TN, 1988), 11.

20. *Ibid.*, 7.

21. Paul Vignaux, 'Nominalisme', an article in *Dictionnaire de Théologie Catholique*, Tome 13, Première Partie, A Vacant et al., eds. (Paris: Librarie Letourzey et Ane, 1936), 743.

Ultimately, this perspective leaves us with nothing but a collection of words. Vignaux asks the right question: 'What do we know? Propositions, composed of terms, which are signs of things.'[22] One could say then that true, external relations between various realities are replaced by relations between words (in a sort of verbal algebra, as Vignaux suggests). Statements of Occam in Distinction XXX of Book I of his *Commentaries on the Sentences* (Question 1, S) indicate that relations spoken of in human words '... have no proper reality outside the mind'.[23]

Nominalism of course is an evasion of 'realism' (which rests on the assumption of a real relation between literary text and historical facts, events and persons pointed to by that text).[24] As Berthoud writes elsewhere, 'In the aesthetics of the Bible (and in the great literature based upon it), form is married to truth, and truth always commands form.'[25] Concerning this sort of nominalist evasion of reality (or 'the truth of being'), T. F. Torrance crisply states in his *Theological Science*:

> The problem posed here is whether truth is primarily concerned with the reference of statements to the reality of things beyond them, or whether it is concerned rather with the logico-syntactical relations of statements to one another and therefore to be discerned in ideological complexes. A double error appears to lurk here: (a) the reduction of truth to ideas, which rests on the mistaken notion that we can express in ideas how ideas are related to being; (b) the reduction of truth to statements, which rests on the mistaken notion that we can state in statements how statements are related to what is stated. The one implies the 'conversion' of universals into abstract entities, and the other implies that in the last resort science is about propositions.

---

22. *Ibid.*, 747.

23. *Ibid.*

24. Thomas F. Torrance has suggested that nominalism gains influence when the culture operates with a damaged relation between existence and language. Discussing the realist use of symbolic systems in science, Torrance states: 'Everything goes wrong, however, if the formal language does not prove to be an appropriate system of representation, or if the relation between the symbols we employ and the realities upon which they are meant to bear is damaged, for then the symbolic systems break loose from the objective control of reality and bear upon it only in an indirect, ambiguous, and misleading way' (*Reality and Evangelical Theology*, 62). Nominalism so focuses on the form of the words themselves (which are held to represent only individual phenomena, not universal realities or actual classes) that their reference to the reality above them can only be indirect. But with realism, 'Signs or words fulfill their semantic function properly when we attend away from them to the realities they signify or intend. Through their correlation with those realities they cease to be objects of attention in themselves but serve as transparent media through which those realities show themselves' (*Ibid.*, 96). See his discussion of realism (as opposed to nominalism and idealism) in Chapter 2 of *Reality and Evangelical Theology*, and Chapter 10 ('Theological Realism') of *The Philosophical Frontiers of Christian Theology*, eds. B. Hebblethwaite and S. Sutherland (Cambridge University Press: Cambridge, 1982).

25. From the periodical, *Positions Créationistes*, No. 11, February 1990.

This represents a mutation from intuitive knowledge of the real to abstractive knowledge either of the ideal or the symbolic, and in both introduces a lapse from the truth of being.[26]

As far as realism and the dualist interpretation which distinguishes between 'literal' and 'literary' in the early chapters of Genesis are concerned, we must not forget that any philosophical assumption, especially when it controls exegesis, must be questioned in light of the Scriptures. Do the Scriptures themselves operate on the basis of this sort of assumption, or do they function in terms of a different presupposition? Professor Meredith Kline is certainly right when, after proposing his framework theory, he states: 'In distinguishing simple description and poetic figure from what is definitively conceptual the only ultimate guide, here, as always, is comparison with the rest of Scripture.'[27]

Elsewhere in Scripture, elegant literary form (such as the strophic or hymnic structure of Philippians 2:5–11, for example) does not appear to vacate the literal, historical significance of the great stages in the humiliation and exaltation of Christ. If there is no dichotomy there between literary form and historical, chronological facts, why should there be in Genesis 1 and 2? Is it not something from outside Scripture that introduces such a dichotomy, rather than internal hermeneutical considerations?

Moreover, the way the New Testament mentions Genesis 1–11 not only fails to suggest any dichotomy between the literary form of those chapters and their literal, chronological and historical veracity, it definitively precludes such procedure. The *Bibliographical and Technical Notes* of this chapter surveys this matter.

This chapter has suggested that it must be some factor from outside the Scripture itself that has caused distinguished Christian exegetes to bring in such a tortured mode of interpretation of texts, which though rich in literary form, have always been understood to furnish a clear reference to historical, chronological realities. Dr Hugh Ross is clear about what this outside factor is.

> I see the community of scientists, including astronomers and astro-physicists, as an *ethnos*. God calls us to reach out to them as He does to every other group on the planet. And though He warns that the childlike simplicity of trusting in Jesus will be a stumbling block for many, we have unwittingly placed another barrier in their path: the dogma of a few-thousand-years-old earth. I cannot imagine a notion more offensive to this group...[28]

---

26. Thomas F. Torrance, *Theological Science* (London: Oxford University Press, 1969), 142, 143.
27. Kline, *op. cit.*, 82.
28. Ross, *op.cit.*, 71, 72.

In similar fashion, Dr Blocher speaks of those who question received naturalistic opinions of ancient origins with their accompanying thesis of evolutionary development as the intellectual equivalent of kamikaze pilots crashing into the academic world.[29] Hence, to avoid offense to 'the community of scientists' and to keep out of the ranks of kamikaze volunteers, conservative Christian writers have imported an alien philosophical procedure into the interpretation of Scripture; an unnecessary dichotomy between literary form and historical truth.

It would be wrong not to commend such scholars for their sincere Christian desire to reach unconverted intellectuals with the minimum of offense. One must also recognize that they have no intention to lessen the truth claims of Scripture.[30] But, it would seem that when their approach is weighed in the balances by comparing how Scripture uses Scripture, it is 'found wanting'. While appreciating the genuine quality of their faith and efforts to reach the lost, one cannot follow them for two good reasons. First, by importing an alien interpretative procedure into Scripture (the dichotomy between form and fact), they unwittingly obscure the pure light God's Word shines into our understanding of space/time reality as well as of the transcendent realm controlling it. And secondly, they do a severe disservice to naturalistic science, precisely because such an obscuring of the full light of divine truth fails to call those in darkness to a full-fledged, repentant restructuring of their whole intellectual world at the deepest level.[31]

This volume is written in the belief that there is a better way: one based on a realistic (not nominalistic) reading of Scripture, and one prepared to raise both presuppositional and empirical questions about widely received (though less so than formerly), naturalistic theories of origins. Our next chapter on the age of the universe is a step in that direction.

---

29. Blocher, *op. cit.*, 17, 18.
30. The evangelical proponents of the Framework Hypothesis would never go so far as some of the classical nominalists in disconnecting the meaning of the text from external reality. That is not their intention, and in that sense they are certainly not 'nominalists'. My only concern is to suggest that their evacuation of the clear temporal significance of the six days unwittingly opens the door, epistemologically and hermeneutically, to this kind of abuse, if carried to its logical conclusion.
31. Abraham Kuyper devoted Chapter II of *Principles of Sacred Theology* to the subject 'Science Impaired by Sin'.

TECHNICAL AND BIBLIOGRAPHICAL NOTES FOR CHAPTER SIX

Does Genesis 2:5 Imply a Non-Chronological Reading of Creation Week?

Professor Kline in his article 'Because It Had Not Rained' discusses the implications of Genesis 2:5: 'And every plant of the field before it was in the earth, and every herb of the field before it grew: for the LORD God had not caused it to rain upon the earth, and there was not a man to till the ground.'

He argues that this observation of Moses of the dependence of plants on water (whether by 'rain' or irrigation by man) implies that '... works of providence ... were part of the divine government of the world in so far as that world was already existent before each new creative act occurred .... If the arrangement of Genesis 2 were not topical it would contradict the teaching of Genesis 1 (not to mention that of natural revelation) that vegetation preceded man on the earth... Embedded in Genesis 2:5ff. is the principle that the *modus operandi* of the divine providence was the same during the creation period as that of ordinary providence at the present time.'[32]

Kline then argues that the Genesis 2:5 allusion to the working of God's normal providence within the created order precludes its having taken place within six twenty-four hour days:

> In contradiction to Genesis 2:5, the twenty-four-hour day theory must presuppose that God employed other than the ordinary secondary means in executing his works of providence. To take just one example, it was the work of the 'third day' that the waters should be gathered together into seas and that the dry land should appear, and be covered with vegetation (Gen. 1:9-13). All this according to the theory in question transpired within twenty-four hours. But continents just emerged from under the seas do not become thirsty land as fast as that by the ordinary process of evaporation. And yet according to the principle revealed in Genesis 2:5 the process of evaporation in operation at that time was the ordinary one.
>
> The results, indeed, approach the ludicrous when it is attempted to synchronize Genesis 2:5 with Genesis 1 interpreted in terms of a week of twenty-four-hour days. On that interpretation, vegetation was created on what we may call 'Tuesday'. Therefore, the vegetationless situation described in Genesis 2:5 cannot be located later than 'Tuesday' morning. Neither can it be located earlier than that for Genesis 2:5 assumes the existence of dry land which does not appear until the 'third day'.... Hence the twenty-four-hour theorist must think

---

32. Kline, *art. cit.*, 147, 149, 151.

of the Almighty as hesitant to put in the plants on 'Tuesday' morning because it would not rain until later in the day![33]

In sum, Professor Kline holds that 'Genesis 2:5 assigns natural reasons for the absence of vegetation' and that 'having been confronted with the evidence of ordinary providential procedure' one is 'bound to reject the rigidly chronological interpretations of Genesis 1 for the reason that they necessarily presuppose radically different providential operations for the creation period. If Genesis 2:5 obviates certain traditional interpretations of Genesis 1, by the same token it validates the not so traditional interpretation which regards the chronological framework of Genesis 1 as a figurative representation of the time span of creation and judges that within that figurative framework the data of creation history have been arranged according to other than strictly chronological considerations.'[34]

A Response

A more careful look at the purposes for which Genesis 1 and Genesis 2 were written and their consequent relationship will, perhaps, remove the apparent contradiction between the work of the third day in Genesis 1 and the observation of Genesis 2 concerning the status of plants and water in the created order. And this should remove the grounds for the theory that the six days of creation are to be interpreted other than chronologically.

First, we must note that within the context of the early chapters of Genesis itself, there is no indication that two different stories of creation have been cobbled together (one in the first chapter and the other in the second chapter), leaving various inconsistencies, so that either (with the liberals) one must posit two different and conflicting documentary sources (i.e. 'P' and 'J'), or (with many evangelicals) one must take Chapter One as a literary framework, rather than a serious chronological sequence. Professor Umberto Cassuto wisely reminds us, 'who are accustomed to the Hellenic process of thought' to keep in mind 'the Semitic way of thinking'.[35]

Cassuto delineates the Hebraic way of writing history in this principle: 'first state the general proposition and then specify the particulars.'[36] The divergencies between the accounts in Genesis 1 and 2 are explained if one realizes that 'In accordance with the prevailing method, a general statement is followed here [in Genesis 2:4ff.] by a

33. *Ibid.*, 151, 152.
34. *Ibid.*, 153, 154.
35. Umberto Cassuto, *A Commentary on the Book of Genesis: Part I From Adam to Noah*, Translated by Israel Abrahams (Jerusalem: The Magnes Press, The Hebrew University, 1961), 91.
36. *Ibid.*, 20.

detailed description.'[37] That is to say, Genesis 1 alone constitutes a cosmogony, whereas Genesis 2:4ff. isolates certain details of interest for the story of mankind and the entrance of evil, and then expands on their significance.

> When we read the Torah as we have it, as a continuous narrative, we find no discrepancy between the earlier statement that at first the world was a mass of water, and what we are told about the dry land at the beginning of the present section. Relying on the account of the first stages of creation above, our section does not recapitulate the story; it depicts simply the position as it was at the *closing phase* of creation when man alone was wanting. An incongruity presents itself only if we separate the conjoined passages and treat our section as an independent narrative; then, of course we need to find in it the beginning of the creation story. The contradiction appears, therefore, only when we regard as proven what the contradiction is supposed to prove; a clear example of begging the question! The theory that the two sections are not a unity does not help us to resolve the inherent problem of the text but creates instead an otherwise non-existent problem.[38]

In place of the Hellenic kind of thinking which invents problems by assuming two conflicting accounts, Cassuto shows that the 'second account' is not another cosmogony at all. Genesis 2:4 is, as we saw from E. J. Young, not a 'subscription' to Genesis 1, but a 'superscription'; a pointer to a different logical section. As Cassuto states, Genesis 2:4 is 'a brief, general outline ... an account of the making of *one of the creatures* of the material world, and the second at length and in detail, as the story of the creation of the *central being* of the moral world... such a repetition was consonant with the stylistic principle of presenting first a general statement and thereafter the detailed elaboration, which is commonly found not only in Biblical literature but also in the literary works of the rest of the ancient East.'[39] Cassuto quotes in this regard, *The Midrash of R. Eliezer b. R. Jose the Galilean*, Enelow's edition, p. 24 (cf. Rashi on ii 8): 'The listener may think that this is another narrative, whereas it is only the elaboration of the first.'[40]

    With this understanding of Genesis 2:4 ff. in view, the statement in Genesis 2:5 ('Now no thorns of the field were yet in the earth and no grain of the field had yet sprung up, for the LORD God had not caused it to rain upon the earth, and there was no man to till the ground') harmonizes perfectly with the plain, chronological reading of the

---

37. *Ibid.*, 89.
38. *Ibid.*, 90.
39. *Ibid.*, 91.
40. *Ibid.*, 92.

six days' work of creation in Genesis 1. It does not provide another explanation of creation week. Rather, it focuses on one aspect of the already created order and expands the details relative to it. Concerning the first clause of verse 5 ('Now no thorns of the field were yet in the earth and no grain'), Cassuto explains:

> The narrative begins with a description of the conditions existing prior to the creation of man. There was no *siah* of the field yet, and the *'esebh* of the field had not yet sprung up; the word *terem* means: 'not yet'...
>
> What is meant by the *siah of the field* and *the 'esebh of the field* mentioned here? Modern commentators usually consider the terms to connote the *vegetable kingdom as a whole*; thence it follows that our section contradicts the preceding chapter, according to which vegetation came into being on the third day.... All interpretations of this kind introduce something into the text that is not there, in order to create the inconsistency. When the verse declares that these species were missing, the meaning is simply that *these* kinds were wanting, but *no others*. If we wish to understand the significance of the *siah of the field* and the *'esebh of the field* in the context of our narrative, we must take a glance at the end of the story. It is stated there, in the words addressed by the Lord God to Adam after he had sinned: THORNS AND THISTLES *it shall bring forth to you; and you shall eat the 'esebh of the field* (iii 18). The words *'esebh of the field* are identical with the expression in our verse; whilst *thorns and thistles*, which are synonymous with the *siah of the field*, are a particularization of the general concept conveyed by the latter (cf. *one of the sihim*, in Gen. xxi 15). These species did not exist, or were not found in the form known to us, until after Adam's transgression, and it was in consequence of his fall that they came into the world or received their present form. Man, who was no longer able to enjoy the fruits of the garden of Eden, was compelled *to till the ground* (iii 23 – the same phrase as in our verse here) in order to *eat bread*; and the clause quoted above, *and you shall eat the 'esebh of the field* (iii 18), corresponds to the words immediately following: *In the sweat of your face* YOU SHALL EAT BREAD (iii 19). Thus the term *'esebh of the field* comprises wheat and barley and the other kinds of grain from which *bread* is made; and it is obvious that fields of wheat and barley and the like did not exist in the world until man began *to till the ground*. In the areas, however, that were not tilled, the earth brought forth of its own accord, as a punishment to man, *thorns and thistles* – that *siah of the field* that we see growing to this day in the Land of Israel *after the rains*.... Here we must point out that the two reasons given in our verse [for the absence of thorns and grain] follow the same order as the two preceding clauses that they come to explain: no thorns of the field were yet in the earth, because the Lord God *had not caused it to rain* upon the earth, and the grain of the field had not yet sprung up, because *there was no man to till the ground*....
>
> Scripture stressed again and again that the world of vegetation, as it was formed on the third day, was composed of those trees and herbs

that naturally reproduce themselves by *seed* alone. Those plants that needed something else, in addition to seed, were excluded: to this category belonged, on the one hand, all species of corn, which, even though isolated specimens might have existed here and there from the very beginning, were not found in the form of fields of grain until man began to till the ground; and on the other hand, thorns and thistles, or *siah* of the field, whose seeds are unable to propagate and grow fresh plants until it rains. After man's fall and expulsion from the garden of Eden, when he was compelled to till the ground and the rains began to come down, there spread through the earth thorns and thistles and fields of wheat – the *siah of the field* and the *'esebh of the field*.[41]

Henri Blocher's *Révélation des origines* follows Kline in abandoning the chronological reading of Genesis 1 in favor of 'the framework hypothesis' as the best way to explain Genesis 2:5. In response to Blocher, Dr Serge Rambert offers an exegesis of Genesis 2:5 somewhat similar to that of Cassuto (but independent of it), to which readers of French are referred.[42]

Did Augustine hold to an early form of the Framework Hypothesis?

Even a superficial reading of St. Augustine's works on the six days of creation will show that his understanding of 'day' is different from, for instance, his mentor, St. Ambrose of Milan, who holds day to mean a twenty-four hour period pure and simple.[43] Some have suggested that therefore Augustine might be placed in the category of Framework Hypothesists.[44] The evidence of what Augustine actually wrote, however, does not seem to justify his inclusion into the 'day-age' school (or its more sophisticated variant in the Framework Hypothesis).

In *The Literal Meaning of Genesis*, Augustine deals particularly with the difficulty of understanding the physical meaning of 'let there be light' and the succession of day and night.[45] He seems especially concerned to make sense of two related facts, which at first glance would seem contradictory: first, when God speaks physical reality into existence, it would apparently occur within a split second of time, and yet according to the Genesis text, it takes six days for the whole work to be performed.

---

41. *Ibid.*, 100, 101, 102.
42. *Positions Créationnistes* No.11, Fevrier 1990, *Révélation des Origines: Une Réponse* (A.C.B.S. Case postale no. 4, CH 1001 Lausanne), 5, 6.
43. Ambrose, *op. cit.*, 42, 43.
44. See Hugh Ross, *Creation and Time*, 45.
45. See particularly Book One, Chapters 9 -12 ; Book Four, Chapters 14-35, and Book Five, Chapters 1-23 of Augustine, *The Literal Meaning of Genesis*.

He suggests as a possible solution the symbolic significance of the 'perfect number' six ('perfect' because it is the sum of its 'aliquot' parts – that is, one can divide the number into parts, and then add them up without remainder[1+2+3=6].[46] This means that somehow the six days' work of creation expresses God's perfect way of seeing and projecting reality in a mode that His creatures (especially the angels) can contemplate. In Book Four, he writes:

> The more likely explanation, therefore, is this: these seven days of our time, although like the seven days of creation in name and in numbering, follow one another in succession and mark off the division of time, but those first six days occurred in a form unfamiliar to us as intrinsic principles within things created. Hence evening and morning, like light and darkness, that is, day and night, did not produce the changes that they do for us with the motion of the sun. This we are certainly forced to admit with regard to the first three days, which are recorded and numbered before the creation of the heavenly bodies.[47]

It seems that Augustine holds that everything was actually created in one day (or perhaps a split second of it): 'And in this way we must picture the world, when God made all things together which were made in it and with it when day was made,'[48] and 'Thus, in all the days of creation there is one day, and it is not to be taken in the sense of our day...'[49] But at the same time he definitely maintains a six-fold repetition of the one creative day:

> In this narrative of creation Holy Scripture has said of the Creator that He completed His works in six days; and elsewhere, without contradicting this, it has been written of the same Creator that He created all things together. It follows, therefore, that He, who created all things together, simultaneously created these six days, or seven, or rather the one day six or seven times repeated.[50]

Where all of this leads Augustine will be even more surprising to us than his speculation on the significance of the 'alioquot parts' of the number six. He then suggests that the primary meaning of the coming of light and the creation of all on one day, with its sixfold repetition in the physical universe in the days following, relates to the knowledge the angels have of God's perfect work.[51]

---

46. See 'Notes' of Augustine, *The Literal Meaning of Genesis*, John H. Taylor, Trans., p. 247, n. 3.
47. *Ibid.*, Book Four, Chapter 18, 125.
48. *Ibid.*, Book Five, Chapter 23, 175.
49. *Ibid.*, Book Four, Chapter 26, 134.
50. *Ibid.*, Book Four, Chapter 33, 142.
51. See especially Chapters 22 to 35 of Book Four, *Ibid.* for what he means by knowledge the angels have of light and created reality in terms of one and six.

John H. Taylor's summary of the entire position of Augustine on this complex question seems accurate:

> The days of creation, he suggests, are not periods of time but rather categories in which creatures are arranged by the author for didactic reasons to describe all the works of creation, which in reality were created simultaneously. Light is not the visible light of this world but the illumination of intellectual creatures (the angels). Morning refers to the angels' knowledge of creatures which they enjoy in the vision of God; evening refers to the angels' knowledge of creatures as they exist in their own created natures.[52]

Hence, whatever else Augustine may have understood by 'day', he did *not* take it to mean (as Taylor reminds us above) a long period of time (which would be essential for the Framework Hypothesis). Indeed, elsewhere (in *The City of God*) he clearly indicates an understanding of the world's duration from Adam to the Flood as consisting of 2,262 years.[53]

Augustine's real concern appears to be not how long creation took, but rather the desire to think through the relationship of two very different approaches to reality: on the one hand the Neo-Platonic concept of pure intelligences (e.g. angels) contemplating absolute essences or forms (e.g. as these are manifested in things that appear during the six days), and on the other hand the Hebraic concept of the sudden but orderly divine creation of the various 'kinds' out of nothing. His peculiar approach to the six days is evidently the result of his attempt to combine these two disparate philosophies, in a way that is, in his view at least, 'literally' faithful to the teachings of Genesis 1 and 2. It would be anachronistic to assume that he wishes to reinterpret 'day' in order to make it ages long so that gradual development would have time to take place. If anything, he shortens the duration of actual creation time (to one day or even an instant), rather than lengthening it to ages.[54]

---

52. *Ibid.*, 9
53. Augustine, *City of God*, Book 15, Ch. 20.
54. Without discussing the details of the question here, we may note that attempts to enlist Augustine into the ranks of theistic evolutionists are as anachronistic as the attempts to make him maintain the Framework Hypothesis. Again, given his background in Neoplatonism, Augustine tries to interrelate the Platonic theory of 'seminal causes' (or rational forms) with Hebraic created 'kinds'. In relating these two diverse concepts, Augustine emphasizes the biblical idea of instantaneous creation of 'fully seeded' various 'kinds' or species (or 'seminal causes'). He seems to leave no room for age-long evolutionary development from one kind or seminal cause to another. What he does is leave room for the normal growth of plants and other living things (or seminal causes) 'after their kinds'. He writes in *The Literal Meaning of Genesis*, Book Four, Chapter 33: 'For through Wisdom all things were made, and the motion we now see in creatures, measured by the lapse of time, as each

The New Testament Assumes the Chronological, Historical Veracity of Chapters 1 and 2 of Genesis

Those who accept the authority of the New Testament will consider the usage its twenty-seven books make of Genesis 1–11 to be of paramount importance for a correct interpretation of the primal text. A careful study of the scattered allusions of the New Testament to the first eleven chapters of Holy Scripture will reveal no trace of any sort of 'Framework Hypothesis' among the apostolic writers. Instead, with one accord they clearly assume a plain, historical/chronological reading of these early texts; a 'literal' rather than 'literary' reading, so to speak.

Hubert Thomas has collated a good deal of relevant evidence in his booklet *Mentions de la création (Ge. 1–11) dans le Nouveau Testament*.[55] His introduction states:

> In effect three main points are demonstrated by reading the list we provide. These three points confirm that the New Testament can in no case whatsoever be appealed to in order to sustain any sort of evolutionary theory. First, without exception, references to creation and especially the citations of Genesis 1 to 11 point to historical events. It is no different than the historical death of the Lord Jesus Christ on Golgotha. As far as the New Testament is concerned, creation ex-nihilo and the creation of Adam and Eve, Cain and Abel, Noah and the Flood, there is no legend and no parable; all deal with persons and events of historical and universal significance.
>
> Second, without exception creation is always mentioned as a unique event which took place at a particular moment in past time. Creation took place; it was accomplished. Events occurred which corrupted the world, and now it awaits a new creation which will take place in the future at a given moment.
>
> Third, the details and recitations of creation given in Genesis 1 to 3 are considered to be literally true, historical and also of surpassing importance. The New Testament doctrine based upon these citations would be without any validity and even erroneous if the primeval events were not historically true. For instance: consider the entry of sin

---

one fulfills its proper function, comes to creatures from those causal reasons implanted in them, which God scattered as seeds at the moment of creation when *He spoke and they were made, He commanded and they were created.* Creation, therefore, did not take place slowly in order that a slow development might be implanted in those things that are slow by nature; nor were the ages established at the plodding pace at which they now pass. Time brings about the development of these creatures according to the laws of their numbers, but there was no passage of time when they received these laws at creation' (*op. cit.*, 141, 142). This subject is carefully discussed in Henry Woods, *Augustine and Evolution: A Study in the Saint's De Genesi ad litteram* (New York, 1924).

55. Hubert Thomas, *Mentions de la Création (Ge. 1–11) dans le nouveau Téstament* (Association Création, Bible et Science: Lausanne, 1993).

into the world. If Adam were not the head of the whole human race, then Jesus Christ [the last Adam] is not the head of the new creation.[56]

Thomas then lists six categories of references to Genesis 1–11 in the New Testament:

1. The Creator and Creation of the World

Matthew 13:35: 'I will utter things which have been kept secret from the foundation of the world.'

Mark 13:19: 'For in those days shall be affliction, such as was not from the beginning of the creation which God created unto this time, neither shall be.'

John 1:3: 'All things were made by him; and without him was not any thing made that was made.'

Acts 4:24: '...Lord, thou art God, which hast made heaven and earth, and the sea and all that in them is:'

Acts 14:15: '...that ye should turn from these vanities unto the living God, which made heaven and earth, and the sea, and all things that are therein:'

Romans 1:20: 'For the invisible things of him from the creation of the world are clearly seen, being understood by the things that are made, even his eternal power and Godhead; so that they are without excuse:'

2 Corinthians 4:6: 'For God, who commanded the light to shine out of darkness, hath shined in our hearts, to give the light of the knowledge of the glory of God in the face of Jesus Christ.'

Colossians 1:16: 'For by him were all things created that are in heaven and that are in earth, visible and invisible, whether they be thrones or dominions or principalities or powers: all things were created by him and for him:'

Hebrews 1:10: 'And thou, Lord, in the beginning hast laid the foundation of the earth; and the heavens are the works of thine hands:'

Hebrews 11:3: 'Through faith we understand that the worlds were framed by the word of God; so that those things which are seen were not made of things which do appear.'

2. Creation of man and woman

Matthew 19:4-6: 'And he answered and said unto them, Have ye not read that he which made them at the beginning made them male and female...'

Mark 10:6: (the same)

---

56. No pagination. My translation from the French.

Matthew 19:8: 'He saith unto them, Moses because of the hardness of your hearts, suffered you to put away your wives: but from the beginning it was not so.'

Acts 17:26: 'And hath made of one blood all nations of men for to dwell on all the face of the earth, and hath determined the times before appointed, and the bounds of their habitation...'

1 Corinthians 6:16: 'What! Know ye not that he which is joined to an harlot is one body? for two, saith he, shall be one flesh.'

1 Corinthians 11:8-9: 'For the man is not of the woman; but the woman of the man. Neither was the man created for the woman; but the woman for the man.'

Ephesians 5:31: 'For this cause shall a man leave his father and mother, and shall be joined unto his wife, and they two shall be one flesh.'

1 Timothy 2:13, 14: 'For Adam was first formed, then Eve. And Adam was not deceived, but the woman being deceived was in the transgression.'

Revelation 2:7: '...To him that overcometh will I give to eat of the tree of life, which is in the midst of the paradise of God.'

Revelation 22:2 and 14: 'the tree of life...'

3. The Fall

Romans 5:12: 'Wherefore, as by one man sin entered into the world, and death by sin; and so death passed upon all men, for that all have sinned...'

Romans 5:14: 'Nevertheless death reigned from Adam to Moses, even over them that had not sinned after the similitude of Adam's transgression, who is the figure of him that was to come.'

Romans 5:17: 'For if by one man's offense death reigned by one: much more they which receive abundance of grace and of the gift of righteousness shall reign in life by one, Jesus Christ.'

Romans 5:19: 'For as by one man's disobedience many were made sinners; so by the obedience of one shall many be made righteous.'

Romans 8:19-20: 'For the earnest expectation of the creature waiteth for the manifestation of the sons of God. For the creature was made subject to vanity, not willingly, but by reason of him who hath subjected the same in hope.'

1 Corinthians 15:21-22: 'For since by man came death, by man came also the resurrection of the dead. For as in Adam all die, even so in Christ shall all be made alive.'

2 Corinthians 11:3: 'But I fear, lest by any means, as the serpent beguiled Eve through his subtilty, so your minds should be corrupted from the simplicity that is in Christ.'

Revelation 20:2: '... that old serpent, which is the devil, and Satan...'

4. The Patriarchs

Matthew 23:35: 'That upon you may come all the righteous blood shed upon the earth, from the blood of righteous Abel unto the blood of Zacharias, son of Barachias...'

Luke 11:52: (same)

Luke 3:34-38: 'Which was the son of Jacob, which was the son of Isaac, which was the son of Abraham ... Shem which was the son of Noah ... son of Enoch ... son of Seth ... son of Adam, which was the son of God.'

Hebrews 11:4-7: 'By faith Abel offered unto God a more excellent sacrifice than Cain .... By faith Enoch was translated that he should not see death .... By faith Noah, being warned of God of things not seen as yet, moved with fear, prepared an ark to the saving of his house .... By faith Abraham, when he was called to go out ...'

Hebrews 11:23: 'By faith Moses, when he was born...'

Hebrews 12:24: 'And to Jesus the Mediator of the new covenant, and to the blood of sprinkling, that speaketh better things than that of Abel.'

1 John 3:12: 'Not as Cain, who was of that wicked one, and slew his brother...'

Jude 11: 'Woe unto them! for they have gone in the way of Cain, and ran greedily after the error of Balaam for reward, and perished in the gainsaying of Core.'

Jude 14: 'And Enoch also, the seventh from Adam, prophesied of these, saying, Behold, the Lord cometh with ten thousand of his saints...'

5. The Flood

Matthew 24:37: 'But as the days were, so shall also the coming of the Son of man be.'

Luke 17:26: 'And as it was in the days of Noah, so shall it be also in the days of the Son of man.'

1 Peter 3:20: ' ... in the days of Noah, while the ark was a preparing, wherein few, that is, eight souls were saved by water.'

2 Peter 2:5: 'And spared not the old world, but saved Noah, the eighth person, a preacher of righteousness, bringing in the flood upon the world of the ungodly...'

2 Peter 3:5-6: 'For this they willingly are ignorant of, that by the word of God the heavens were of old, and the earth standing out of the water and in the water...'

6. Allusions to Creation

Ephesians 3:9: '...the mystery, which from the beginning of the world hath been hid in God, who created all things by Jesus Christ...'

James 3:9: 'Therewith bless we God, even the Father: and therewith curse we men, which are made after the similitude of God.'

Revelation 3:14: '...These things saith the Amen, the faithful and true Witness, the beginning of the creation of God...'

Revelation 4:11: 'Thou art worthy, O Lord, to receive glory and honor and power: for thou hast created all things, and for thy pleasure they are and were created.'

Revelation 10:6: 'And sware by him that liveth for ever and ever, who created heaven, and the things that therein are, and the earth, and the things that therein are, and the sea, and the things which are therein, that there should be time no longer...'

Revelation 14:7: '...worship him that made heaven, and earth, and the sea, and the fountains of waters.'

Romans 1:25: '... and worshipped and served the creature more than the Creator, who is blessed for ever. Amen.'

Romans 16:25: '... according to the revelation of the mystery, which was kept secret since the world began...'

1 Timothy 4:4: 'For every creature of God is good...'

Hebrews 2:10: 'For it became him, for whom are all things, and by whom are all things...'

Hebrews 4:10: 'For he that is entered into his rest, he also hath ceased from his own works, as God did from his.'

Hebrews 9:26: 'For then must he often have suffered since the foundation of the world...'[57]

In none of these references, nor in any of the larger contexts in which they are located, is there the slightest indication of anything other than the literal, chronological understanding of the six days of creation and the succeeding patriarchical history. The loose, 'anti-literal' atmosphere of the 'literary' Framework Hypothesis is not suggested by the New Testament writers. Nor does a careful exegesis of Genesis 1 and 2 reveal it. It must have come from somewhere outside the scriptural world-view. Our next chapter may indicate its true origins.

---

57. Useful reference may also be made to an article by David C. C. Watson, containing twelve New Testament references indicating a straight-forward historical reading of the early chapters of Genesis (i.e. Matt. 13:35; Luke 1:70; 11:50, 51; Heb. 4:3, 4; 9:26; Mark 10:6; 13:19; Rom.1:20; Acts 3:21; John 9:32) in *Creation ex Nihilo*, Vol. 10, No. 3, June-Aug., 1988.

QUESTIONS FOR STUDY

1. What are the two major differences between Biblical Christianity and secular Naturalism?

2. What does the word 'day' generally signify in Scripture?

3. Name instances in Scripture where 'day' does not mean a twenty-four hour, or solar day.

4. Give reasons why it is logical to interpret all of the six creation days as being twenty-four hour days.

5. Why do some maintain that the Sabbath day of Creation week is not yet finished, and how would you answer this?

6. How did St. Ambrose of Milan interpret 'day'?

7. What might be the reason why God created the world in six days (rather than in a shorter or longer time)?

8. Since the sun was only placed in the heavens on the fourth day, does this mean that the previous days could not have been solar, twenty-four hour days? Why or why not?

9. What is Dr Hugh Ross's argument for an extended day, and how would you answer it?

10. What is the 'Framework Hypothesis'?

11. Why did it appear to be an attractive option?

12. Does 'literary refinement' rule out 'literal reading'? Why or why not?

13. Why is the theory that 'literary refinement' precludes a 'literal reading' dangerous for a correct interpretation of other parts of the Bible?

14. What is the basic difference (for purposes of biblical interpretation) between Nominalism and Realism?

Chapter Seven

The Age of the World and the Speed of Light

THIS volume deals with the truths of Genesis in light of shifting paradigms or world models in the scientific realm. In terms of Thomas Kuhn's theory, it is not possible to be certain that a major 'paradigm shift' or change in explanatory world picture has taken place until some decades after its occurrence. In the middle of such a shift it would still be unclear whether the alternative explanation of a large field of reality would later be widely accepted as forward looking and accurate, or was merely a mistaken and reactionary attempt to challenge a valid paradigm. In this author's opinion, the Western scientific culture is in the beginning phases of a serious challenge to the chronological paradigm that assumes high antiquity for the solar system. Only time will tell whether this challenge is merely a reactionary effort to re-establish the rejected biblical world view, or constitutes the wave of future scientific thought that will eventually supplant contemporary chronological assumptions.

In the nature of the case, this chapter and the next one are much more tenuous than the rest of the book. One could entirely skip them and still have a basic understanding of the Genesis teaching on the six days of creation. The various methodologies employed to assess the age of the solar system (whether employed by advocates of an ancient or young world) are characterized by imprecision and uncertainty, since origins and the passage of long ages are not repeatable experiments. Discussions of the chronology of the cosmos are somewhat problematical. Reasons for avoiding this question entirely, especially when one wishes to plead for the possibility of a young world, are not hard to find.

First, no matter how imprecise dating methods may be, the vast majority of contemporary scientists accept as fact the high antiquity of the universe. Dr David Wilkinson in his critique of Stephen Hawking states fairly and realistically the weight of informed opinion against all scientific attempts to argue for a young earth:

> Arguments used for such a young universe include a decay in the speed of light, problems with ages derived from solar clusters and problems with the Big Bang. These are supplemented by evidence for a young Earth, apparently shown by changes in the magnetic field strength, problems with radioactive dating, the explanation of the fossil record by means of the effects of a global flood and arguments against evolution. Some of these arguments do point to some inadequacies in current scientific theories, but have not convinced the vast majority of the scientific community that our picture of the origin of the universe is mistaken.[1]

Second, even Christian scholars in the evangelical tradition generally accept the opinions of the broader scientific community regarding the age of the cosmos, and are quick to dissociate themselves from attempts to question widely received views of a universe billions of years old. Respected authors such as Professors Davis A. Young[2], Pattle P. T. Pun[3] and Dr Hugh Ross[4] could be mentioned.

However, the very point of a paradigm shift consists in the challenges raised against the older, established model. According to Kuhn, a minority of thinkers raise the preliminary challenge, although their alternative explanation is generally unwelcome by the majority at the time it is made. If truth is on their side, however, their explanation will eventually supplant the older, majority paradigm.

Such a challenge is now to the fore in the area of the chronology of the cosmos, and should be welcomed by those who believe that

---

1. David Wilkinson, *God, the Big Bang and Stephen Hawking: An Exploration into Origins*(Monarch: Tunbridge Wells, 1993), 145.
2. e.g. Davis A. Young, *Creation and the Flood* (Baker: Grand Rapids, Mich., 1977) and *The Biblical Flood: A Case Study of the Church's Response to Extrabiblical Evidence* (William B. Eerdmans: Grand Rapids, Mich., 1995).
3. e.g. Pattle P. T. Pun, 'A Theory of Progressive Creationism', in *Journal of the American Scientific Affiliation* 39 (March 1987).
4. e.g. Hugh Ross, *op. cit.*, and *The Creator and the Cosmos* (NavPress: Colorado Springs, Co, 1993).

Holy Scripture is as true when it speaks of space, time and material reality, as it is when it speaks of 'religious' or 'spiritual' matters. This volume looks sympathetically at scientific efforts to reconcile the age of the universe with the 'young' date indicated by biblical chronology with full awareness of the tentative nature of these still early attempts at harmonization. To question the high antiquity of the universe on the basis of Scripture, seems no more unreasonable than to have questioned biological evolution on the same basis. After all, since scientific research has rendered macroevolution implausible (through a fuller understanding of such matters as the first two laws of thermodynamics and the irreducible complexity of living structures), it has at least indirectly pointed to the viability of something like biblical creation. What could be more rational than to assume that the same Word is just as true in the realm of chronology as it was in the realm of 'intelligent design', even before possessing unquestionable empirical validation of it? Such an assumption is not intended to preclude fullest scientific discussion and critique of various chronological theories, from whatever point of view they may emanate.

Those who believe that the early chapters of Genesis mean exactly what they say, will be inclined to favor new models that challenge the ancient world paradigm for the following reason. The biblical documents seem clearly to indicate a relatively young earth and solar system. Genesis chapters one and two speak, as we have already seen in this volume, of a completed creation within the space of six days as we know them from an earthly perspective. Then the genealogies of chapters ten and eleven of Genesis, and those of Matthew chapter one and Luke chapter three all concur in indicating a date of human and terrestrial history in terms of something less than ten thousand years since creation.

In the seventeenth century two famous Hebraic scholars, Archbishop James Ussher and Dr John Lightfoot, attempted to work out an exact date from these textual evidences. Ussher dated creation at 4004 BC and Lightfoot formulated a fairly similar date, even suggesting the month of October as the terminus *a quo*.[5] While it is certainly true that the Bible itself never gives us anything approaching an exact date of creation week, the procedure of Ussher and Lightfoot does not seem inherently unreasonable, since the genealogies are central to the unfolding of both creation and redemption.

Even apart from post-nineteenth century assumptions of vast ages of the physical cosmos, however, considerable caution is called for in any attempt to fix a date for creation. Nineteenth-century Princeton

---

5. See James Ussher, *Annales Veteris et Novi Testamenti* (1650-54).

Seminary scholar, William Henry Green, a believer in scriptural inerrancy (though also accepting ancient ages for the cosmos), reassessed the scriptural genealogies in a way very different from Ussher and Lightfoot.[6] By comparing the various genealogies of the Bible, Green noted that various generations were at times omitted, and that 'father' and 'begat' could bear the meaning of more remote ancestor. Green's successor at Princeton, Professor B. B. Warfield, wrote articles that agreed with him (and indeed, Warfield, though a conservative evangelical Calvinist, also accepted some form of theistic evolution and ancient earth).[7]

Professor Charles Hodge, who had taught both Green and Warfield at Princeton, while opposing Darwinian evolution in his famous 1874 *What Is Darwinism*, still was prepared to accept geological arguments for an ancient earth.[8] The famous Dutch Calvinist scholar, Abraham Kuyper, who was a contemporary and friend of Warfield, critiqued Warfield's teacher, Hodge, for his defective methodology in relating Scripture to contemporary scientific theories (which unwittingly gave ground to evolution).[9]

A careful study of the biblical genealogies does not appear to support Green and Warfield in their endeavor to harmonize the biblical time scale with the long ages required for evolution. Green argued that because of symmetry in these family trees a sort of literary arrangement was intended instead of chronological accuracy. But this argument is no more convincing than the 'framework hypothesis' discussed in Chapter Six of our work. It is true that an exact date is not given, and that fact alone should make us hesitant to be more exact than the inspired text itself. Nonetheless, historical and chronological considerations do seem part and parcel of the scriptural message. As Jean-Marc Berthoud has pointed out,[10] it is illegitimate to divorce literary style from historical intention.

---

6. William Henry Green, 'Primeval Chronology', *Bibliotheca Sacra* 47 (1890), 285-303. Reprinted in Walter C. Kaiser, ed., *Classical Evangelical Essays in Old Testament Interpretation* (Grand Rapids: Baker Book House, 1972).

7. See for instance B. B. Warfield, 'On the Antiquity and Unity of the Human Race' in *Biblical and Theological Studies* (New York: Oxford University, 1932), 235-258. Warfield's views on theistic evolution are discussed in Stanley W. Bamberg, 'Our Image of Warfield Must Go', *Journal of the Evangelical Theological Society*, Vol. 34, No. 2 (June 1991), 229-241, and Mark A. Noll, *The Princeton Theology 1812-1921* (Grand Rapids: Baker, 1983), see especially p.298.

8. See John C. Wells, *Charles Hodge's Critique of Darwinism: The Argument To Design* (Yale University PhD. published by University Microfilms International: Ann Arbor, MI, 1986), 56-61.

9. Abraham Kuyper, *Principles of Sacred Theology* (Wm. B. Eerdmans Publ. Co.: Grand Rapids, Mich., 1954), 318-319.

10. See Chapter Six of this work.

Even if Green and Warfield were correct in positing gaps within the genealogies of the Bible, the most generous assigning of gaps between various generations could not add more than several hundred, or at the most, a thousand or so years to Ussher's and Lightfoot's chronologies. Indeed, a more careful look at these gaps will indicate that they really do *not* change the overall Biblical chronology for the following reason. The writer of Genesis defined the length of the patriarchal age in terms of the time between the births of the patriarchs who are actually listed; not in terms of how many other descendants there may have been who are not listed. James B. Jordan explains:

> Anyone who opens the Bible to Genesis chapters 5 and 11 will notice that the age of each father is given for the time of his son's birth. Adam was 130 years old at the birth of Seth, who was 105 years old at the birth of Enosh, and so forth. Thus we appear to have an unbroken chronology from Creation to Abraham. There are no gaps in the sequence: son follows father in strict succession, it seems. The link between Genesis 5 and Genesis 11 is established by Genesis 6:7 and Genesis 11:10 – Arphaxad was born in Noah's 602nd year. Thus at first glance there appears to be good reason to accept the chronologies of Genesis 5 and 11 at face value.[11]

Moreover, the gaps mentioned by Green and Warfield can actually be filled in from elsewhere in Scripture, so that the biblical chronology as defined by Ussher is not really affected by them. As Arthur C. Custance noted:

> We are told again and again that some of these genealogies contain gaps; but what is never pointed out by those who lay the emphasis on these gaps, is that they only know of the existence of these gaps because the Bible elsewhere fills them in. How otherwise could one know of them? But if they are filled in, they are not gaps at all! Thus, in the final analysis the argument is completely without foundation.[12]

But even if the gaps in certain genealogies could not be filled in, very little would be gained, for such relatively minor stretching could in no way begin to approach the millions of years required by evolutionary theory. It is better to be honest and face the facts of the case: a straightforward reading of Holy Scripture teaches an earth only a few thousand years old. This is irreconcilable with the vast ages posited by the evolutionary hypothesis.

---

11. James B. Jordan, 'The Biblical Chronology Question: An Analysis' in *Creation and Social Science and Humanities Quarterly*, Vol. II, No. 2 (Winter 1979), 9.
12. Arthur C. Custance, *The Genealogies of the Bible*, Doorway Papers No. 24 (Ottawa, 1967), 3.

Chronological Conflicts and Paradigm Shifts

The irreconcilability of biblical chronology with evolutionary age hypotheses will be as stoutly resisted by theistic-evolutionary evangelicals, as it is openly admitted by liberals.[13] It is crucial to note here that for all their profound theological differences, evolutionary evangelicals and theological modernists do share one thing in common: both of these opposing parties stand on the same side of the older philosophical, 'scientific' model, based on the assumption of evolution and a vastly ancient solar system.

To return to Thomas S. Kuhn's terminology, neither the liberals nor evolutionary evangelicals have undergone 'a paradigm shift'. That is, on the point of chronology at least (though not in most other ways), both presuppose that evolutionary ascent in an ancient cosmos is the only responsible reading of scientific evidence. Hence, 'progressive creationists' (another term for evangelical evolutionists) grant the essential validity of the reigning evolutionary paradigm, particularly as regards chronology (though they profoundly differ from it in terms of divine purpose, intervention and meaning).

Thus, progressive creationists deny a straight-forward reading of the Scriptural implications for chronology of the world, for the same reason that liberals (or Modernists) affirm a plain reading: both assume a cosmos billions of years old, and a human race millions of years old. Their goals are entirely contrary: liberals are pleased to show that the Scriptures teach a young earth in order to 'liberate' people within the church from bondage to historical and scientific truth claims of Scripture (since its chronology is thereby seen to be scientifically incredible), while evolutionary evangelicals deny a plain reading in order to re-interpret the Scriptures in hopes of accommodating the same chronological assumptions held by the secular culture (thereby hoping to render more credible the historical reliability of most of Scripture outside Gen: 1-11). In other words, in both cases, the reigning secular paradigm prevents both modernists and many evangelicals from allowing the plain teachings of Holy Scripture to provide basic principles for an alternative world model (or scientific paradigm) as regards the chronology of the solar system as well as the human species.

It is the concern of this volume to argue that the time has indeed come for a major paradigm shift in the interpretation of origins. A sceptical questioning and systematic intellectual reorganization of the inadequate dogma of evolutionary development and chronology is now occurring in both scientific and theological quarters. The

---

13. Compare and contrast Hugh Ross' theistic-evolutionary *Creation and Time*, for instance, with Chapter 3 of James Barr's liberal theological critique, *Fundamentalism*.

dilemma of either a plain reading of Genesis, teaching a young earth (which liberals admit, but thereby reject scripture's truth claims), or an affirmation of the historicity of scripture (which evangelical evolutionists affirm, but at the price of allegorizing and thereby evading the straightforward teaching of the first eleven chapters of Genesis) is unnecessary. A deep and broad rethinking of both philosophical, theological presuppositions and empirical evidences is currently taking place concerning how the world was brought into being, how old it is and how it functions.

The still dominant evolutionary model (or paradigm) is being radically challenged across a broad field of studies by a contrary creationist model with a chronology antithetical to that of the older paradigm. This presuppositional conflict in world models or paradigms must be kept in mind as we consider theories bearing on the age of the solar system, the earth, and humankind.

Keeping this contemporary conflict between conflicting paradigms in mind will provide the appropriate background for contrasting and evaluating the evolutionary paradigm with its ancient chronology over against the creationist paradigm with its recent chronology. That is to say, evidences are inevitably interpreted within a larger intellectual framework or world picture in order to make sense of them. Not to recognize the connection between the larger world picture ('paradigm' or 'system of presuppositions') and the evaluation of evidences within that system is to be blinded to a factor crucial to the discovery of truth. On the contrary, an awareness that empirical evidences are accepted (or perhaps excluded) and then explained in terms of deeper, non-empirical (or faith) assumptions can liberate the mind to approach the whole field of reality from a different point of view: one that critically questions generally unspoken philosophical (or faith) assumptions, methodologies, interpretations of facts and resulting world pictures – even when what is being questioned commands a hitherto impressive majority.

This chapter and the next one, building on what others have done for the last three decades, attempt to do just that. Hence, in the interests of the discovery of truth (which, we believe, will always be found to lie in the direction of the general principles of the Word of God written), we must in this chapter discuss a central question involved in a scientific endeavor to establish a natural chronology: the speed of light and the age of the universe. In Chapter Eight we shall discuss various geological or biological chronometers and their bearing on the age of the earth.[14]

---

14. The author wishes to state candidly at the outset of this discussion that he has no expertise in scientific chronology, and has used secondary resources, rather than primary ones in both of these chapters. Dr Walter Brown, to whom considerable reference is made in this volume, has done careful research in primary scientific monographs, as may be seen in the sixth general edition of his work, *In the Beginning*.

The Speed of Light and the Age of the Solar System

The speed of light (c) is generally accepted as being 299,792.458 kilometers per second. A 'light year' is the distance light travels in a year. Thus a star might come into being a million light years away from earth but could not actually be observed until a million years later because it would take that long for the starlight to reach the earth from outer space. If this is the case, then the solar system would have to be immensely older than the few thousand years indicated by the Genesis chronologies. This fact would seem to remove the biblical chronology from serious consideration in constructing a scientifically valid world picture.

But there are weighty reasons – empirically based – not to be hasty in drawing such a conclusion. For a number of physicists who hold to the chronological validity of the Genesis genealogies (and thus to a young earth) have proposed alternative models that maintain a recent creation and, at the same time, accept the correctness of Einstein's General and Special Theories of Relativity, which give central emphasis to the significance of the speed of light. Of several proposals that have been made, we shall mention only two as meriting serious consideration in this chapter.

First, arguments that the speed of light has been slowing down (and thus traveled much more rapidly in the past), if correct, would indicate a very young universe, in terms of thousands rather than billions of years. This matter has been debated since the 1980s. Barry Setterfield, an Australian scientist, proposed the decay in the speed of light in *The Velocity of Light and the Age of the Universe*.[15] According to Setterfield, the first careful measurement of the speed of light was made by a Danish astronomer, Roemer, in 1675, and then by the English astronomer, Bradley, in 1728. It has been measured many times since then, and is said to have reached an equilibrium of 299,792.458 kilometers per second by 1960 (since which time atomic clocks have been used).

These data indicate that the speed of light in 1675 was around 2.6% higher than today, and that it continued to decline until 1960 (when atomic clocks began to be employed). Setterfield charted a rate of about 5.7 kilometers decrease in velocity per second between 1675 and 1728 and 2.5 kilometers per second decrease between 1880 and 1924, etc.[16] He then worked out a curve (a log sine curve) tracing the decay of the velocity of light. He postulates that at the time of creation the speed of light was 5×10^{11} faster than now, so that light once traveled

---

15. Published by Creation Science Association (Inc.): Adelaide, S. A., 5001, Australia, 1983.
16. Setterfield, *op.cit.*, 12.

about seven million times faster than it does at present.[17] On this basis, Setterfield figures that the earth was created about 4040 BC, plus or minus one hundred years.[18]

If he is correct, then previous measurements of light speed (which assume that it has never changed its rate) would yield a date vastly too old for the solar system, rather like the difference in speed and time between a man sailing in a small craft from London to New York, and flying there in the Concorde. If one measured the time it took to cross the Atlantic to New York in a slow boat (comparable to the speed of light at present, according to Setterfield), it would require much longer than flying in the supersonic Concorde (comparable to the speed of light at the time of creation). Hence, to continue the illustration, previous measurements of the vast age of the universe are said to be immensely too long because they have been charted at 'boat speed' rather than 'jet speed' (my analogy; not Setterfield's). Therefore, to the point of this chapter, if the speed of light has indeed decayed in terms of Setterfield's charts, then the most basic empirical measurement of the age of the solar system would fit precisely into the genealogical chronologies of Genesis, yielding a date not much more than six thousand years ago.

Moreover, this – assuming it is correct – might explain why the dates derived from various types of radioactive measurements on physical, geological elements (such as the half-life of Uranium 238 decaying into Lead over millions of years) suggest a time frame vastly older than the true creation.[19] As Setterfield writes, '...the velocity of the electron in its orbit is proportional to the speed of light. This is an expected result because whatever mechanism causes the speed of light to decrease with time is going to act in a precisely similar way causing the decrease in speed of all other propagations of mass-energy.'[20] Hence, '...radiometric ages in rocks, meteorites and other astronomical objects in conventionally allocated years can all be predicted by the high initial value of c and accommodated within a 6,000 year framework.'[21] That is why '...the 1/2-lives of the radioactive elements are proportional to $1/c$ and so were much shorter in the past. The vast ages conventionally allocated to rocks dated by radioactive methods, are based on the assumption of virtually fixed decay rates

17. *Ibid.*, 17.
18. *Ibid.*
19. Regardless of these arguments for the decay of the velocity of light, a number of other significant factors must be taken into account in assessing the validity of radiometric dating. This matter will be addressed in Chapter Eight.
20. Setterfield, *op.cit.*, 34.
21. *Ibid.*, 17.

and a constant c. Ignoring this high initial value of *c* and its subsequent decay, inevitably results in these vast conventional ages.'[22]

A seminar to discuss Setterfield's work was held at Stanford University on October 24, 1989, and was reported in *The Pascal Centre Notebook* the next year.[23] Reports of this seminar show that two other physicists have also suggested a decay in the speed of light (independently of Setterfield). French astronomer M. E. J. Gheury de Bray first proposed the decay in light speed in articles published in *Science* (1927) and in *Nature* (1931, 1934).[24] A contemporary Russian scientist, V. S. Troitskii of the University of St. Petersburg, has also argued for the decay of light speed.[25]

This proposed 'paradigm shift' of such great proportions has not gone without serious challenges. Some have suggested that a decay in the speed of light would call into question Einstein's almost universally accepted equation: $E=mc^2$.[26] However, Setterfield states that a decay in light speed does not run counter to Einstein's equation: 'Einstein's theory of relativity requires *c* to have the same value at any point in time throughout the universe, but says nothing about the value of *c* being constant with respect to time itself.'[27] Dr Walter T. Brown supports him in this:

> Does the decrease in the speed of light conflict with the statement frequently attributed to Albert Einstein that the speed of light is constant? Not really. Einstein's theory of special relativity assumes that the speed of light is independent of the velocity of the light source. This is called Einstein's Second Postulate. Many have misinterpreted this to mean that 'Einstein said that the speed of light is constant'. Imagine two spaceships traveling away from each other. An astronaut in one spaceship suddenly shines a flashlight at the other spaceship. Einstein claimed that the beam will strike that spaceship at the same speed as it would if the two spaceships were travelling toward each other. This paradox has some experimental support. Setterfield, on the other hand, says that while the speed of light has decreased, at any instant all light beams travel at the same speed, regardless of the velocity and location of their sources.[28]

22. *Ibid.*, 31.
23. Volume One, Number One, July, 1990 (Toronto); presented by Lambert Dolphin, Ph.D. in physics and electrical engineering (of Stanford), Senior Research Physicist for SRI International, and reported by Nancy Pearcey, contributing editor to the *Pascal Centre Notebook*.
24. See *Pascal Centre Notebook*, Vol. One, No. One, 1.
25. V. S. Troitskii, 'Physical Constants and the Evolution of the Universe,' in *Astrophysics and Space Science*, Vol. 139, No. 2, December, 1987, 389-4ll.
26. e.g. Hugh Ross, *Creation and Time*, 98-99.
27. Setterfield, *op.cit.*, 8.
28. Walter T. Brown, *In the Beginning: Compelling Evidence for Creation and the Flood* (Center for Scientific Creation: Phoenix, AZ, sixth general edition, 1995), 160. For further observations on the non-contradictory nature of the decrease in light speed and Einstein's Relativity Theory, see note 13, p. 162 of Brown.

A second, more serious, criticism of the validity of Setterfield's statistics has been offered by scientists from both the theistic-evolutionary[29] and young-earth creationist sides.[30] These critics question the accuracy of the seventeenth and early eighteenth-century astronomical instruments employed to measure the speed of light at that time. Eugene Chaffin in 1992 stated in a paper[31] that:

> '[One measurement of]... the speed of light in the 17th century was within 0.4% of today's value. That value is within the experimental error of the early instruments used, and it is considerably below the 2.6% value Setterfield used.'[32]

However, Humphrey's (and Chaffin's) dismissal of evidence for the decay in the velocity of light seems premature. Dr Walter T. Brown has pointed out that even if one excludes the seventeenth and eighteenth century measurements, still from the time of unquestionably accurate charting of the speed of light (as with Michelson in the 1920s and others down to 1960),[33] definite and measurable decrease in the velocity of light is empirically indicated.[34] Dr Brown states:

> In the seven instances where the same scientists measured the speed of light with the same equipment years later, a decrease was always reported. The decreases were often several times greater than the reported experimental errors. I have conducted other analyses that weight (or given significance to) each measurement according to its accuracy. Even after considering the wide range of inaccuracies, it is hard to see how anyone can claim with any statistical rigor, that the speed of light has remained constant.[35]

Dr Brown has stated that of five atomic 'properties' known to be directly dependent upon the velocity of light, four have already been demonstrated to indicate decrease.[36] He writes:

> If atomic frequencies are decreasing, then five 'properties of the atom', such as Planck's constant, should also be changing. Statistical studies of the past measurements of four of the five of these 'properties' support both the magnitude and direction of this change.[37]

---

29. Hugh Ross, *op.cit.*, 97-99.
30. D. Russell Humphreys, *Starlight and Time: Solving the Puzzle of Distant Starlight in a Young Universe* (Master Books: Colorado Springs, Col., 1995), 46-49.
31. E. F. Chaffin, 'A determination of the speed of light in the seventeenth century,' *Creation Research Society Quarterly*, 29:3 (1992), 115-120.
32. Chaffin's conclusion as summarized by D. R. Humphreys, *op.cit.*, 48.
33. See Setterfield, *op. cit.*, 13 and 27.
34. Brown, *op. cit.*, 158-162.
35. *Ibid.*, 158.
36. In a personal communication to me on January 18, 1996.
37. Brown, *op. cit.*, 159.

Of crucial importance to the assessment of the thesis that light speed has been slowing down is the correct observation that this decrease appears to have stopped by the early 1960s. But as we noted earlier in this chapter, it was at this time that atomic clocks began to be widely used. The major point here is that since the velocity of an electron around the proton of an atom is proportional to the speed of light, then as light speed decreases, the atomic clocks used to measure them also decrease![38] Being directly dependent on the speed of light (and slowed down as it slows down), they are therefore unable to show its decrease.

Recent research carried out by T. C. Van Flandern at the U. S. Naval Observatory is consistent with the slowing of atomic clocks.[39] He has compared them to orbital clocks, based on the orbiting of celestial bodies, particularly that of the earth around the sun year by year. Dr Brown summarizes the position:

> Before 1967, one second of time was defined by international agreement as 1/31,556,925.9747 of the time it takes the earth to orbit the sun. Atomic clocks are based on the vibrational period of the atom, especially the cesium-133 atom. In 1967, a second was redefined as 9,192,631,770 oscillations of the cesium-133 atom. Van Flandern showed that if atomic clocks are 'correct', then the orbital speeds of Mercury, Venus, and Mars are increasing; consequently, the gravitational 'constant' should be changing. However, he noted that if orbital clocks are 'correct', then the gravitational constant is truly constant, but atomic vibrations and the speed of light are decreasing. The drift between the two types of clocks is only several parts per billion per year. But again, the precision of the measurements is so good that the discrepancy is probably real.[40]

A decrease in the velocity of light does appear to deserve serious consideration. Whether Setterfield's conclusions will be confirmed remains to be seen. If his concept of decay in the speed of light finds wider acceptance, it should be expected to play a major role in the change from the evolutionary paradigm of antiquity to the creationist one of youth. In that case, it may later be deemed inappropriate to have stretched the clear Scriptural meaning of the six days of creation and a few thousand years of earth history into vast aeons of time to

38. Professor Frederick N. Skiff and Dr Carl B. Fliermans have both raised questions about Setterfield's point (in personal communications to this author). Professor Skiff, in particular, has addressed this matter in a recent communication (28 December 1996), which is reproduced in *Technical and Bibliographical Notes* for this Chapter.
39. T. C. Van Flandern, 'Is the Gravitational Constant Changing?', *Precision Measurement and Fundamental Constants II*, editors B. N. Taylor and W. D. Phillips, National Bureau of Standards (U.S.A.), Special Publication 617, 1984, pp. 625-627. Referred to in Brown, *op.cit.*, 161, 162.
40. Brown, *op. cit.*, 158-159.

suit a failing paradigm. But much more data must be presented if this concept is to be rendered credible.

The Distortion of Time in White Holes

Another approach to the question of how billions of light-years can be accommodated within the framework of an earth only a few thousand years old is found in the recent work of Dr D. Russell Humphreys.[41] Although he discounts (perhaps prematurely?) evidence for the decay in the speed of light, he offers an alternative solution to the problem of recent creation and ancient starlight. In terms of Einstein's General Theory of Relativity, he notes that gravity affects time. Clocks at a low altitude (as the Royal Observatory in Greenwich) tick a few microseconds slower per year than identical clocks at high altitudes (as the National Bureau of Standards in Boulder, Colorado).[42] This confirmed reality of 'gravitational time dilation' means, according to the hypothesis of Dr Humphreys, that in the early universe: '... while a few days were passing on earth, billions of years would have been available for light to travel to earth.'[43] He offers support for this scenario by rejecting a central assumption of 'Big-Bang' cosmology; that the universe has no boundary (called the 'cosmological' or 'Copernican principle'[44]). He holds that since this unboundedness of the universe is definitely an arbitrary assumption, one could more reasonably (especially in terms of the centrality of the history of redemption on planet Earth) posit a bounded universe with a center.[45]

The significance of this model so different from that of the Big-Bang is as follows: '... if the universe is bounded, then there would be a center of mass and a net gravitational force, and we could begin to consider the time-distorting effects of gravity on a massive scale. In such a universe, clocks at the edge of the universe would be ticking at a rate different from clocks at the center...'[46] He then discusses the question of the expansion of the universe, and the effects of that on time. He theorizes this mighty expansion of the early created elements in terms of a Black Hole running in reverse, also known as a White Hole[47] (or in J.-P. Luminet's words, a 'light fountain'[48]). Humphreys writes of the Black Hole (also true of

41. Humphreys, *op. cit.*
42. *Ibid.*, 11.
43. *Ibid.*, 13.
44. *Ibid.*, 18.
45. *Ibid.*, 18, 19.
46. *Ibid.*, 19, 20.
47. *Ibid.*, 22-25, 106-108.
48. *Ibid.*, 108.

its reverse, the White Hole): 'This ... is where time is massively distorted.'[49] He adds:

> 'Like a black hole, a white hole would also have an event horizon... the equations of GR [Einstein's General Relativity Theory – ed.] require that light and matter inside the event horizon of a white hole must expand outward.'[50]

Following (though from opposite premises) Stephen Hawking's *A Brief History of Time*, Humphreys states that 'Strange things happen to time near an event horizon.'[51] Specifically:

> '...according to GR, time effectively stands still at the event horizon. Clocks and all physical processes at that location are stopped, and near that location they run very slowly (relative to clocks away from it)... If you were standing on the earth as the event horizon arrived, distant objects in the universe could age billions of years in a single day of your time. And there would be ample time for their light to reach you.'[52]

More research remains to be carried out on Dr Humphreys' alternative paradigm to the Big-Bang (and he invites others to join him in this work[53]). But if these preliminary indications of the decay of the velocity of light, as well as the rather different research of Humphreys on White Holes and the distortion of time, were to gain a broad hearing, then the widely accepted paradigm of an ancient solar system would be more open than ever to radical question on empirical scientific grounds.

In the nature of the case, humanly derived cosmologies (whether naturalistic or creationist) cannot be taken with the same seriousness as the clear teaching of the divinely inspired Scriptures on origins. It is never wise to identify in an absolute fashion the plain teachings of the Word of God with even the most compelling contemporary scientific, and especially, cosmological theories. Nevertheless, with this warning in mind, since the Scriptures do speak to the space/ time cosmos, one must inevitably seek for an approach which seems to make the best sense of both realms. And on these grounds, one can welcome scientific challenges to the assumption of an ancient cosmos, without asserting the truth of such challenges until much more data are available.

---

49. *Ibid.*, 23.
50. *Ibid.*, 24.
51. *Ibid.*, 27.
52. *Ibid.*, 28, 29. See also pp. 37-38, 70-71, and 126.
53. *Ibid.*, 127.

TECHNICAL AND BIBLIOGRAPHICAL NOTES FOR CHAPTER SEVEN

Chronologies of Genesis and the Date of Creation

Various contemporary scholars, who take seriously both the most recent scientific research as well as the chronological viability of Genesis, have sought to find an approximate date for the creation of the world. Some of their efforts are merely listed here, without claiming any authoritative assessment of them. Research in primary sources, as well as fresh types of analysis and experimentation are called for, in order to strengthen the case one way or the other.

1. Barry Setterfield

Barry Setterfield by plotting the decay curve in the velocity of the speed of light holds that the speed of light was 391,966 Km. per second at 1 AD; at the time of the Great Flood (accepted as 2,384 BC) 1,621,908 Km./sec. and in Creation Week approximately 5×10^{11} greater than at present.[54] Thus he charts the approximate date of creation to be around 4040 BC plus or minus twenty years.

Problems with Setterfield's Theory of the Decay of the Speed of Light

Professor Frederick N. Skiff has discussed some of the difficulties involved in Setterfield's proposal as follows:

> I see that Setterfield does indeed propose that Planck's constant is also changing. Therefore, the fine structure constant 'a' could remain truly constant and the electron velocity in the atom could then change in a fashion proportional to the speed of light. His hypothesis is plausible. My concern was that if you say
>
> 1) The speed of light is changing. And
> 2) The electron velocity in the atom is proportional to the speed of light, then you will generate an immediate objection from a physicist unless you add
> 3) Planck's constant is also changing in such a way as to keep the fine structure 'constant' constant.
>
> The last statement is not a small addition. It indicates that his proposal involves a certain relation between the quantum theory (in the atom) and relativity theory (concerning the speed of light). The relation between these theories, in describing gravity, space and time, is recognized as one of the most important outstanding problems in physics. At present these theories cannot be fully reconciled, despite their many successes in describing a wide range of phenomena. Thus, in a way, his proposal enters new territory rather than challenging current theory. Actually,

---

54. Setterfield, *op. cit.*, 16, 17.

the idea has been around for more than a decade, but it has not been pursued for lack of proof. My concerns are the following:

The measurements exist over a relatively short period of time. Over this period of time the speed changes by only a small amount. No matter how good the fit to the data is over the last few decades, it is *very* speculative to extrapolate such a curve over thousands of years unless there are other (stronger) arguments that suggest that he really has the right curve. The fact is that there are an infinite number of mathematical curves which fit the data perfectly (he does not seem to realize this in his article). On the other hand, we should doubt any theory which fits the data perfectly because we know that the data contain various kinds of errors (which have been estimated). Therefore the range of potential curves is even larger, because the data contain errors. There is clearly some kind of systematic effect, but not one that can be extrapolated with much confidence. The fact that his model is consistent with a biblical chronology is very interesting, but not conclusive (there are an infinite number of curves that would also agree with this chronology). The fact that he does propose a relative well known, and simple trigonometric function is also curious, but not conclusive.

The theoretical derivation that he gives for the variation of the speed of light contains a number of fundamental errors. He speaks of Planck's constant as the quantum unit of energy, but it is the quantum unit of angular motion. In his use of the conversion constant b he seems to implicitly infer that the 'basic' photon has a frequency of 1Hz, but there is no warrant for doing this. His use of the power density in an electromagnetic wave as a way of calculating the rate of change of the speed of light will not normally come out of a dynamical equation which assumes that the speed of light is a constant (Maxwell's Equations). If there is validity in his model, I don't believe that it will come from the theory that he gives. Unfortunately, the problem is much more complicated, because the creation is very rich in phenomena and delicate in structure.

Nevertheless, such an idea begs for an experimental test. The problem is that the predicted changes seem to be always smaller than what can be resolved. I share some of the concerns of the second respondent in the *Pascal Notebook* article.[55] One would not expect to have the rate of change of the speed of light related to the current state-of-the-art of

---

55. A reference to 'Decrease in the Velocity of Light: Its Meaning For Physics' in *The Pascal Centre Notebook*, Vol. One, Number One, July, 1990. The second respondent to Setterfield's theory was Dr Wytse Van Dijk, Professor of Physics and Mathematics, Redeemer College, who asked (concerning Professor Troitskii's model of the slowing down of the speed of light): 'Can we test the validity of Troitskii's model? If his model is correct, then atomic clocks should be slowing compared to dynamic clocks. The model could be tested by comparing atomic and gravitational time over several years to see whether they diverge. I think such a test would be worthwhile. The results might help us resolve some of the issues related to faith and science' (p. 5).

measurement (the graph of page 4 of *Pascal Notebook*[56]) unless the effect is due to bias. Effects that are 'only there when you are not looking' can happen in certain contexts in quantum theory, but you would not expect them in such a measurement as the speed of light.

These are my concerns. I think that it is very important to explore alternative ideas. The community which is interested in looking at theories outside of the ideological mainstream is small and has a difficult life. No one scientist is likely to work out a new theory from scratch. It needs to be a community effort, I think.[57]

2. E. W. Faulstich

Eugene Faulstich, a computer expert, has extensively studied biblical chronology in terms of ancient ways of reckoning time, and then programmed this information into his computer in order to plot backwards precise dates of major scriptural events. While I feel unable to evaluate competently the results of his work, I believe it is worth summarizing here, for those who wish to pursue it.

First, he notes the difference between 'modern' (post-Roman) calendars and those of the ancients:

> We are presently using a calendar system developed by the Romans in about 50 BC. It has been modified from time to time, but is not the same as the calendar used by the ancients.... The ancient Hebrew calendar always began the new year with the first sighting of a new moon after evidence that spring had arrived. There are not exactly twelve lunar months in a solar year, so the first day of the year would float back and forth within a month. The second and very important part of time keeping was the seven-day week. This was to be kept on penalty of death, so it has never been lost over the centuries. Time depended on three factors, therefore, the solar year, the lunar month, and the seven-day week. Contained within one solar year were 365.24199 days and 12.36826748 lunar months, and 52.177457 weeks. If we were to multiply them, we would find that it would take 235.707 years to come close to the starting location. Each year would begin with a different day of the week, and the sequence would be completely random. We can, therefore, look to the spring of any specific year, then over to the first new moon, determine the day of the week, and begin our computer calculations backward using the above numbers.
>
> Looking at illustration I, we might compare these forces as three wheels rolling forward with timing marks on them. The solar year has a range from the 15th of March until the 7th of April in which the new year may begin. The lunar cycle must always start on the timing mark, the week has no reference point, and will repeat at random. By

---

56. *This graph consists of a correlation of accuracy of measurements of speed of light (c) with the rate of change in c between 1740 and 1980'*.

57. Second Personal Communication from Professor Skiff to the author, 28 December 1996.

knowing the position of these three motions in respect to each other today, we can go back to any day in history, and tell the day of the week on which it happened. This is a very important characteristic, for if the Bible is correct, we should be able to turn back the clock to a number of years corresponding to creation, and show that it happened on the first day of the week. We should be able to determine that Christ died on the sixth day of the week, etc. If we know that an event took place on a Saturday, as an example, and we know the date, but are not certain of the year, the reconstructed computer calendar will give us the information we need...[58]

On the basis of this computer methodology, Faulstich finds that the Flood occurred 1656 years after creation; Abraham was born 1950 years after creation; the Exodus took place 2540 years after creation; David was born 2975 years after creation; Judah fell 3413 years after creation (or 587 BC), and Christ was born 3995 years after creation.[59]

3. Walter T. Brown

Dr Brown has a careful chart based on the biblical values of the length of lives of the patriarchs from Adam to Joseph. He shows the beginning of the Flood, 1656 years after creation, the birth of Abraham in 2008 after creation, and the death of Joseph 2369 years after creation.[60] He succinctly discusses traditional problems raised with these numbers; particularly the differences between the Masoretic and Septuagintal and Samaritan texts, as well as the question of rounding of numbers, the age of Terah at Abraham's birth and gaps in the genealogical lists.[61]

In summary, it is interesting to observe that contemporary endeavors such as these to establish the basic chronology of ancient times are relatively close to the classical work of seventeenth scholars, Ussher and Lightfoot. Even amidst the still prevailing Darwinian chronology, a straight-forward reading and acceptance of the ancient Genesis chronologies as accurate historical guideposts is being argued for by one strand of scientific research, which finds sufficient empirical data to justify such research. Some of their findings are addressed in Chapter 8. Though still a minority reading, such research will play a part in challenging the humanist paradigm of an ancient universe in favor of a new one, consistent with a biblical world picture.

---

58. Eugene W. Faulstich, 'God's Perfect Timing: A Computerized Verification of Time in the Bible', *Repossess The Land: Essays and Technical Papers, 15th Anniversary Convention – Bible-Science Association* (Bible-Science Association: Minneapolis, Minnesota, 1979), 91.
59. *Ibid.*, 93, 94.
60. Brown, *op. cit.*, 192.
61. *Ibid.*, 193.

Questions For Study

1. What biblical material outside Genesis 1 and 2 appears to require a 'young earth'?

2. How serious are the 'gaps' in the Biblical genealogies?

3. Why do the 'progressive creationists' believe it is necessary to lengthen the chronology of the world?

4. How does the current paradigm with its evolutionary suppositions exclude scientific evidence which points in a direction compatible with the Biblical account of creation?

5. What is meant by a 'light year'?

6. How does the passage of a light year appear to support a very old universe?

7. What is the significance for the age of the world of Barry Setterfield's assertion that the speed of light has slowed down since creation?

8. How does he support this idea?

9. What are some of the criticisms against Setterfield's theory?

10. How could a decay in the speed of light (if true) affect radioactive measurement of the age of geological specimens?

11. What implications does this relationship of the speed of light with radioactive specimens have for estimating the age of the earth?

12. Explain the apparent cessation of the slowing down of the speed of light since the early 1960s.

13. How does Humphreys back his argument that clocks proceed at different rates?

14. How do both Setterfield's and Humphreys' hypotheses provide examples of the kind of 'paradigm shift' discussed on page 142f. of this chapter?

15. How do they offer a scientific view that attempts to explain creation without compromising a straightforward interpretation of Genesis 1?

16. Why is it unwise to identify too closely the truth of Scripture with various cosmological theories (even creationist ones)?

Chapter Eight

The Age of the World and Physical Chronometers

THE length of time it takes light to travel from stars to earth, though of prime importance, is not the only factor relevant to dating the age of the world. For well over a century significant attempts have been made by a vast host of research scientists and others to measure the age of rocks, fossils and other geological formations. Although this has been an inexact science, its conclusions have nevertheless commanded, until recently, almost universal assent in Western culture.

The various physical chronometers used to establish the age of the earth and solar system are generally understood to indicate a date reaching back many billions of years. These conclusions of historical geology impacted other fields of study, and disrupted the traditional, plain interpretation of Genesis nearly two centuries ago. For the most part, Christian interpreters by the first half of the nineteenth century beat a hasty retreat into varying sorts of allegorical readings of Genesis 1–11, in order to avoid conflict between the straight-forward meaning of the text with the new and imposing paradigm of an ancient cosmos.

It is clear that such questions enter directly into the viability of the Genesis account and thus into its interpretation. Therefore, in this chapter we must address some of the central principles involved in dating the earth. In doing so we shall find the results of such dating methodology to have come under significant questioning.

Decrease in the Speed of Light and Geological Dating

Chapter Seven discussed Setterfield's theory of the direct effects of decrease in the speed of light upon the aging of physical elements.[1] This does not call for recapitulation other than to note that, if Setterfield is correct, the velocity of an electron in its orbit around the proton of the atom is directly proportional to the speed of light. Consequently, if he is correct in maintaining that the speed of light has in fact been slowing down, then so has the velocity of the electron in the atomic structure of matter. Hence any attempt to date the elements of a rock which assumes that the rate of decay from one element to another has remained the same in the past as it is today (a rate said to be based upon the speed of light) will result in an age too great.

An illustration of this process would be the decay occurring during the 'half life' of uranium 238 into its daughter element of lead 206. If the speed of light were constant across the millennia, then this particular half-life would demonstrate millions of years involved in the final stable product of a particular rock formation (e.g. in the case of U238 to Pb 206, 4.5 billion years are assumed to be required). But if the speed of light were much faster in the past, then the half-life decay would have occurred with greater rapidity, thus rendering an age in the thousands, not millions. This would be true for all radioactive elements, since matter is a function of energy (and all energy is related to the speed of light).

If sufficient data should be presented to confirm Setterfield's approach, a far-reaching reassessment of all geological and biological dating would be in order. But even apart from the foundational question of changes in the speed of light, there are other empirical facts that many scientists believe bear witness to the relative youth, rather than the high antiquity, of the geological and biological formations of our planet.

Important Assumptions in Radiometric Dating

Robert E. Kofahl has called attention to three basic assumptions for any kind of valid radiometric dating. It is important that we be aware of these sometimes hidden assumptions in this supposedly

---

1. But see the question raised by Frederick Skiff concerning Setterfield's theory of the connection of the speed of light and the decay of physical elements in *Technical and Bibliographical Notes* for Chapter Seven.

neutral scientific methodology, for as we saw in our last chapter, the assumptions implicit in the framework or paradigm in which we interpret a given set of facts are very influential in how we explain their meaning.

Kofahl shows that the assumptions underlying radiometric dating are much like the requirements for a normal clock to measure time correctly: 'a) the clock must run at a known rate; b) the clock must be set correctly at the beginning of the time period being measured; c) the clock must not be disturbed during the time period being measured.'[2]

Using the example above (of U238/Pb206), Kofahl then illustrates how these three necessary assumptions function in this particular geological time measurement: '... a) the rock contained no daughter lead at time zero; b) no parent uranium or daughter lead was either added to or taken from the rock since; and c) the rate of radioactive decomposition has not varied.'[3]

He concludes that 'the radiometric dating methods do not fulfill all of the requirements for a reliable clock,'[4] and shows why none of these three necessary requirements for chronological accuracy can be assumed in radiometric dating:

a. The evidence generally supports the view that the rates of radio-active decay are constant within narrow limits.... It is possible that unusual conditions such as exposure to neutrino, neutron, or cosmic radiation could greatly have changed isotopic ratios or the rates at some time in the past [Although this is not probable, ed.].

b. The daughter products of the various systems are all found widely distributed in the earth's crust, e.g., Pb-206, Pb-207, Pb-208, argon-40, and strontium-87. It is not possible to be sure that some daughter product atoms were not present in the rock at time zero [Although for some techniques this assumption seems safe, *ed.*].

c. Finally, all of the parent and daughter atoms can move through the rocks. Heating and deforming of rocks can cause these atoms to migrate, and water percolating through the rocks can transport these substances and redeposit them. These processes correspond to changing the setting of the clock hands.... From the above facts it can be seen that the radiometric dating methods do not in general fulfill all of the requirements for a reliable clock.[5]

2. Robert E. Kofahl, Ph.D., *Handy Dandy Evolution Refuter* (Beta Books: San Diego, 1980), 109, 110.
3. *Ibid.*, 110.
4. *Ibid.*, 111.
5. *Ibid.*, 111, 112.

Reassessment of Dating Methods that Indicate Antiquity of Physical Structures

A large and growing number of technical, scientific studies has been conducted in the last thirty years (especially since the publication of Morris and Whitcomb's *The Genesis Flood* in 1961[6]), reassessing on empirical grounds conventional methodology which yielded vast ages for the earth. Most of these studies have been conducted by creationists, and have not as yet commanded widespread acceptance in the general scientific community Only a few high points need be mentioned here.

1. Appearance of Age

According to Genesis, God created within six days a full grown universe. It had an appearance of many years' maturity when it was but a few days old. Adam, for example, was a full grown man the first hour he was created, although he would have presumably appeared to be eighteen or twenty years old. It would be the same for oak trees, geological structures and animals. From our perspective, we would have judged the mature oak to be hundreds of years old. A New Testament illustration of this reality would be Christ's turning the water into wine: a process requiring a few years was compressed into a moment of time. To attempt to measure the age of the earth without taking this fact into account would mean starting off with a falsely inflated chronology.[7]

2. The Uniformitarian Thesis Versus Catastrophism

Much of modern historical geology is based upon a philosophical, 'faith' assumption which runs counter to biblical testimony, and has not been clearly demonstrated by operational science: the uni-formitarian thesis. By the early nineteenth century the central presupposition of uniformitarianism that 'the present is the key to the past' had been popularized by James Hutton and Charles Lyell (who in turn influenced Darwin).

> Uniformitarianism is the belief that the origin and development of all things can be explained exclusively in terms of the same natural laws and processes operating today.... Uniformitarianism has been the backbone of modern historical geology and is responsible for

---

6. Henry M. Morris and John C. Whitcomb, Jr., *The Genesis Flood*, Presbyterian And Reformed Publishing Company: Philadelphia, Penn., 1967).

7. In the nature of the case, there are certainly limits to this. It is one thing to realize that Adam was created full grown, but quite another to hypothesize that distant stars were created with a pathway of light shining all the way to earth (perhaps indicating the historical explosion of a supernova, which – according to this theory – never actually occurred). The former follows from a sensible reading of the text of Genesis; the latter does not.

the current widespread assumption that the earth is billions of years old.... [The Uniformitarians] insist that all geological features and formations, once attributed to geologic cataclysms, can now be satisfactorily explained by ordinary processes functioning over long periods of time.[8]

But creationists have argued on the contrary that '...geological evidences support a universal hydraulic cataclysm'.[9] Morris and Whitcomb marshalled evidence from known natural processes (including 'the hydrodynamic drag' of flood water) to demonstrate the necessity of a universal flood to explain the present geological structures of the earth, which cannot be explained from present slow processes.[10] Many more recent studies appear to have confirmed their work.[11] Widespread geological phenomena such as a heavy preponderance of sedimentary rocks and structures all across earth's surface, including sea shells on the tops of highest mountains; rapid deposit of fossils and extremely large and deep fossil graveyards as well as the pressurized formation of coal and gas all point to a watery catastrophe, not slow natural processes such as we experience today.

Scott M. Huse summarizes some of this evidence:

> Creationists maintain that uniformitarian principles simply cannot account for most of the major geologic features and formations. For instance, there is the vast Tibetan Plateau which consists of sedimentary deposits, which are thousands of feet thick, located presently at an elevation of three miles above sea level. The Karoo formation of Africa contains an estimated 800 billion vertebrate animals! The herring fossil bed of California contains approximately one billion fish within a four-square mile area. The uniformitarian concept is equally incapable of explaining the Columbia Plateau in northwestern United States which is an incredible lava plateau several thousand feet thick covering an area of 200,000 square miles. Uniformitarianism also fails to offer a reasonable explanation for important geological concepts such as mountain building....
>
> It is believed that the Flood was accompanied by massive and violent earth movements, volcanic action, and dramatic changes in climate and topography... which helps to explain how sedimentary strata (formed during the Flood) have come to be lifted thousands of feet above sea level in the mountainous regions of the earth.... The universal presence

8. Scott M. Huse, *The Collapse of Evolution* (Baker Book House: Grand Rapids, Mich., 1988), 7, 8.
9. *Ibid.*, 9.
10. Morris and Whitcomb, *op. cit.*, chapters 3 to 6.
11. e.g. see Walter T. Brown, *op.cit.*, Part II; R. L. Wysong, *The Creation-Evolution Controversy* (Inquiry Press: Midland, Mich., 1976), Chapter 20, and a continuing stream of articles in *Creation Research Society Quarterly*.

of fossils in sedimentary deposits is, indeed, conclusive proof of rapid burial and formation. Rapid burial and lithification are essential for the formation and preservation of fossils; otherwise, they would decay or be destroyed by scavengers. The fact that large scale fossilization is not occurring anywhere in the world today is a serious problem for uniformitarian geologists....

According to Dr Henry M. Morris, hydraulic analysis shows that, in most formations, the individual stratum has been formed within a few minutes time. Furthermore, there is evidence to suggest each subsequent stratum began to be deposited immediately after the preceding one. This suggests that the geologic column was formed rapidly, not gradually over aeons of time. Thus, the geologic evidence supports a cataclysmic interpretation rather than a uniformitarian explanation.[12]

The uniformitarian assumption that millions of years of geological work (extrapolating from present slow, natural processes) would be required to explain structures such as the American Grand Canyon for instance, is called into serious question by the explosion of Mount St. Helens in the state of Washington on the 18th of May 1980. Massive energy equivalent to 20 million tons of TNT destroyed 400 square kilometers of forest in six minutes, changing the face of the mountain and digging out depths of earth and rock, leaving formations not unlike parts of the larger Grand Canyon. Recent studies of the Mount St. Helens phenomenon indicate that if attempts were made to date those structures (which were formed in 1980) on the basis of the uniformitarian theory, millions of years of formation time would necessarily be postulated![13]

Ironically, one of the center-pieces used to demonstrate uniformitarian chronology, the geologic column, on closer inspection actually witnesses to catastrophism. Wysong writes:

The geologic timetable spreads life over about 2 billion years and depicts the least complex and smallest organisms as the youngest. The charts on historical geology are supposedly a representation of the historical record of life as it has been retained for our examination in the form of fossils. The geologic timetable is in chart form what we should find if we dug into the ground and examined the fossils of each successive strata.[14]

But actually, such geologic columns as we have do not represent this smooth transition from simple to complex fossils (as required by the

---

12. Huse, *op. cit.*, 34, 35.
13. See Dr Steve Austin, 'Mount St. Helens and Catastrophism', *Proceedings of the First International Conference on Creationism*, Vol. I (Creation Fellowship: Pittsburgh, PA, 1986).
14. Wysong, *op. cit.*, 348.

ancient chronology demanded by evolutionary theory). As Wysong points out:

> Nowhere in the earth is the complete succession of fossils found as they are portrayed in the chart. For example, if you want to find Pre-Cambrian or Palaeozoic strata you must go to the Grand Canyon. If you want to find Mesozoic you must travel to eastern Arizona. To find Tertiary, you must then travel to New Mexico. In order to find the entire succession, from Cenozoic to Archaeozoic, one would have to turn shovels all over the world flitting from one place to another in order to see the 'proper' geologic column.[15]

When one lays aside the assumption of the evolutionary, uniformitarian theory, and looks at the hard geologic facts, something quite different appears. In fact, it is not at all clear that the classical geologic column of the standard textbooks even exists (as least, as it is portrayed in the charts).[16] Those structures (such as the Grand Canyon) that do provide views of many thick and variegated strata of rock and fossil formations very often show the supposedly primitive fossils hundreds of feet above the supposedly recent fossils (in terms of evolutionary theory). This is the exact opposite of what uniformitarian theory predicts.

Uniformitarian geology has attempted to handle this difficult problem by proposing massive upturning of deeper parts of the earth onto more shallow parts by means of 'overthrusts.' However, granted the massive size of many of the supposed overthrusts (such as the 400 mile long 'thrust fault' in Glacier Park[17]), this proposal seems to be more in the realm of fiction than empirical fact. In a study of rock strata and fossils, John G. Read and C. L. Burdick have shown the illusory nature of some 'overthrusts' and the nonconcordance of the location of actual fossils with evolutionary, uniformitarian theory.[18] Wysong asks the right question: 'If the complete sequence of fossils is not found in the rocks as it is portrayed on the geologist's paper, upon what basis do geologists make the time scale?'[19] The obvious answer is a manifest example of circular reasoning. 'The assumption of evolution is used to arrange the sequence of fossils, then the resultant

---

15. *Ibid.*, 348, 349.
16. See John Woodmorappe, 'The Essential Nonexistence of the Evolutionary Geologic Column: A Quantitative Assessment', *Creation Research Society Quarterly*, Vol. 18, No. 1, June 1981, 46-71.
17. See Clifford L. Burdick, Ph.D., 'Problems in the Geologic Column', *Repossess The Land*, *op. cit.*, 53-55.
18. John G. Read and C. L. Burdick, *Fossils, Strata and Evolution* (Scientific–Technical Presentations: Culver City, CA, 1979).
19. Wysong, *op. cit.*, 350.

sequence is advanced as proof of evolution.'[20] Or as R. H. Rastall says in *Encyclopaedia Britannica*,

> It cannot be denied that from a strictly philosophical standpoint geologists are here arguing in a circle. The succession of organism has been determined by a study of their remains embedded in the rocks, and the relative ages of the rocks are determined by the remains of organisms that they contain.[21]

That is to say: on the one hand geologists date the antiquity of rocks by the fossils in them, and on the other date the fossils by the antiquity of the rock strata in which they are found. Furthermore, when the rock strata do not follow the prescribed uniformitarian succession from simple (in the lower levels) to complex (in the higher levels), then it is stated (on the basis of evolutionary theory) that many square miles of rock material (containing 'ancient' fossils) must somehow have managed to be placed on top of the strata containing more recent fossils. This procedure is evidently based on 'faith', because it has not been demonstrated as being required by empirical facts. Indeed, this uniformitarian, evolutionary 'faith' (or paradigm) seems less able to accommodate hard empirical facts than the creationist paradigm proposed by this book.

Thus, the earth's rock strata (or 'geologic column', insofar as it exists), far from testifying to uniformity, evolution and an ancient earth, actually points to universal hydrological catastrophism, which can more readily be understood in terms of a recent creation and flood.[22] A more scientifically serious model that explains earth's geological (and particularly continental) structures in terms of recent catastrophism of hydroplates, rather than long, slow uniformitarian processes, is offered in Walter T. Brown's recent work, *In The Beginning*.[23]

3. The Significance of Carbon–14 Dating

Since the famous research of W. F. Libby, *RadioCarbon Dating*,[24] it has been widely assumed that life goes back many thousands of years longer than the Genesis chronologies indicate. Dr Robert L. Whitelaw of Virginia Polytechnic Institute has carefully responded to Libby's methodology by working through 15,000 radiocarbon dates. In contrast to Libby, Whitelaw believes that his own research can be interpreted to establish a recent date for creation and the Flood. While the details of Whitelaw's significant research are postponed to the *Technical &*

---

20. *Ibid.*, 351.
21. R. H. Rastall, 'Geology', *Encyclopaedia Britannica*, Vol. 10, 1954, 168.
22. See, for instance, Wysong's demonstration of this in op. cit., 'Fossilization', 355-392.
23. Brown, *op. cit.*, Part II.
24. W. F. Libby, *Radiocarbon Dating* (Chicago, Ill.: University of Chicago, 1952).

Bibliographical Notes for this Chapter, it is appropriate here briefly to consider why this important dating method, when properly pursued, actually bears witness to a young earth. Wysong explains how this procedure works:

1. Radioactive carbon is formed from the action of cosmic rays on nitrogen in the atmosphere.
2. C–14, in turn, combines with oxygen to form carbon dioxide which is then incorporated into plant and animal structures.
3. At death, no more C–14 is assimilated into tissues, and that present in organism decays into nonradioactive materials.
4. Since the present level of C–14 in living tissue is known, and it is also known that 1/2 of the C–14 in a sample will decay in about 5,600 years [actually, 5,700, *ed.*], then to determine the age of a sample of organic material we simply measure the amount of C–14 left.[25]

However for this method to be properly evaluated, it is necessary to bring to the surface an important assumption, namely that the ratio of Carbon–12 to Carbon–14 in the atmosphere was the same in the past as it is today. If this ratio has changed, the measurements are seriously skewed (or, in the words of Robert Kofahl, 'the hands of the clock have been moved'). Walter Brown explains:

> The assumption usually made (but rarely acknowledged) is that the ratio of carbon–14 to carbon–12 in the atmosphere has always been about what it is today – about one in a trillion. But that may not have been true in the ancient past. For example, a worldwide flood would uproot and bury preflood forests. Afterwards, less carbon would be available to cycle between living things and the atmosphere. With less carbon–12 to dilute the carbon–14 that is continually forming in the upper atmosphere, the ratio of carbon–14 to carbon–12 in the atmosphere would slowly begin to increase. If the ratio of carbon–14 to carbon–12 doubled and we did not know it, radiocarbon ages of things living then would appear to us to be one half-life (or 5730 years) older than their true ages. If that ratio quadrupled, organic remains would appear 11,460 (2 x 5,730) years older, etc. Consequently, a 'radiocarbon year' would not correspond to an *actual* year.[26]

Dr Robert H. Brown has carefully discussed the factors that might have changed the concentration of C–14 in the upper biosphere, especially in light of what would have occurred during a universal flood.[27]

The validity of radiocarbon dating is thrown into some doubt by the dates it has yielded of artifacts whose history can be measured in some other way. Instances of high inaccuracy have been carefully charted, such as new wood from actively growing trees has been dated at

25. Wysong, *op. cit.*, 149.
26. Brown, *op. cit.*, 156.
27. Robert H. Brown, 'Interpretation of C–14 Age Data', *Repossess The Land, op. cit.*, 45-52.

10,000 years; mortar from the Oxford Castle in England (built only 785 years ago) was dated by C-14 at 7,370 years, and freshly killed seals have been dated at 1,300 years.[28] Wysong protests with good reason: '...why should we believe dates that have not had their assumptions validated when so many dates that can be checked for accuracy are wrong, sometimes ludicrously so.'[29]

Natural Chronometers that Indicate a Young Earth

The Genesis chronologies appear more viable in light of the contemporary reassessment of the ancient ages yielded by both radiometric dating and the charts based on uniformitarian geology. Their viability is also being argued for by a variety of other modes of chronological measurement of natural phenomena. These other modes of dating the age of the earth appear to have been generally ignored by proponents of the ancient earth in the evolutionary paradigm. But recent studies, especially by creationists, are bringing them to view, perhaps as an early phase of the coming shift from the naturalistic paradigm of evolutionary faith to the creationist paradigm of biblical faith. Several contemporary works discuss some of these chronometers that are held to yield dates of the earth of only a few thousand years. *Technical & Bibliographical Notes* for Chapter Eight makes reference to some of these studies. Here we need mention only a few representative samples of these kinds of chronometers.[30]

Moon Dust

Before man reached the moon, it was assumed by some scientists who were committed to the paradigm involving a moon perhaps 3.5 billion years old, that there would be a very thick layer of dust on the moon. R. A. Lyttleton, astronomer and consultant to the U.S. space program had written in the 1956:

> '... the lunar surface is exposed to direct sunlight, and strong ultra-violet light and x-rays can destroy the surface layers of exposed rock and reduce them to dust at the rate of a few ten-thousandths of an inch per year. But even this minute amount could during the age of the moon be sufficient to form a layer over it several miles deep.'[31]

---

28. Wysong, *op. cit.*, 151.
29. *Ibid.*
30. These studies by creationists are listed here since they do not appear to be widely known in the general intellectual culture. The author has done no primary research in any of these measurements, but believes they may merit further consideration by those who are competent to address them.
31. R. A. Lyttleton, *The Modern Universe* (N. Y.: Harper, 1956), 72. Quoted in Wysong, *op. cit.*, 176.

Astronaut Neil Armstrong was concerned about stepping out of the spaceship into a possibly suffocating layer of dust.[32] But very little was there. '...if the calculations indicating the rate of dust accumulation were accurate, there was not a billion years' worth of dust, nor was there a million years' worth of dust. There was, in fact, only a few thousand years' worth of dust on the moon's surface.'[33]

An article in *Science* by R. Ganapathy and others dealt with some aspects of this question after the Apollo 12 lunar landing.[34] Walter T. Brown has assembled information on both sides of the question.[35]

Oil Gushers

When oil reservoirs are tapped by drilling, the immense pressure in the reservoir forces up a spouting geyser. The great pressure that is still surrounding oil formations is thought by some geologists to testify to a young earth. Dickey and others have published the results of their research on this matter in *Science*:

> Studies show that any pressure built should be dissipated, bled off into surrounding rocks, within a few thousand years. The excessive pressures found within oil beds, therefore, refute the notion of their age being on the order of millions of years and argues for the youthful age (less than about 10,000 years) of the rock formations and the entrapped oil.[36]

Melvin A. Cook has also addressed this matter in *Prehistory and Earth Models*.[37]

The Earth's Magnetic Field

Dr Thomas G. Barnes charted the decay of earth's magnetic field in relation to the age of the earth. He based his figures upon measurements taken from 1835 to 1965 of the half-life of earth's magnetic field (calculated to be 1,400 years).[38] Wysong concluded from the first edition of Barnes' work (1973):

> Calculating the rate of decay of the magnetic field, and extrapolating backwards, the strength of the earth's field at any point in history can be computed. If we extrapolate to just 20,000 years, the Joule heat

32. Walter Brown, *op.cit.*, 68.
33. Paul D. Ackerman, *It's A Young World After All* (Baker Book House: Grand Rapids, MI, 1986), 21.
34. R. Ganapathy *et al.*, 'Apollo 12 Lunar Samples', *Science*, Vol. 170, 30 October 1970, 533-534.
35. Walter Brown, *Ibid.*
36. Wysong, *op. cit.*, 159, referring to M. Cook, (Ref. 24) p. 341; P. Dickey and others: 'Abnormal Pressure in Deep Wells of Southwestern Louisiana', in *Science*, 160 (1968): 609.
37. Melvin A. Cook, *Prehistory and Earth Models* (Max Parrish: London, 1966), 10-14.
38. Thomas G. Barnes, *Origin and Destiny of the Earth's Magnetic Field* (Institute for Creation Research: El Cajon, Calif., 1983, second edition).

generated would probably liquify the earth... Therefore, according to this dating method, the earth cannot be millions or even tens of thousands of years old. Rather, the decay of the earth's magnetic moment speaks to (1) a creation of the earth; and (2) an age for the earth of less than 10,000 years.[39]

Criticisms were properly raised against some opinions in the first edition of Barnes' volume, where he denied the reality of the reversals of earth's magnetic fields. He and other creationists later accepted the correctness of reversals of magnetic fields. Most interpretations of the magnetic fields are still based on an ancient chronology,[40] but a revised model for magnetic reversals has been worked out by Dr Russell Humphreys in terms of a young earth.[41] Dr Hugh Ross denied the validity of all of Barnes' research[42] on the basis of the limitations of his first edition regarding magnetic reversals. But apart from this earlier mistake, which has now been corrected, Dr Russell Humphreys has confirmed the essential correctness of Barnes' research (even though Dr Ross apparently failed to take account of this recent confirmation in his *Creation and Time*[43]).

The Mississippi River Delta

Henry M. Morris did considerable work on the chronological significance of river deltas.[44] Huse summarizes Morris's and other studies, especially as it pertains to the Mississippi delta:

> Approximately 300 million cubic yards of sediment are deposited into the Gulf of Mexico by the Mississippi River each year. By carefully studying the volume and rate of acculumation of the Mississippi River delta and then dividing the weight of the sediments deposited annually into the total weight of the delta, it can be determined that the age of the delta is about 4,000 years old.[45]

39. Wysong, *op. cit.*, 161.
40. e.g. D. W. Strangway, *History of the Earth's Magnetic Field* (McGraw-Hill Book Co.: New York, 1970) and J. R. Dunn and others, 'Paleomagnetic study of a reversal of the earth's magnetic field', Science 172, 840-845.
41. See John D. Morris, *The Young Earth* (Master Books: Colorado Springs, CO, 1994) for the details of Humphreys revision of Barnes' earlier research.
42. Ross, *Creation and Time*, 106.
43. Mark Van Bebber and Paul S. Taylor, *Creation and Time: A Report on the Progressive Creationist Book by Hugh Ross* (Eden Communications: Mesa, Arizona, 1994), 107-108.
44. Morris, *op. cit.*, 303-330.
45. Huse, *op. cit.*, 23.24.

Salinity and Chemical Composition of the Oceans

Henry Morris has also studied in detail the salinity of the oceans, and found in it an evidence of a young age of the earth.[46] From his work and that of several others, Wysong has concluded:

> The uranium, sodium, nickel, magnesium, silicon, potassium, copper, gold... molybdenum and bicarbonate concentrations (and many others) in the oceans are much less than would be expected if these elements and compounds were being added to the oceans at the present rate for thousands of millions of years. Some, for example nitrates and uranium, do not break down or recycle like salt. Their small concentrations are then taken as an accurate indicator that the oceans are a few thousand years old.[47]

The Poynting-Robertson Effect

Articles in *The Astrophysical Journal*[48] and in *Nature*[49] have discussed 'The Poynting-Robertson Effect.' Creationists have understood this phenomenon as bearing witness to a young earth. Paul Ackerman explains why creationists believe this phenomenon indicates a young world. He calls it 'the solar janitor'.[50] He compares its effect in space to the rain hitting one's windshield. Photons (light radiations from the sun) slow down the forward movement of objects in space.[51] Wysong summarizes the results of this solar process:

> The solar drag force exerted upon micrometeoroids in the solar system causes the particles to spiral into the sun. This is called the Poynting-Robertson effect. The sun is thus vacuum sweeping space at the rate of about 100,000 tons per day. If the solar system is billions of years old, there should no longer be any significant quantities of micrometeoroids since there is no known source of significant replenishment. On the contrary, however, the solar system is abundant in micrometeoroids. This speaks for solar youth.[52]

Harold S. Slusher concluded (on the basis of Whipple's research on the sorting effect according to size of the Poynting-Robertson phenomenon, which yielded no dispersion whatsoever in any of the meteor streams studied):

46. Morris, *op. cit.*, 385-387. See also S.A. Austin and D.R. Humphreys, 'The sea's missing salt: a dilemma for evolutionists', Proceedings of the Second International Conference on Creationism, 1990, Vol. II, pp. 17-33.
47. Wysong, *op. cit.*, 163.
48. Stanley P. Wyatt, Jr. and Fred L. Whipple, 'The Poynting–Robertson Effect on Meteor Orbits', *The Astrophysical Journal*, Vol. 3, January 1950, 134-141.
49. David A. Weintraub, 'Comets in Collision', *Nature*, Vol. 351, 6 June 1991, 440-441.
50. Ackerman, *op. cit.*, see chapter 3.
51. *Ibid.*, 32, 33.
52. Wysong, *op. cit.*, 171.

If there is not this dispersion, this spreading out of material into smaller and smaller orbits, how can meteor streams be more than 10,000 years old? Meteor showers do not show the dispersion effect that the Poynting-Robertson effect predicts; therefore they cannot be old.[53]

Radiohalos

Dr Robert Gentry has done original work upon rapidly decaying radioactive elements, particularly polonium radiohalos, which confirms a young earth. Gentry's *Creation's Tiny Mystery*[54] argues for a sudden creation, and one of his articles in *Science* is also relevant to this question.[55] Huse discusses its significance for a correct chronology:

Polonium 218 has been considered a daughter element of the natural decay of uranium, but through the works of Dr Gentry and other researchers, polonium halos have been found in mica and fluorite without any evidence of *parents*. In other words, it was primordial – present in the original granite from the very beginning. Also, and most significantly, polonium halos should not exist at all because of their extremely short half-lives. Polonium 218 has a half-life of only 3 minutes. If the evolutionist's interpretation was correct and the rock formations gradually cooled over millions of years, the polonium would have decayed into other elements long ago.

Thus, the evidence clearly points to an instantaneous crystallization of the host basement rocks of the earth concurrent with the formation of the polonium. Simply stated, the presence of polonium radiohalos is one of the greatest blows to evolutionary thinking because it speaks so eloquently of instantaneous creation.[56]

Although Hugh Ross has denied the validity of Gentry's work,[57] Van Bebber and Taylor have questioned the methodology involved in Ross's critique, and stated that Gentry had already given convincing answers to such objections.[58]

Population Growth

In *Biblical Cosmology And Modern Science*, Henry M. Morris devotes chapter six to 'World Population and Bible Chronology'.[59] In painstaking detail with the aid of mathematical equations, he shows how the world population is an indication of a young chronology of the

53. Harold S. Slusher, 'A Young Universe', Bible–Science Newsletter, 13 January 1975, 1 ff., quoted in Ackerman, *op. cit.*, 34.
54. Robert V. Gentry, *Creation's Tiny Mystery* (Knoxville, TN: Earth Science Associates, 1986).
55. Robert V. Gentry *et al.*, 'Differential Lead Retention in Zicrons: Implications for Nuclear Waste Containment', *Science*, 16 April 1982, 296-298.
56. Huse, *op. cit.*, 26, 27.
57. Ross, *Creation and Time*, 108-110.
58. Van Bebber and Taylor, *op. cit.*, 106-107.
59. Baker Book House: Grand Rapids, MI, 1970, 72-83.

earth. In a later work, *Scientific Creationism*, he shows that an extremely conservative average population growth of only ½ per cent per year (just ¼ of our present rate) would add up to the entire present population of earth in only 4,000 years.[60]

Biblical Cosmology And Modern Science argues against the possibility of an ancient earth in terms of human population, stating that:

> *It begins to be glaringly evident that the human race cannot be very old!* The traditional Biblical chronology is infinitely more realistic than is the million-year history of mankind assumed by the evolutionist. If the above very conservative assumptions were made (x = 1, c = 1.5) [In Morris' formula, x= the average span of life in terms of a generation, and c = the average number of children per family] for the over 28,600 generations assumed in a supposed million years of man's life on earth, the world population should now be over 10^{5000} people.... Even if we eventually are able to colonize other worlds, and to build space cities everywhere in the inter-stellar spaces, it can be shown that a maximum of no more than 10^{100} people could be crammed into the entire known universe!
>
> The Ussher chronology, on the other hand, based on a literal acceptance of the Biblical histories, gives the date of the Flood as about 4300 years ago. The present population of the world has come originally from Noah's three sons (Genesis 9:19). To be ultra-conservative, assume that one generation is 43 years and thus that there have been only 100 generations since Noah. To produce a world population of 3 billion persons (still assuming x = 1), equation (4) [equation 4 is explained on p. 73 of Morris, op.cit.] is solved for c as follows:
>
> $$3,000,000,000 = 2 \ (c)^{100} \text{ from which:}$$
>
> $$c = (1,500,000,000)^{.01} = 1.24, \text{ or approximately } 1\ 1/4.$$

Thus, the average family must have had 2.5 children in order to bring the population to its present magnitude in 100 generations. This is eminently reasonable, though conservative, and is strong confirmation of at least the order-of-magnitude accuracy of the Ussher chronology. However, a period of human history much greater than indicated by the post-Deluge chronology of the Bible is evidently rendered improbable in a very high degree by the facts of population. A million years even at this rate would produce a population of 102700 people.'[61]

---

60. Morris, *Scientific Creationism* (Creation-Life Publishers: San Diego, CA, 1976), 277.
61. Morris, *Biblical Cosmology And Modern Science*, 75, 76.

TECHNICAL AND BIBLIOGRAPHICAL NOTES FOR CHAPTER EIGHT

Chronometrical Studies Indicating A Young Earth

Of the large number of contemporary scientific studies which discuss natural phenomena indicating a young earth, only a few of the major ones will be listed here.

1. Henry M. Morris

The pioneering study on young earth chronometers was by Henry M. Morris and John C. Whitcomb, *The Genesis Flood*. Chapter VII, 'Problems in Biblical Geology', deals particularly with indications of young chronology. Such matters as: meteoritic dust, meteorite radioactivity, tektites, disintegration of comets, atmospheric comets, atmospheric helium, salt in the sea, juvenile water and crystal accretion are addressed.[62]

2. Walter T. Brown

The sixth edition of Dr Walter Brown's *In the Beginning: Compelling Evidence for Creation and the Flood* discusses a large sample of chronometers that suggest an earth only a few thousand years old. Among these evidences of physical youth are: helium, lead and helium diffusion, excess fluid pressure (of oil, gas and water), volcanic debris, river sediments, continental erosion, dissolved metals, shallow meteorites, meteoritic dust, magnetic decay, molten earth, moon recession, moon dust and debris, crater creep, hot moon, young comets, small comets, young rings (around Saturn, Uranus, Jupiter and Neptune), hot planets, solar wind, Poynting-Robertson effect, solar fuel, shrinking sun, star clusters, unstable galaxies, and galaxy clusters.[63]

He concludes:

> All dating techniques, especially the few that suggest vast ages, presume that a process observed today has always proceeded at its present rate.This assumption may be grossly inaccurate. Projecting presently known processes far back in time is more likely to be in error than extrapolation over a much shorter time. For the many dating 'clocks' that show a young earth and a young universe, a much better understanding usually exists for how they work.[64]

---

62. See Morris and Whitcomb, *op. cit.*, 378-391.
63. Walter Brown, *op. cit.*, 26-31.
64. *Ibid.*, 31.

3. R. L. Wysong

R. L. Wysong's *The Creation-Evolution Controversy* devotes part of Chapter Ten to 'Methods Showing Youth'.[65] He discusses several of the evidences for a short chronology which I have already listed above. In addition to these, he mentions: Carbon–14 disintegration versus production, large stars, dendrochronology, sea ooze, earth spin, mutation load, stellar radiation, cosmic dust velocity, earth heat, lunar inert gases, short-lived lunar isotopes, and atmospheric oxygen.

4. Paul D. Ackerman

Ackerman's *It's A Young World After All: Exciting Evidences for Recent Creation* discusses in a clear and helpful way a number of the evidences for a recent creation (and flood) as are listed above. Of particular interest is his comment on the American space program:

> The evidence of our space probes indicates that the solar system, despite its reputed antiquity, is active and alive. For evolutionist scientists the main outcome of our space exploration has been *surprise*. Phrases such as 'apparent paradox' and 'seems to violate known laws of physics' have abounded. Yet there is nothing in the finds that does not square fully with basic laws of physics, as long as one is willing to give up the idea of vast ages. The data are abundantly clear: the creation is not old; it is young.[66]

5. Dr Robert L. Whitelaw

Robert L. Whitelaw, Professor of Nuclear and Mechanical Engineering, Virginia Polytechnic Institute, has made an important study of 'Time, Life and History in the Light of 15,000 Radiocarbon Dates.'[67] In sum, he notes that '...the method could give measurable dates only to about 50,000 years before the present, since the radio-activity from anything older would be scarcely detectable.'[68] After studying 15,000 radiocarbon dates, he notes this (among several other conclusions): 'Practically every specimen of once-living material is found to be datable within 50,000 years.... To fully appreciate the significance of this, it must be emphasized that if Lyellian geology and evolutionary time are valid, if living matter has been accumulating and dying upon earth over supposed eons of time, then such a world-wide random sampling of buried organic matter should yield 20,000 undatable specimens for each one datable! Granted that many investigators

---

65. Wysong, *op. cit.*, 158–179.
66. Ackerman, *op. cit.*, 45.
67. Robert L. Whitelaw, 'Time, Life and History in the Light of 15,000 Radiocarbon Dates' in *Creation Research Quarterly* (June 1970), 56–71, 83.
68. *Ibid.*, 59.

were looking for specific ancient cultures.... Nevertheless, all were still dated within 50,000 years *to the maximum depth of any deposit!* The great preponderance of samples, moreover, related to vegetation, shells, pollen, peat bogs, buried trees, fossiliferous clay, ocean-bottom cores, buried bones and cultural charcoal beds – *most* of which should have been undatable. Yet, all had measurable radiocarbon activity!'[69]

Professor Whitelaw then goes on to consider the traditional biblical dates for creation and flood (less than 7,000 years ago) in light of these findings in radiocarbon dating of thousands of samples from throughout the geological world. He notes that of course a creation some 7,000 years ago is still very different from the radiocarbon suggestions of 50,000. However, he discusses two assumptions on which radiocarbon dating is based: '(1) the rate of production of C–14 in the atmosphere by cosmic rays is assumed equal to its rate of decay in living matter, at a value of 16.0 dpm/gm, and (2) this equilibrium is assumed to have been reached eons ago, so that all once-living matter datable by radiocarbon possessed this same activity when it died, namely 16.0 dpm/gm.'[70]

Whitelaw points to an imbalance between the decay rate of C–14 in living matter today (i.e. 16.0) and a production rate of about 19.0 of almost 20%. 'This imbalance, to use Libby's own phrase, points to a recent "turning on" of cosmic radiation...'[71] As Whitelaw works out the appropriate calculations, 'The "turning on" date, T, comes out less than 16,000 years ago!'[72]

Furthermore, Whitelaw shows that: 'A second inescapable consequence of this imbalance is that the *true* age, T, of any specimen will always be *less than* the measured age, L, using Libby's assumptions (as published in *Radiocarbon*) since the latter is calculated as if *no imbalance exists*.... The error... clearly becomes progressively worse as age increases. Thus the underlying data on which the radiocarbon clock is built compel us to acknowledge (1) a recent creation, and (2) a reduction in all published ages.'[73]

Using statistical methods, to which the reader is referred in Whitelaw's article, he calculates approximate dates of creation at about 7,000 years ago and the flood at around 4,950 years ago.[74]

Representative works of evangelical scholars who deny the implications of any or all of these evidences for a young world may

---

69. Ibid., 59, 62.
70. Ibid., 63.
71. Ibid., 64.
72. Ibid.
73. Ibid.
74. Ibid., 65.

be found in Professor Davis A. Young and Dr Hugh Ross,[75] as well as Dr Robert C. Newman and Herman J. Eckelmann, Jr.[76] Their writings may be consulted along with some of the creationist interactions with them.[77]

Chapters Seven and Eight may be succinctly summarized: those who are willing to look outside the uniformitarian, evolutionary paradigm which posits a solar system over four billion years old, will find several strands of empirical evidence that seem to point to a universe which may eventually prove to be not much more than six thousand years old. This is still a very minority reading of the evidence among scientists, but it indicates a new insistence on submitting previously unchallenged authority viewpoints to radical questioning. Those who questioned the truth claims of Scripture are now having their own truth claims questioned. This should be good for all who desire the advancement of truth. It appears less necessary than formerly automatically to abandon a plain, historico-literal reading of the earliest texts of Holy Scripture in order to accommodate a temporal paradigm that is now under radical question.

---

75. Davis A. Young, Creation and the Flood: An Alternative to Flood Geology and Theistic Evolution (Baker Book House: Grand Rapids, Mich., 1977) and The Biblical Flood: A Case Study of the Church's Response to Extrabiblical Evidence (Eerdmans: Grand Rapids, Mich., 1995); Hugh Ross, The Creator and the Cosmos (NavPress: Colorado Springs, CO, 1993) and Creation and Time (NavPress: Colorado Springs, CO, 1994).
76. Robert C. Newman and Herman J. Eckelmann, Jr., Genesis One and the Origin of the Earth (Interdisciplinary Biblical Research Institute: Hatfield, Penn., 1989).
77. For instance, Mark Van Bebber and Paul S. Taylor, op.cit.

QUESTIONS FOR STUDY

1. What are three basic assumptions in radioactive dating for it to be accurate?

2. What would cause radioactive dating to be inaccurate?

3. What is meant by creation with 'an appearance of age'?

4. What is 'uniformitarianism'?

5. Name some of the problems with this theory.

6. List some geological evidences for a universal flood.

7. How does Mount St. Helens volcanic action present a problem for the uniformitarianist's dating process?

8. What is the geologic column and what does evolutionary theory hold that it proves?

9. Do rock strata and fossil formations in any locations actually support their theory? Why or why not?

10. What is meant by 'overthrusts'?

11. Show how some geologists employ circular reasoning for their time scale.

12. Explain the basic concept of radio-carbon dating.

13. Assess its likelihood of accuracy.

14. What are some natural 'chronometers' that appear to bear witness to a young earth?

Chapter Nine

Days Two and Three of Creation: Separations Resulting in Air and Dry Land

THE second and third days of creation are both marked by the work of separation: that of the second day resulting in the firmament, and that of the third, in dry land.

The Second Day of Creation

Genesis 1:6-8 describes the work of the second day of creation in terms of a separation which would play a major part in making the world habitable for plant and animal life:

> And God said, Let there be a firmament in the midst of the waters, and let it divide the waters from the waters. And God made the firmament, and divided the waters which were under the firmament from the waters which were above the firmament: and it was so. And God called the firmament Heaven. And the evening and the morning were the second day.

This is the second of two essential separations to make earth a livable place. The first separation was *temporal*, as Cassuto points out, 'and was due to recur at regular intervals; the second was *spatial* and was destined to remain unchanged for ever.'[1]

---

1. Cassuto, *op. cit.*, 33, 34.

Thus on the second day of creation the world was something like an undifferentiated mass, or 'original amorphous matter'.[2] Perhaps it would be comparable to having a room full of mud and water and heat, pulsating like a moving blob. In it there would have been no breathing space. In other words, all the material elements were present as well as energy, but the dividing (or separating) and organizing of these elements which would be necessary to make the earth habitable had not yet occurred. It was, to use the old Greek concept, a chaos, and not yet a cosmos.

What happened on Day Two is that God by His creative activity, by His very speaking, divided out this uninhabitable mass of gasses, 'mud' and energetic elements, thus producing open breathing space or something like 'atmosphere.' The concept of 'firmament' or 'expanse' (Hebrew *raqia'*) comes from a Hebrew verb form meaning 'to strike or to stamp'. 'The root of the word is the same as that of *way^{e}raqq^e'u* ["and they did hammer out"] in Exodus 39:3: "And they did hammer out gold leaf"; the term signifies a kind of horizontal area, extending through the very heart of the mass of water and cleaving it into two layers, the one above the other – the upper and lower layers of waters.'[3] 'From [vs. 8 – "And God called the firmament Heaven"] ...we may infer that immediately after its formation, the firmament occupied of its own accord the place appointed for it by the will of God, which is the site of the heavens as we know it.'[4]

Morris describes the significance of the stretching out of the 'firmament':

> The earth had originally been 'standing out of the water and in the water' (2 Peter 3:5), indicating the preeminent importance of the marvelous compound H_2O, in the earth's composition and sustenance. All life and practically all earth processes depend upon water. The primeval deep which enveloped the earth (Gen. 1:2) had been divided into two segments on the Second Day: the waters *above* the firmament (i.e. atmosphere), very likely in the vapor state, extending far into space and providing the earth with a wonderful protective canopy under which to dwell, with a most pleasant climate and healthful environment; and the 'great deep' of subterranean waters, vast reservoirs from which were fed artesian springs and rivers, locked under pressure inside the crust.[5]

---

2. Cassuto, *ibid.*, 31.
3. *Ibid.*
4. *Ibid.*
5. Morris, *Biblical Cosmology And Modern Science*, 32.

Morris and Whitcomb[6] and others[7] have suggested that this stretched out firmament originally included a massive canopy of water vapor, extending high up into the atmosphere. If so, it has been argued that it may have been the source for much of the water volume that fell during the Flood of Noah (perhaps condensed by the dust of volcanic activity). But the text of Genesis does *not* specifically state the formation of a canopy of water vapor in the firmament on the second day, and more recent work by scientists who believe in both creation and flood suggests a rather different explanation of 'waters above the expanse'. This newer model for explaining the position of the primeval waters and the possible mechanics of the great Flood a few thousand years later seems to avoid some of the problems in the canopy hypothesis.

Some of the severe problems that render the Vapor Canopy theory untenable have been discussed by Robert L. Whitelaw[8] and Walter T. Brown.[9] Brown summarizes these difficulties as: 'The Heat Problem' (a large vapor or ice canopy would so increase heat that it would 'roast' all living things); 'The Light Problem' (starlight 'for signs and seasons' could scarcely have been seen, and sunlight could not have reached through with sufficient heat to support tropical plants); 'The Pressure Problem' (a vapor canopy holding more than 40 feet of water would increase such high pressure at its base that its temperature would exceed 220 degrees F); 'The Support Problem' (neither vapor, liquid nor ice canopy could have physically survived for the many centuries between creation and the flood. It would condense, evaporate or vaporize); 'The Ultraviolet Problem' (A canopy surrounding the atmosphere would not have been protected from ultraviolet light, which would have disassociated water into hydrogen and oxygen, thus destroying the canopy).[10]

In addition to some of these problems, Whitelaw argues cogently that the Canopy Theory cannot account for the sudden decrease in the specific production rate of C–14 immediately after the Flood (for a canopy would have caused a lower specific reduction rate, rather than higher.) Whitelaw's work with 15,000 radiocarbon dates points to a higher, not lower, specific reduction rate of C–14 before the Flood,

6. Morris and Whitcomb, *op. cit.*, 243-258.

7. e.g. Donald Patten, 'The Pre-Flood Greenhouse Effect', *Symposium on Creation II* (Grand Rapids: Baker Book House, 1970), 11-41.

8. Robert L. Whitelaw, 'The Fountains of the Great Deep and the Windows of Heaven: A Look at the Canopy Theory, and of a Better Alternative' in *Science at the Crossroads: 1983 National Creation Conference Proceedings* (Minneapolis, Minn., 1983), 95-104.

9. Walter T. Brown, *In The Beginning: Compelling Evidence for Creation and the Flood* (Sixth General Edition: Center For Scientific Creation: Phoenix, AZ, 1995), 174-179.

10. *Ibid.*, 175-177.

and this renders the Canopy Theory untenable from the perspective of C–14 dating.[11]

The proposed physical mechanism for explaining the world-wide catastrophe of Noah's Flood is not our concern in this volume (since we deal only with the first two chapters of Genesis). However, the interested reader is referred to Whitelaw's proposal of 'Ocean Floor and Terrestrial Evidence of a "Recent" Global Catastrophe in conjunction with related Evidence for Catastrophe in the Solar System' (i.e. a coincidence of Earth, Mars, Ceres and Jupiter).[12] Brown discusses at length and in careful empirical detail 'The hydroplate theory' – an explanation based on the discovery in the 1950s of the Mid Oceanic Ridge. The concept rests upon the catastrophic division of the various plates on which the continents and oceans of earth ride. The continents are believed to have quickly slidden east and west from what is now the Mid-Atlantic Ridge and come to their present positions owing to massive volcanic disturbances associated with the beginning of the Great Flood, when vast amounts of water burst forth from deep within the earth, thus inundating the entire world.[13]

Whitelaw describes the results of these movements:

> Magnified by these vast continental motions, the world ocean, raised some 3,000 feet by the Pacific floor upheaval, surges back and forth across each of the subsided moving continents in waves over 10,000 feet high. The titanic hydraulic forces they generate roll up vast areas of vegetation and sediment with each pass, burying them in successive strata at enormous pressure. Hence the worldwide fossil beds all in sedimentary strata, inexplicable by uniformitarian geology, but clearly implied in the Biblical phrase, 'And the waters prevailed (Hebrew *gabar* – to become mighty) exceedingly upon the earth' (Gen. 7:19).[14]

Genesis 1 and 2 of course do not yet go into these matters (that is reserved for chapters 6 and following). What the text does clearly teach here about the second day of creation, however, is that it was marked by a divine separation between the waters, which resulted in a livable atmosphere on earth. Brown and Whitelaw appear to be correct Biblically and scientifically in suggesting that the 'waters above the earth' simply means those above the earth's crust as opposed to the subterranean waters beneath it (masses of which extruded at the beginning of the Flood).

---

11. Whitelaw, *op. cit.*, 97, 98.
12. *Ibid.*, 98-103.
13. Brown, Sixth edition, *op. cit.*, 75-105; 184-186.
14. Whitelaw, 'The Fountains of the Great Deep...', 102.

The Third Day of Creation: Dry Land

Another separation was performed by God on the third day of creation. This separation was also essential to future life on earth, and indicates a further step in preparing the earth for habitation. Genesis 1:9 tells us that God separated the waters under the heavens into one place so that the dry land appeared. The water recedes into the seas and subterranean caverns and the dry land is raised up. The 'stage' was now being developed for plant, animal – and then human – life to inhabit the planet.

In other words, until the third day, the earth was completely covered by water, as though it were a shoreless ocean with nowhere for a boat to land. It was, of course, not yet a habitable environment. So God by His mighty power caused the continents to be formed, and perhaps mountain ranges to be pushed up (though even more of this architectonic building may have occurred during the cataclysm of the great Flood).

Psalm 104:7-9 speaks poetically of the division of the sea from the land:

> At thy rebuke they fled; at the voice of thy thunder they hasted away. They go up by the mountains; they go down by the valleys unto the place which thou hast founded for them. Thou hast set a bound that they may not pass over; that they turn not again to cover the earth.

This third separation occurring on Day Three of Creation brought about what we might call a completion of infrastructure, and its accomplishment is noted by God calling it 'good'. 'Now that the work of the water was completed and the world had assumed its proper tripartite form of Heaven, Earth and Sea, it is possible to declare, *that it was good.*'[15]

Immediately after this third separation, God introduced plant life into the earth, as though to point to the purpose for which the various separations have been made. In the words of Cassuto:

> On the selfsame day, as soon as the inanimate matter, which serves as a foundation for plant-life, had been set in order, there were created, without delay, the various kinds of vegetation. Similarly on the sixth day: immediately after the formation of vegetable and animal, which, in turn are the basis of human life – on the same day – man was created.[16]

Unlike the Deism of western culture, which separates the living God from the real world, Genesis 1:11 shows God speaking ('Let the earth bring forth grass...'), and Genesis 1:12 shows the immediate, *physical*

---

15. Cassuto, *op. cit.*, 40.
16. *Ibid.*

response: 'And the earth brought forth grass, and herb yielding seed after his kind, and the tree yielding fruit, whose seed was in itself, after his kind: and God saw that it was good.' As Aalders reminds us: 'When it is stated that the earth "produced" these plants, this does not mean that the power for this lay within the earth itself. It merely indicates that the divine will caused plants to sprout forth from the earth.'[17]

Genesis 1:12 indicates something of crucial importance about the trees and plants that God created on the third day: they were full grown at the beginning, with their seed in them. That is, vegetable life was formed with the capacity to reproduce itself through seed 'after its kind,' so as to pass on its living characteristics in orderly fashion for that future, which God had in store for the natural order.

The biblical picture presented here by Genesis is of a living God who creates out of nothing, and then orders, beautifies and interacts with what He created so as to guide it to His intended purposes for it. Cyril of Alexandria, writing against the fourth-century form of Hellenistic dualism that separated God from the natural world, constantly emphasizes the genuine interaction between the transcendent God and the physical world. Cyril refers to God's direct intervention at every stage of creation week in such a way that God immediately determines the physical laws governing each creature, including plant and animal life.[18]

How different this is from the secularist paradigm which in its earlier phase pictured a remote deity who somehow brought the machine into being, but then remains distant and cut off from it, as an absentee landlord, allowing it 'to run on its own steam' without personal interaction with it! It is, if possible, even further from the contemporary phase of the secular world model, which portrays nature more as an organism than a machine; a complex that became alive on its own and developed its own structures and reproductive capacities, out of eternally existing matter. The scientific implausibility of the literally incredible thesis of abiogenesis (living structures forming themselves out of matter which somehow 'came to life' – or 'abiogenesis') is discussed in *Technical & Bibliographical Notes for Chapter Nine*.

There is a sobriety about the biblical account of the origins of plant life which is far removed from the mythological guesswork of the evolutionary paradigm. The few, but illuminating details given in the brief Genesis text on this question must now be more closely considered.

---

17. Aalders, *op. cit.*, 63.
18. Cyril of Alexandria, *Contra Iulianum Imperatorem* in Migne, *Patrologia Graece*, 76, 585.

First, there is a distinction between types of vegetable life, 'Let the earth bring forth grass, the herb yielding seed, *and* the fruit tree yielding fruit after his kind, whose seed is in itself...' (v. 11). Although the English version might appear to posit three types of vegetation, Cassuto's explanation is convincing, that 'grass' [*dese'*] 'refers to vegetation generally' and that the classification is twofold, not threefold: that is, 'plants' [*'esebh*] and 'trees' [*'es*].[19] In Aalders' view, the two categories of plant life depend on whether they are 'seed-bearing' or 'fruit-bearing'. 'The obvious distinction was whether the seed was inside a fruit or not.'[20]

Secondly, this small text in one sense might be said to provide the underlying foundations of the science of genetics in the pregnant phrase: 'yielding seed after his kind' (v. 12). Cassuto notes that the importance of 'seed after his kind' is emphasized by the recurrence of some form of the stem *zr'* ['seed, to yield seed'] no less than ten times (in Genesis 1:11, 12 and again in 29): 'as though it wished to draw the reader's attention to the fact that the plants that were created on the third day were capable of reproducing themselves after their likeness by means of the seed.'[21]

The meaning of 'seed' can be grasped with more exegetical and scientific precision than 'kind'. 'Seed' is clearly the ability to reproduce a form of life 'in its own likeness'. Genetically, this means precisely what Henry Morris points out:

> Implanted in each created organism was a 'seed', programmed to enable the continuing replication of that type of organism. The modern understanding of the extreme complexities of the so-called DNA molecule and the genetic code contained in it has reinforced the Biblical teaching of the stability of kinds. Each type of organism has its own unique structure of the DNA and can only specify the reproduction of that same kind. There is a tremendous amount of variational potential within each kind, facilitating the generation of distinct individuals and even of many varieties within the kind, but nevertheless precluding the evolution of new *kinds*! A great deal of 'horizontal' variation is easily possible, but no 'vertical' changes.[22]

The exact limits of 'kind' is a more difficult question. Aalders explores its Biblical usage:

> In the Old Testament it is applied only to living organisms and then usually to animal life. This is the only place it is used to denote plant

19. Cassuto, *op.cit.*, 40
20. Aalders, *op. cit.*, 62.
21. Cassuto, *op. cit.*, 41.
22. Morris, *The Genesis Record*, 63.

life. If we examine the passages in which the word occurs, no clearly defined meaning of the word comes through. In verse 21 of this chapter it is used to distinguish such broad groups as water creatures and birds. In verses 24-25 it likewise applies to broad groups such as cattle and creeping things. In Genesis 6:20 and 7:14 it is used of birds, cattle, and creeping things, and in Ezekiel 47:10 of fish. Over against this, in Leviticus 11:13-19 and in Deuteronomy 14:12-18, the word is used to designate specific kinds of birds. In Leviticus 11:29-30 it refers to all kinds of lizards, while in Leviticus 22 only certain kinds of edible grasshoppers are designated. It is obvious, therefore, that there is no justification for concluding that the word indicates a certain definite classification that would meet the standards of botanists or biologists. These are not 'species' as they are generally understood in these sciences. All we can say is that the word 'kind' indicates that, from the day of creation, an abundance of variety was displayed in the world of plants.[23]

Hebrew word usage certainly indicates that Aalders is right in stating that 'kind' is often much broader than modern understandings of 'species'. Morris suggests that probably 'kind' [*min*] 'often is identical with the "species," sometimes with the "genus," and possibly once in a while with the "family". Practically never is variation possible outside the biologic family.'[24] In sum, 'Whatever precisely is meant by the term "kind" (Hebrew *min*), it does indicate the limitations of variation.... In any case, the evolutionary dogma that all living things are interrelated by common ancestry and descent is refuted by these Biblical statements, as well as by all established scientific observations made to date.'[25]

Scientific evidence for essential genetic stability of 'the kinds' (though *not* narrowly defined 'fixity of species') is discussed in *Technical & Bibliographical Notes*. Hence, separation of sea and land and genetic stability of newly created plant life were the great divine works of the third day, preparing the world for the introduction of animal life, and finally, all would be ready for mankind: the crown of God's creation. On this remarkable day, the text states twice the phrase: 'And God saw that it was good' (vv. 10 and 12), for 'two works were performed on the third day, the separation of the sea from the dry land and the creation of plants; hence the formula *that it was good* is uttered twice on this day.'[26]

---

23. Aalders, *op. cit.*, 62.
24. Morris, *op. cit.*, 63.
25. *Ibid.*, 63, 64.
26. Cassuto, *op. cit.*, 41.

TECHNICAL AND BIBLIOGRAPHICAL NOTES FOR CHAPTER NINE

1. Abiogenesis (Chemical Evolution): A Failing Theory of Origins

The teaching of Genesis 1:11-12 is that the origin of plant life was by a creative act of God on the third day of creation, and that this life reproduces its likeness in subsequent generations by the genetic coding passed on in its 'seed'. Because of its anti-theism, the philosophy (or paradigm) of evolutionary materialism of necessity had to replace God and His creative act with something else.

A. The Alleged Mechanism of Abiogenesis

On the basis of what must be called a type of 'faith' (which, as we shall directly see runs contrary to known scientific principles), evolutionary theorists rehabilitated the ancient Greek concept of the spontaneous generation of life from eternally existing material elements. But this very old theory of spontaneous generation of life (as an alternative to divine creation out of nothing) had already been discredited by experiments of Francesco Redi in 1668 and by work of Louis Pasteur in the 1860s. But it was given a new lease on life in the 1920s, when a Russian scientist, A.I. Oparin, proposed that life gradually arose in a series of stages from non-living matter. Simple chemicals were alleged to have combined to form organic compounds, such as DNA and so on upwards. Oparin's theory is called prebiotic evolution or chemical evolution.

His theory claimed support by Miller and Urey, American biochemical researchers, who became famous in 1953 for experiments in which they mixed simple gases together, exposed them to energy sources, and seemed to have come up with some amino acids. But the experiment was flawed as a true model of origins because the workers had to eliminate oxygen in order to produce these acids. There is strong evidence that there has always been plenty of oxygen in the earth's atmosphere (found in oxides in rocks). As Michael Behe states concerning Miller's experiment: 'Since he thought amino acids would be the most interesting chemicals to find, he jiggled the apparatus around in hopes of producing them.'[27] His assessment of later 'prebiotic chemical' experiments of later scientists such as Sidney Fox on 'proteinoids' is no more positive: '... a heavy odor of investigator involvement hangs over proteinoids.'[28]

---

27. Behe, *op. cit.*, 169.
28. *Ibid.*, 170.

The fascinating details of this unsuccessful (though still popular) attempt to give scientific credence to an old Greek myth is found in *Of Pandas and People: The Central Question of Biological Origins* (pp.3-7 and 41-58).[29] The authors evaluate abiogenesis on a scientifically empirical basis, and their research indicates that complex structures of coded information (essential to life) are far more likely to be the product of intelligent design by a Higher Power, than mere chance in a prebiotic soup, in which there were oxygen and other factors against the production of DNA. As Dr Carl Fliermans has pointed out, if a code is involved, there must be a decoding system already in place to understand the code.[30]

One of the authors of *Of Pandas and People*, Charles B. Thaxton, has (along with Walter L. Bradley) elsewhere written a penetrating chapter on this same theme: 'Information and the Origin of Life.'[31] In it they chronicle how, following the work of T. R. Cech, abio-geneticists hoped that discoveries in the structure of RNA '...might provide a bridge from simple chemical building blocks such as amino acids and sugars to the highly complex DNA-based cells found in modern organisms.'[32]

But 'the veracity' of this model was 'seriously challenged by new research findings in the 1980s. RNA has been found to be exceedingly difficult to synthesize under the conditions that likely prevailed when life originated. Furthermore, it has been established that RNA cannot easily generate copies of itself. To make matters worse, even Miller's seminal experiments have been found suspect due to atmospheric physicists' newly emerging consensus that the early earth's atmosphere never contained significant amounts of ammonia, methane or hydrogen.'[33]

They further note that 'The conceptual bankruptcy of Oparin's "soup theory" was highlighted in a debate held at the international ISSOL symposium in Berkeley, California, in 1986.'[34] Thaxton and Bradley conclude: 'In the light of the foregoing analysis we consider that it is reasonable to doubt whether prebiological evolution occurred, and we suggest intelligent design as an alternative.... The general persistence in defending prebiotic evolution is based on philosophical commitment quite apart from experience.'[35]

---

29. P. Davis, D. H. Kenyon & C. B. Thaxton, *Of Pandas and People: The Central Question of Biological Origins* (Haughton Publishing Company: Dallas, TX, 1989).
30. Personal communication to the author, 18 December 1996.
31. Chapter 5 in J. P. Moreland, ed., *op. cit.*
32. *Ibid.*, 175.
33. *Ibid.*
34. *Ibid.*, 193.
35. *Ibid.*, 197.

Michael Behe devotes two chapters of his recent book to showing that as more is learned about the amazing complexity of cellular structures (as well as that of their building blocks), the theory of chemical evolution becomes ever more impossible.[36] He refers to Gerald Joyce and Leslie Orgel – two scientists who have worked long and hard on the origin of life problem – [who] call RNA 'the prebiotic chemist's nightmare.'[37]

B. The Underlying Assumption and Circular Methodology of Abiogenesis

Another significant volume that shows the nonempirical and 'religious' nature of the theory of abiogenesis is by Canadian Medical Professor, Magnus Verbrugge, *Alive: An Enquiry into The Origin and Meaning of Life* (Ross House Books: Vallecito, CA, 1984). Dr Verbrugge writes:

> Our Christian scientists must be equipped to show the utter weakness of the materialistic position: that it rests on a primitive religion which began in the mists of Greek mythology ... abiogenesis is science fiction, not to be taken seriously even by humanistic scientists. Its major consequence is that life is merely a modified form of 'dead' matter. Abiogenesis declares that *life is death*. In contrast, Christ brings the good news of *life*, also in science.[38]

His volume demonstrates that '...materialism is in flagrant conflict with the pertinent data, and that abiogenesis is a myth, that it has no basis in reality.'[39] Underlying the materialist explanation of origins is a severe category mistake:

> The tragedy of Western science is its tendency to 'promote adjectives to the rank of substantives,' to make *functors* [defined by Verbrugge as 'An entity which can function just like an actor can act. Functions do not exist except as a property of a functor' – p. 153] out of *functions*. By this confusion between functor and function we 'barter understanding for voodoo formulas'. It all goes back 2500 years to Greek metaphysics. Modern scientists have so far refused to update their philosophy in keeping with their rapidly expanding body of information. Animism still reigns.
>
> Herman Dooyeweerd published a penetrating critique of this Greek legacy, so fatal to our understanding of the real world, in a series of articles in *Philosophia Reformata* between 1943 and 1946. He pointed out

---

36. Behe, *op. cit.*, chapters 7 and 8.
37. *Ibid.*, 171.
38. Magnus Verbrugge, *Alive: An Enquiry into The Origin and Meaning of Life*, 7, 8.
39. *Ibid.*, 7.

that Aristotle used to abstract a function such as life from a functor and then endow it with a substance called anima or soul.[40]

Verbrugge demonstrates that this primitive animism (which turns 'function' into 'functor') became important to modern science as a substitute for the God whom the European Enlightenment rejected:

> As soon as man rejected the Creator, he replaced Him with a substitute. In that way animistic belief gained access to a branch of science. And immediately speculation and fiction would enter through the back door, complete with circular reasoning and other flaws in logic.[41]

Throughout his book, he unveils the fact that circular reasoning (*not* empirical or operational science) is the underlying methodology used 'to prove' abiogenesis. For instance, Jacques Monod makes a god out of chance,[42] and Harold Blum makes a god out of time.[43] Verbrugge replies to them both:

> [Monod] declares chance to be the non-dependent agency on which all else depends for its existence. So he makes this abstract concept into something divine, endowed with the power to create...[44] [And] Blum ignores the question of whether inorganic matter *has* given birth to living things. He talks himself quickly past the question of *how* inorganic matter could have done so. He just walks around these hurdles and addresses the question of whether it could *possibly* have happened.... This is of course loose talk. *Father Time* solves no problems, just as *Mother Nature* does not give birth to things. Time is not a functor that can make it probable for the properties of living organisms to appear. Time is not an agent that can make possible what clashes with the laws of physics and chemistry. Time is not even an agent. It is a concept. Blum raises the abstract concept of time to the position of a spiritual power to 'create' the conditions necessary for life.[45]

Thus it is clear that the work of I. A. Oparin and those who have followed him assumed a sort of animism, and then 'proved' it by means of circular reasoning. Verbrugge illustrates how Lawrence S. Dillon in this way justified the work of Oparin, Miller and Urey.[46]

First, he quotes Dillon: 'Life is the capacity of synthesizing proteins ... it becomes amply evident that living things are chemical entities, whose fundamental properties are describable in ordinary physico-

---

40. *Ibid.*, 19.
41. *Ibid.*, 137.
42. *Ibid.*, 117.
43. *Ibid.*, 118.
44. *Ibid.*, 117.
45. *Ibid.*, 118.
46. L. S. Dillon, *The Genetic Mechanisms and the Origin of Life* (New York: Plenum Press, 1978).

chemical terms. Hence, to this degree *the prevailing mechanistic view of the organic world is firmly supported.*'[47]

Then, Verbrugge demonstrates that his proof is nothing but a species of circular reasoning:

1. Living things are chemical entities.
2. Their properties are describable in physico-chemical terms.
3. This firmly supports our viewing them as chemical mechanisms.

'Stripped of redundant verbiage' this means:

1) Living things are chemical entities.
2) They have chemical properties.
3) This firmly confirms the view that they are chemical entities.

It is legitimate to ask why such a celebrated scientist can come up with such a naive and unscientific specimen of circular reasoning. His first premise already contains the conclusion. It begs the question. It is 'petitio principii'.[48]

Verbrugge goes beyond Dillon, and concludes that this sort of circular reasoning applies to scores of other scientists who assume chemical evolution and abiogenesis:

They all say the same thing:

1) First there was only inanimate matter on earth.
2) Today we observe many species of living beings.
3) These clearly arrived on the scene after the earth was formed.
4) Since *there is nothing but physical forces* that could have produced them, we *must* hold these forces responsible for their appearance.

If proposition 1 and 2 are true, No. 3 follows logically from them. Any Bible-believer will agree: God created them after the earth. But proposition 4 is entirely unrelated to the other three. It is not based on observation. It too is based on a revelation: it is a 'must', whether you like it or not. It is revealed to us by the imagination of the Greeks and repeated over and over by modern materialists. But verbal repetition brings no proof to a proposition. Like all forms of humanism, materialism is a religion. It cannot be proved but must be believed. And it needs the theory of abiogenesis in order to explain life's origin.[49]

As Verbrugge frequently says, given the empirical and logical bankruptcy of materialistic abiogenesis, a different paradigm is called for: '... fresh winds have begun to blow. Voices are being raised, asking

47. *Ibid.*, 426.
48. Verbrugge, *op. cit.*, 118, 119.
49. *Ibid.*

for a new paradigm...'[50] This volume, in company with many others, hopes to make a contribution in that direction.

2. The Genetic Stability of 'the Kinds'

Genesis 1:11 and 12 deal not only with the origin of vegetable life, but also with its orderly continuation in the future. As we have seen, this is by means of stable 'kinds' who by virtue of their seed pass their likeness to succeeding generations. Genetic studies indicate that while there is wide variation possible within the broad groups known as 'kinds', there has never yet been demonstrated one kind evolving into another, or a more primitive kind developing itself into a higher, more complex form.

The belief that they do, although widely held by impressive numbers of persons and great institutions for well over a century, is still – scientifically speaking – nothing but that: a belief. It is a fundamental plank in the humanist platform (or paradigm) of materialistic monism, and has to be assumed (just as abiogenesis) in order to be proven.

The Darwinian faith in constant change within living organisms by means of genetic instability is one of the weakest planks in the entire evolutionary edifice. *Of Pandas and People* carefully surveys the empirical evidence against large scale genetic change.[51] They note that 'while Darwin was constructing his theory, an Austrian monk named Gregor Mendel was conducting experiments [to account for changes or new traits within organisms]':[52]

> Mendel discovered that traits could be lost in one generation only to reappear in a later generation. For example, when he crossed a pea plant bearing wrinkled seeds, all the offspring in the first generation had round seeds. Was the wrinkled trait lost? Not at all; it reappeared in the next generation of pea plants.
>
> Mendel concluded that heredity is governed by particles (later called genes) passed from parent to offspring. A trait might disappear temporarily, but the gene that codes for the trait remains present within the organism and is passed on to its offspring.[53]

The contrast between Mendel's empirical work and Darwin's largely hypothetical work is great:

> The irony is that Darwin was developing a theory of constant change at the same time Mendel was demonstrating that living things are remarkably stable....

50. *Ibid.*, 18.
51. See especially 8-14 and 59-76 in *Of Pandas and People*.
52. *Ibid.*, 8.
53. *Ibid.*, 8, 9.

Yet Mendelian genetics has proved to be a mixed blessing for evolutionary theory. On the one hand, it provides the stability necessary for a trait to become established in a population. On the other hand, stability is just what evolution doesn't need if change is to be so far-ranging as to produce the whole complex web of life from a single-celled organism.[54]

The real question here is evidence for the breadth of *change* amongst living kinds. Evolutionary theory has argued that even variation within a species is evidence for the massive change of evolution from one species to another. As Davis *et al.* state:

> Scientists sometimes give the impression that any change is evidence for evolution. But evolution is not just any kind of change. It is a very special kind – the transformation of one type of organism into another.... The change produced by breeders is horizontal change, the flowering and elaboration of a single branch on that tree (biologists call this adaptive radiation). What is needed, however, is vertical change leading up the evolutionary tree and creating a new branch.
>
> To put it another way, breeders can produce sweeter corn or fatter cattle, but they cannot turn corn into another kind of plant or cattle into another kind of animal. What breeders accomplish is diversification within a given type, sometimes called *microevolution*. What is needed is the origin of new types, or *macroevolution*.
>
> Neo-Darwinism assumes that microevolution leads to macro-evolution. To put that into English, it assumes that small-scale changes will gradually accumulate and produce large-scale changes. The genetic sources of change in living things are mutation and recombination.[55]

But, do we have evidence to demonstrate that such has actually occurred? First, experimental genetic studies show that *recombination* has definite limits (as for instance the infertility of too highly bred animals). This is still a horizontal sort of change. 'The natural tendency in living things is to stay within definite limits. Although recombination is often cited as a source for evolution to work on, it does not produce the endless, vertical change necessary for evolution.'[56]

The second type of mechanism said to make macroevolution possible is *mutation* within the gene pool; a change in the DNA structure. 'Gene mutations occur when individual genes are damaged from exposure to heat, chemicals, or radiation. Chromosome mutations occur when sections of the DNA are duplicated, inverted, lost, or moved to another place in the DNA molecule.'[57]

54. *Ibid.,* 9.
55. *Ibid.,* 10, 11.
56. *Ibid.,* 11.
57. *Ibid.*

Thus, '... the central mechanism of evolution [is] mutations.'[58] Therefore, a great deal of work has been done with mutations for the last fifty years to see if they establish evolutionary theory. The fruit fly in particular has been studied intensively with this idea in view:

The fruit fly... has been the subject of many experiments because its short life-span allows scientists to observe many generations. In addition, the flies have been bombarded with radiation to increase the rate of mutations. Scientists now have a pretty clear idea what kind of mutations can occur.

Mutations do not create new structures. They merely alter existing ones. Mutations have produced, for example, crumpled, oversized, and undersized wings. They have produced double sets of wings. But they have not created a new kind of wing. Nor have they transformed the fruit fly into a new kind of insect. Experiments have simply produced variations within the fruit fly species.

Mutations are quite rare. This is fortunate, for in virtually all instances they are harmful. Recall that the DNA is a molecular message. A mutation is a random change in the message, akin to a typing error. Typing errors rarely improve the quality of a written message; if too many occur, they may even destroy the information contained in it. Likewise, mutations rarely improve the quality of the DNA message, and too many may even be lethal....

How likely is it that random mutations will come together and coordinate to form just one new structure? Let's say the formation of an insect wing requires only five genes (a very low estimate). Most mutations are harmful, and scientists estimate that only one in 1,000 is not. The probability of two non-harmful mutations occurring is one in one thousand million million. For all practical purposes, there is no chance that all five mutations will occur within the life cycle of a single organism. So far, we have discussed the possibility of the random formation of only one structure. Yet, an organism is made of many structures that must appear at the same time and working together in an integrated whole.[59]

The French zoologist, P.-P. Grassé, has studied mutations in generations of bacteria, which reproduce much more rapidly than even fruit flies. One bacterial generation lasts approximately 30 minutes. Hence they multiply 400,000 times faster than human generations. Researchers, therefore, can trace mutational change in bacteria in relatively brief compass equivalent to 3,500,000 years of change within the human species. But Grassé has found that these bacteria have not essentially changed during all these generations.[60] In view of this empirical fact,

58. *Ibid.*
59. *Ibid.*, 11, 12, 13.
60. P.-P. Grassé, *Traité de zoologie*, Tome VIII (Masson, 1976).

is it reasonable to maintain that humankind has evolved during the same equivalent time period in which bacteria have been stable?

Thus, hard genetic facts militate against evolution being possible through either recombination or mutations. The concept of the upward evolutionary scale of life is not grounded in empirical science, it is actually contrary to it. This means that the theory of evolution is really philosophy, not operational science. In the words of the French biologist, Rémy Chauvin, Professor in the Laboratory of Animal Sociology at René Descartes University in Paris:

> I say, and underline the fact that if this mass of preconceived ideas did not exist, everyone would admit that since those forms of animal life which mutate very rapidly have remained the same during tens of millions of generations, mutation could not be considered the motor of evolution. This is a matter of good sense, but given the strength of prejudice within science as everywhere else, good sense loses its case in court.[61]

Chauvin seems fully justified in stating that evolutionary theory 'follows its own path without worrying about the facts'.[62] According to Michael Behe, John Maynard Smith accused one of his former students, who is an 'origin of life' chemist, of practicing 'fact-free science'.[63] In other words, evolution is a matter of faith, not fact. Materialist evolutionary philosophy cannot even account for the origin of the complex system of life in the present world, much less for the hypothetical upward development of life forms in some past world.

> Evolution locates the origin of new organisms in material causes, the accumulation of individual traits. That is akin to saying the origin of a palace is in the bits of marble added to the tool shed. Intelligent design, by contrast, locates the origin of new organisms in an immaterial cause: in a blueprint, a plan, a pattern, devised by an intelligent agent.[64]

Genesis 1:1-12 shows us that this 'intelligent agent' is the living God, who on the third day of creation, separated the land from the sea, and caused plant life to sprout from the land, bearing their seed in them, so that their own likenesses would be replicated to the end of time. Known principles of genetic studies support the testimony of Genesis and run counter to the hypothesis of evolution.[65]

---

61. Rémy Chauvin, *La biologie de l'esprit* (Editions du Rocher: Monaco, 1985), 23, 24.
62. *Ibid.*, 24.
63. Behe, *op. cit.*, 156.
64. *Of Pandas and People*, 14.
65. There are many other significant contemporary scientific studies demonstrating the nonviability of recombination and mutations as mechanisms for macroevolution. Only a few will be mentioned here. See in particular these chapters of Michael Denton's *Evolution: A*

QUESTIONS FOR STUDY

1. What took place on the second day?

2. What seems to be the meaning of 'firmament'?

3. What main points do Brown and Whitelaw list against the vapor canopy theory?

4. What do they understand 'the waters above the earth' to mean'?

5. What took place on the third day?

6. Why was the third separation on Day Three called 'good'?

7. How does God's interaction with the development of vegetable life differ from the theory of Deism?

8. What is the genetic significance of plants having 'their seeds in them'?

9. What does Genesis appear to mean by 'kind'?

10. Distinguish between chaos and cosmos in the context of Days 2 and 3.

Theory in Crisis: Ch. 9 – 'Bridging the Gaps'; Ch. 10 – 'The Molecular Biological Revolution', and Ch. 11 – 'The Enigma of Life's Origin'. See also the chapter (6) by Kurt P. Wise, 'The Origin of Life's Major Groups', in J. P. Moreland, ed., *op. cit.*, 211-234. Consult Chapter 3 of Phillip E. Johnson's *Darwin on Trial* – 'Mutations Great and Small' (32-44), and the following chapters in Thaxton, Bradley and Olsen, *The Mystery of Life's Origin: Reassessing Current Theories* (Philosophical Library: New York, 1984): Ch. 1 – 'Crisis in the Chemistry of Origins', 2 – 'The Theory of Biochemical Evolution', 3 – 'Simulation of Prebiotic Monomer Synthesis', 5 – 'Reassessing the Early Earth and its Atmosphere', and 10 – 'Protocells'. Two chapters (7 & 8) explore the essential connection of 'open systems thermodynamics' and DNA, showing the heavy weight of evidence against the possibility of genetic development apart from 'information' (or 'intelligent design') to direct it. This is the exact opposite of what would be predicted by evolutionary theory. This last volume is a demonstration of how true 'operational' science shows that the evolutionary theory of the 'chance' origin of life is a 'faith' (see pp. 5, 202, 205-208), which proceeds on the basis of circular reasoning (see pp. 77, 86, 148, 152, 196), without evidence of what it seeks to prove (see pp.65, 83), and hence is rapidly weakening with the advances of 'operational' science, as opposed to 'origins' science (see p.185).

Chapter Ten

Days Four and Five of Creation: Additions to the Created Order – Luminaries, Fish and Fowl

WITH the work of Days Four, Five and Six, we enter into what Cassuto has aptly termed 'the second phase of the six days of creation'.[1] That is to say, there is a certain parallelism between the work of the first three days and that of the second three days, marked by both balance and further development:

> In the first stage were created the three sections of the inanimate world, followed by vegetation, that is, all the created entities that cannot move by themselves. In the second there were made, in precisely parallel order to that of the first, the mobile beings, to wit, on the fourth day the luminaries, the moving bodies in which the light formed on the first day is crystallized; and on the fifth and sixth days, in like manner, the creatures that correspond to the works of the second and third days.[2]

Cassuto demonstrates this parallelism as follows:

DAY 1	Light	DAY 4	Luminaries
DAY 2	Sea and Heaven	DAY 5	Fish and Fowl
DAY 3	Earth (with its plants)	DAY 6	Land creatures and Man[3]

---

1. Cassuto, *op. cit.*, 42.
2. *Ibid.*
3. *Ibid.*, 17. He argues that the symmetry of this parallelism 'provides a completely harmonious balance' (*ibid.*) and is strong evidence against the liberal Higher Critical theory of these verses being a later conflation of different primitive documents. The theory (advanced by holders of 'the Framework Hypothesis') that this literary parallelism precludes straightforward chronological meaning was dealt with in Chapter Six (pp. 112-120).

Day Four of Creation: The Addition of Lightbearers

While the three earlier days were marked by a series of 'separations' to make earth habitable, the three latter days are characterized by 'additions' to complete this process of rendering the earth a place of beauty and order suitable for animal and human life. Luminaries, then fish and fowl, and animals are added, as the cosmos is made ready for them. Finally, all is prepared for God's image-bearer, mankind to inhabit the newly made world.

> And God said, Let there be lights in the firmament of the heaven to divide the day from the night; and let them be for signs, and for seasons, and for days, and years: And let them be for lights in the firmament of the heaven to give light upon the earth: and it was so. And God made two great lights; the greater light to rule the day, and the lesser light to rule the night: he made the stars also. And God set them in the firmament of the heaven to give light upon the earth, And to rule over the day and over the night, and to divide the light from the darkness: and God saw that it was good. And the evening and the morning were the fourth day (Gen. 1:14-19).

Day Four sees the addition of the light bearers: sun, moon and stars, whose functions impart clarity, beauty and order to the natural realm, thus making it a fit home for the various forms of created life. This creation of the luminaries on the fourth day confronts us with a mystery in that light was already shining before the formation of the sun and other stars.

From the perspective of our present solar system, it is unclear, for instance, how the process of photosynthesis could have operated in plants before the sun was in place. Cassuto's comments are sensible:

> The question has also been raised: how could the plants grow on the third day without sun? This is not a difficult problem. Seeing that light was there already, and where there is light there must be heat, the requisite conditions for plant-life were already in existence.[4]

To obviate this difficulty, other commentators[5] have suggested that the luminaries were already in existence; the fourth day merely saw the clearing of the atmosphere so that they could then be perceived from earth. Somewhat more plausibly, the great German commentator, Leupold, suggests that the sun was in existence as a nonluminous body, and on the fourth day something happened that caused it to begin to shine.[6] But neither of these solutions of the difficulty works in terms of the clear teaching of the text: on the fourth day God actually

---

4. Cassuto, *op. cit.*, 44.
5. e.g. Robert C. Newman and Herman J. Eckelmann, Jr., *Genesis One and the Origin of the Earth* (Interdisciplinary Biblical Research Institute: Hatfield, PA, 1977), 80.
6. Leupold, *op. cit.*, 71.

created these luminaries. They were *not* already in existence (whether luminous or nonluminous).

Claus Westermann simply denies that the text means what it says: 'P [i.e. the hypothetical "Priestly writer"] does not mean that the heavenly bodies were not created until after the light.'[7] How he knows that 'the Priestly writer' did not mean what he says is not explained. However, Von Rad, even though he shares the 'higher critical' premises of Westermann, candidly lets this text speak for itself: 'Evidently the stars are not creators of light, but only mediating bearers of a light that was there without them and before them.'[8] In this way he gives us the key to approach the difficulty of light before sun and stars, 'the stars are not creators of light.' God is light and He alone creates light. He had already spoken it into existence on the very first day (Gen. 1:3, 4), and then, to use the attractive expression of Cassuto, He 'crystallizes' it into the moving bodies formed on the fourth day.[9] John Calvin faithfully, but with careful reserve, describes what happened:

> God had before created the light, but he now institutes a new order in nature, that the sun should be the dispenser of diurnal light, and the moon and stars should shine by night.... For Moses relates nothing else than that God ordained certain instruments to diffuse through the earth, by reciprocal changes, that light which had been previously created. The only difference is this, that the light was before dispersed, but now proceeds from lucid bodies; which, in serving this purpose, obey the command of God.[10]

We are not given the slightest suggestion in this text – or in any other – how all of this took place. The creation scientist, Dr D. Russell Humphreys, has written in some detail of what he thinks may have occurred on the fourth day to focus the light into the luminaries, in terms of the occurrence of 'an event horizon' in 'a black hole' running in reverse (or, in other words, 'a white hole').[11] Perhaps further research may confirm that there is something to commend this idea, but in the meantime it seems best to admit our ignorance of 'the mechanics' of light on the first and fourth days. In sum, the thought of Henry Morris that the light source before the creation of the sun 'may well have emanated from the theophanic presence of God Himself'[12] seems sound, as long as we keep in balance both 'the otherness' of

---

7. Westermann, *op. cit.*, 10.
8. Von Rad, *op. cit.*, 56.
9. Cassuto, *op. cit.*, 42.
10. John Calvin, *A Commentary on Genesis* (The Banner of Truth: Edinburgh, 1975 reprint), 83.
11. Humphreys, *op. cit.*, 78-9, 83, 98, 126.
12. Henry Morris, *The Remarkable Birth of Planet Earth* (Dimension Books: Minneapolis, Minn., 1972), 69.

the creation from God and its continual dependence upon Him (as Polkinghorne properly reminds us).[13]

These newly created luminaries were assigned three functions: first, to separate the day from the night; second, to be for signs and for seasons and for days and years; and third, to be luminaries in the heavens, giving light upon the earth. This first function, as Cassuto points out, does not mean that 'the sun is the *cause* of daytime, for the latter is to be found without the former. This is an empirical concept based on the observation that light pervades the atmosphere even before sunrise and also after sundown.'[14] What the text does indicate is that the sun and moon are called into being *to distinguish* the two periods of day and night.

> ...when He created the luminaries He handed over to them the task
> of separation, that is He commanded that the one should serve by day
> and the others should serve at night, and thus they would all become
> signs for distinguishing the two periods of time.[15]

The second function of the luminaries was 'to serve' (as Cassuto translates the verb *wᵉhayu*- 'and let them be') 'as signs for the determination of the seasons... and for the division of time'.[16] The idea of their serving as signs for the division of time is easily grasped: days and years 'are respectively the shortest and the longest measures of time definitely fixed by the movement of the heavenly bodies'.[17] In the context of days and years, the luminaries also indicate 'seasons', probably referring to seed time and harvest.[18]

Though imprecise and in a different category from modern meteorology, the fourth century *Hexameron* of St. Basil still constitutes a thought-provoking meditation on the luminaries and their function as markers of 'signs and seasons':

> The signs which the luminaries give are necessary to human life....
> Our Lord indicates to us one of the signs given by the sun when He
> says, 'It will be foul weather today; for the sky is red and lowering.'
> In fact, when the sun rises through a fog, its rays are darkened, but
> the disc appears burning like a coal and of bloody red colour. It is
> the thickness of the air which causes this appearance; as the rays of

---

13. John Polkinghorne, *Science and Creation: the Search for Understanding* (SPCK: London, 1993). He writes (in opposition to panentheism, which makes the world part of God): 'Panentheism's defect is its denial of the true otherness of the world from God, which is part of our experience. The classical doctrine of creation, with its assertion of the world's freedom to be itself over against God, but yet of its contingent dependence upon him for its existence, is surely the better understanding' (p.53).
14. Cassuto, *op. cit.*, 44.
15. *Ibid.*
16. *Ibid.*
17. Leupold, *op. cit.*, 74.
18. See Aalders, *op. cit.*, 64.

the sun do not disperse such amassed and condensed air, it cannot certainly be retained by the waves of vapour which exhale from the earth, and it will cause from superabundance of moisture a storm in the countries over which it accumulates. In the same way, when the moon is surrounded with moisture, or when the sun is encircled with what is called a halo, it is the sign of heavy rain or of a violent storm; again, in the same way, if mock suns accompany the sun in its course they foretell certain celestial phenomena. Finally, those straight lines, like the colours of the rainbow, which are seen on the clouds, announce rain, extraordinary tempests, or, in one word, a complete change in the weather...[19]

The meaning of 'signs' (*'othoth*) could also involve such things as navigational aid at sea and measuring land boundaries by lining up one's instruments with the North Star. Presumably the coming of the Wise Men from the East by following a star to Bethlehem (Matt. 2:1-10) would be included in the sign function of the stars.

Granted, however, the strong antipathy of the Old Testament to astrology, Aalders is surely right that 'serving as signs' could *not* imply the pagan practice of fortune-telling by means of the zodiac.[20] Basil in some detail shows the 'ridiculous' nature of the assertions of 'the inventors of astrology' in pretending that being born under certain 'signs of the Zodiac' affects the events of one's life. For this, he says, rests on 'the pretence of arriving at the influence on each other of things which have not the least connexion!'[21] Hippolytus of Rome, an early second-century Christian writer, also ridiculed the pseudo-science of astrology.[22]

The text then states that these light bearers 'rule over' the day and the night (Gen. 1:18). The ancient pagan practice of ascribing personality to the stars as though they were literal rulers is of course excluded by the Old Testament. As Cassuto writes: '...the meaning is simply this: since the luminaries are situated *above the earth*, they appear to be ruling over it, as well as over its days and nights.'[23]

When we draw together the first verb of verse 17 – 'And God set them' (*wayyitten* – literally – 'and He *gave*'[24]) with God's review of the process in verse 18 ('And God saw that it was good'), we have the right perspective on the significance of the luminaries on the fourth day: they are 'one of God's good gifts to mankind'.[25] And from this

19. Basil, *The Hexameron*, Homily VI. 4.
20. Aalders, *op. cit.*, 64.
21. Basil, *op. cit.*, VI. 5, 6.
22. See *Technical and Bibliographical Notes* for this chapter.
23. *Ibid.*, 46.
24. *Ibid.*

perspective as well the progress of Days Three and Four is to be seen: plants are now growing, soon to provide food for the coming crown of God's creation, mankind, and the luminaries are in place to guide and illumine him when he appears.

The work of these days then indicates strong purposive movement in the divine activity: God is preparing the stage with the intended purpose of making a home for His image bearers: Adam and Eve and their descendants. The awe inspiring concept here of sublime and remote celestial bodies existing for the purpose of serving frail humans who dwell on this planet, made the Psalmist cry out: 'When I consider thy heavens, the work of thy fingers, the moon and stars, which thou hast ordained; What is man, that thou art mindful of him? and the son of man that thou visitest him?' (Psalm 8:3, 4).

Day Five of Creation

The fifth day of creation carries the divine purpose of providing a home for humanity even further. Day Four saw the addition of the luminaries, as it were, 'outside the house', and Day Five sees the addition of some new inhabitants (comparable perhaps to 'furnishings') 'inside the house':

> And God said, Let the waters bring forth abundantly [literally – 'swarm with swarming things'] the moving creature that hath life, and fowl that may fly above the earth in the open firmament of heaven. And God created great whales ['the great sea monsters'], and every living creature that moveth, which the waters brought forth abundantly after their kind, and every winged fowl after his kind: and God saw that it was good. And God blessed them, saying, Be fruitful, and multiply, and fill the waters in the seas, and let fowl multiply in the earth. And the evening and the morning were the fifth day (Gen. 1:20-23).

This fifth day sees the earth receiving its first inhabitants:

> All the necessities for living creatures were present on the earth by this time: light, air, water, soil, chemicals, plants, fruits, and so forth. One deficiency yet remained – the earth was still 'void' of inhabitants. However, God had 'formed it to be inhabited' (Isa. 45:18); and the fifth and sixth days were to be devoted to this final work of creation.[26]

The work of this fifth phase of creation may be summarized in two major actions: the creation of conscious life and then the blessing of that life, which would insure the presence of inhabitants in the newly completed 'house'.

---

25. Leupold, *op. cit.*, 76.
26. Morris, *The Genesis Record*, 68.

The Creation of Life

The first occurrence in Holy Scripture of the word translated 'life' is found here in verse 20. It is *nephesh* in Hebrew, often rendered 'living soul'. 'According to the biblical viewpoint plants have no life. But the life of living creatures is present in their "souls," and so they have souls ascribed to them. But this "soul" again is regarded as nothing more than "that which breathes"' (cf. Brown, Driver & Briggs, *Hebrew Lexicon*).[27] Another way to describe this would be 'principle of consciousness', or '...entity of conscious life which would henceforth be an integral part of every animate being, including man.'[28]

Thus on the fifth day the continuing drama of creation reaches new heights as it reaches forward to completion on the sixth day. While the Genesis text does not specifically say so, one would infer that the introduction of 'the moving creature that hath life' is, so far, the highest form of God's creative activity. As Leupold comments:

> But on the whole an entirely new type of being has come into existence, creatures that breathe and are animated and have power of their own volition to go from place to place. To give existence to such is the peculiar prerogative of God and is a monumental, epoch-making achievement that deserves to be described by the verb 'and he created' (*wayyibhra'*) as the opening verse does.[29]

Conscious life (or *nephesh*), therefore, was brought forth by direct creative command of the living God. The English translation of the Authorized Version of Genesis 1:20 gives an incorrect impression, when it reads: 'Let the waters *bring forth abundantly* the moving creature that hath life...' This might appear to imply that animal life came from potencies in the waters. But the actual text teaches otherwise.

As Cassuto shows, the original Hebrew means: 'Let the waters SWARM [*yisrᵉsu*] *with* SWARMING THINGS [*seres*].'[30] The repetition of this word is known as 'paranomasia', and is also found in verse 11, 'Let the earth vegetate with vegetation.' 'God willed that into the midst of the waste and inanimate waters, from one end of the sea to the other, there should now enter a living spirit, and that there should be born in their midst moving, animate beings, subject to no limitation of numbers or intermission of movement.'[31]

Similarly, by creative command – this time, not in the seas, but in the open air – God causes 'flying creatures to fly about the earth...'[32] We cannot fail to notice here a parallel between Day Two and Day

---

27. Leupold, *op. cit.*, 78, 79.
28. Morris, *op. cit.*, 69.
29. Leupold, *op. cit.*, 80 , 81.
30. Cassuto, *op. cit.*, 48.
31. *Ibid.*

Five. On Day Two, the two parts of the natural realm were created: the heavens and the sea, and on Day Five, these two parts begin to be filled with inhabitants: the fish and the fowl.[33]

Commentators have properly found an important theological significance in the statement of verse 21, that 'God created the great sea monsters'. Cassuto discusses both Israelite and pagan traditions of sea monsters, who were often associated with evil and rebellion (e.g. compare Isa. 27:1; 51:9-10; Ps. 74:13-14; Job 7:12; 26:13). He concludes:

> Far be it from any one to suppose that the sea monsters were mythological beings opposed to God or in revolt against Him; they were as natural as the rest of the creatures, and were formed in their proper time and in their proper place by the word of the Creator, in order that they might fulfill His will like the other created beings. Similarly it is stated in Psalm 148:7: *Praise the Lord from the earth,* YOU SEA MONSTERS AND ALL DEEPS. The poet invites all created forms of life to praise the Lord, and among the terrestrial creatures, beneath the heavens, he invites, first and foremost, the sea monsters and the deeps specifically.[34]

Or as Von Rad writes: 'nothing in this realm... is outside the creative will of God. Outside God, there is nothing to fear; even this creature is good in God's sight!'[35]

Evil entered the world later, as the result of Satan's fall and man's first sin. But in all parts of the original creation, there was nothing but goodness. The immense variety of life – in the words of the poet – 'all creatures great and small' were good. Physical life, the realm of nature, the created order were thoroughly good and pleasing to their Creator. That is why, in verse 21, surveying the accomplishments of the fifth day, 'God saw that it was good.'[36]

The Blessing of Life

Genesis 1:22 shows God blessing the life He had created on the fifth day by providing the reproductive capacities for the passing on of that life. As Morris explains:

> Like the various plants, the actual biochemical reproductive systems of the animals were programmed to assure the fixity of the kinds. Physically and chemically, animals are similar to plants. Modern

---

32. Genesis 1:20 does not imply that the fowls were flying as high as the stars, for the Hebrew text literally states 'in the *face* of the firmament'.
33. *Ibid.*
34. *Ibid.*, 50, 51.
35. Von Rad, 56, 57.
36. This crucial theological tenet of Genesis 1-3, Romans 5-6 and elsewhere cannot be reconciled with the thesis of theistic evolution, which introduces evil and death into the created order long before the fall of Satan and sin of Adam.

genetics has shown that all replicating systems function in the framework of the marvelous information program in the DNA molecule. The DNA for each kind is programmed to allow for wide individual variations within the kind, but not beyond the structure of the kind itself.[37]

All of this means that the reproduction of life is the specific blessing of God. Isaiah 9, referring prophetically to the government of Christ, says that 'of the increase of his government, there shall be no end' (v. 7). The Bible frequently speaks of increase as a blessing. Cassuto lists the 'many more expressions of benison, linked with the idea of fecundity... in the book of Genesis, *viz.* 9:1; 17:16, 20; 22:17; 24:60; 26:3-4; 28:3; 35:9-11; 48:3-4; 49:25.' He then compares Genesis 48:15-16: 'AND HE BLESSED *Joseph, and said* ... BLESS *the lads* ... AND LET THEM GROW [*w^{e}yidhgu*; cf. *dagh*, 'a fish'] *in multitude in the midst of the earth.*'[38] As we shall soon see, Genesis 1:28 goes on to link fecundity of offspring amongst humans with the direct blessing of the generous, Creator God.

This is an utterly different attitude from the pagan materialism of our declining Western society, which sees reproductive increase as a curse, rather than a blessing. Because of their departure from Biblical standards (which are based essentially on love of life, God first and one's neighbor next), the Western countries have for some decades experienced a decline in population (except where boosted by immigration from countries which do not see reproductive increase as a curse). This most basic denial of moral law – loving self rather than God and neighbor – is running an epidemic course in the world's richest societies. Its grim symptoms are evidenced in abortion and euthanasia. Only a return to the value Genesis gives to the increase of life, through the redeeming activity of the One through whom 'all things were made, in whom is life...' (John 1:3, 4) can bring healing to the educated and outwardly wealthy, but often dissatisfied and perishing multitudes of the Western world.

So then, Genesis 1:14-23 concludes with 'the house' built, illuminated from above, and some of the first inhabitants moved in to begin furnishing it. All of this creative activity on the first five days of creation is to prepare us for the marvel of Day Six: the creation and presentation of the crown of God's creation: mankind, male and female; the image bearers of the very Creator Himself.

---

37. Morris, *op. cit.*, 70. Part II of *Technical and Bibliographical Notes for Chapter Nine* discusses the bearing of genetic studies on the Genesis teaching of reproduction 'after their kinds.'
38. Cassuto, *op. cit.*, 51, 52.

TECHNICAL AND BIBLIOGRAPHICAL NOTES FOR CHAPTER TEN

Hippolytus of Rome on the Pseudo-Science of Astrology

In his early third-century work, *The Philosophumena* (or *The Refutation of All Heresies*), Hippolytus demonstrates the fictional nature of astrology with its lack of integrity, disconnection from the real world, and self-contradictory claims. Book IV of this work is devoted to uncovering the false premises involved in deducing the events of one's human life from the sign of the Zodiac under which one was born. The untold millions of secularized moderns who rely on their reading of newspaper astrological columns for personal guidance, would do well to read this twenty page section written over 1,700 years ago!

His surprisingly detailed analysis of the preposterous practices of astrologers shows how little their craft has changed since antiquity. One passage should indicate the value of his critique for modern as well as ancient times:

> But since also they frame an account concerning the action of the zodiacal signs, to which they say the creatures that are procreated are assimilated, neither shall we omit this: as, for instance, that one born in Leo will be brave; and that one born in Virgo will have long straight hair, be of a fair complexion, childless, modest. These statements, however, and others similar to them, are rather deserving of laughter than serious consideration. For, according to them, it is possible for no Aethiopian to be born in Virgo; otherwise he would allow that such a one is white, and with long straight hair and the rest. But I am rather of opinion, that the ancients imposed the names of received animals upon certain specified stars, for the purpose of knowing them better, not from any similarity of nature; for what have the seven stars, distant from one another, in common with a bear, or the five stars with the head of a dragon...?' (*Refutation of All Heresies*, IV, vi.)

The preference of otherwise intelligent people in the secularized Western nations for guidance by the stars rather than by the Word of God and prayer, illustrates a basic principle taught by St. Paul in Romans chapters 1 and 2: when men deny God's existence, they are left with a deep vacuum in their finite, limited selves. Inevitably they will try to fill this vacuum by replacing God with something less than God; with some aspect of the created order. In this case, they tragically replace living their lives in the divine presence by looking to the imaginary influence of the stars. In so doing, St. Paul says:

> Because that, when they knew God, they glorified him not as God, neither were thankful; but became vain in their imaginations, and their foolish heart was darkened. Professing themselves to be wise, they became fools, and changed the glory of the uncorruptible God into

an image made like to corruptible man.... Who changed the truth of God into a lie, and worshipped and served the creature more than the Creator, who is blessed for ever. Amen (Rom. 1: 21-23b, 25).

A repentant return to the biblical doctrine of creation could liberate many from superstition, futility and despair.

QUESTIONS FOR STUDY

1. Discuss the parallelism between the work of the first three days of creation and that of the second three days.

2. How are these last three days characterized by additions?

3. What are some different theories on the shining of light before the creation of the sun?

4. What does Genesis seem to indicate about how light could shine before sun and stars?

5. What were the three functions of the newly created luminaries?

6. How do the stars *not* serve as signs?

7. Discuss the additions of Day Five 'inside the house'.

8. Interpret the significance of the original Hebrew text of Genesis 1:20, which is translated in the Authorized Version as: 'Let the waters bring forth abundantly the moving creature that hath life...'

9. In what sense does Genesis 1:22 imply that reproduction of life is a blessing?

Chapter Eleven

Day Six of Creation: Mankind, The Crown of Creation

THE work of the first five days of creation was preparatory for the crowning action of the sixth day: the creation of mankind. We have compared this to the construction of a great mansion in orderly stages. The purpose of that construction is fulfilled only when the inhabitants for whom it was so exquisitely prepared actually move into it. This is what occurs on Day Six of creation.

Creation of the Land Animals

There is one final act of preparation, however, before the beautiful scene is ready for the habitation of humanity, and that is the creation of the land animals. We may, roughly speaking, compare their creation on the first part of Day Six to the concluding placement of needed furnishings. Or, stated more accurately, God creates last those higher animals whose bodies most resemble men, and whose presence is necessary to enable man to fulfill the tasks he will be given (such as horses and oxen for labor and cattle for milk).

> And God said, Let the earth bring forth the living creature after his kind, cattle, and creeping thing, and beast of the earth after his kind: and it was so. And God made the beast of the earth after his kind, and cattle after their kind, and every thing that creepeth upon the earth after his kind: and God saw that it was good (Gen. 1:24-25).

We have previously noted a parallelism between the first three days of creation and the last three:

> The sixth day corresponds to the third: on the third day the earth was created, and on the sixth the living creatures of the earth were made; on the third day, immediately after the organization of inanimate nature had been completed, the plants, whose dominion extends throughout the earth, were brought into being; so, too, on the sixth day, when vegetation and animal life had been fully established, man, who bears rule over all created life upon earth, was formed forthwith.'[1]

These land animals (or 'living creatures') are divided into three basic sorts, and in these three sorts all animals of the earth are included. 'These are: *cattle*, that is, living creatures whom man can domesticate or tame; *creeping things*, to wit, small creatures that creep about on the ground, or even big animals that have no legs, or have very short legs, so that they appear to be walking on their bellies; *beasts of the earth*: four-legged creatures that can never be domesticated or tamed.'[2]

The Creation of Man

In Genesis 1:26 there is a notable shift in language, indicating the highest stage in all the week's creative activity, the solemn act for which purpose all the rest had been merely a preparation.

> And God said, Let us make man in our image, after our likeness: and let them have dominion over the fish of the sea, and over the fowl of the air, and over the cattle, and over all the earth, and over every creeping thing that creepeth upon the earth. So God created man in his own image, in the image of God created he him; male and female created he them. And God blessed them, and God said unto them, Be fruitful, and multiply, and replenish the earth, and subdue it: and have dominion over the fish of the sea, and over the fowl of the air, and over every living thing that moveth upon the earth (Gen. 1:26-28).

John Calvin appositely comments on this shift in language in verse 26: 'Hitherto God has been introduced simply as commanding; now, when he approaches the most excellent of all his works, he enters into consultation... This is the highest honor with which he has dignified us...'[3] For the first time in the work of creation, the one God uses the plural form – 'Let us'. Earlier when He was making the creatures, both inanimate and animate (which are less than man), He spoke in the singular form of the verb. That form of language is called 'fiat' (from the Latin, meaning 'Let there be'). It is an impersonal form of the verb.[4]

---

1. Cassuto, *op. cit.*, 53, 54.
2. *Ibid.*, 55. One would assume that before the Fall all animals were essentially tame, but even then not necessarily intended for domestication.
3. Calvin, *op. cit.*, 91.
4. The actual Hebrew *y'he* is in the jussive form, which is an affirmative command in the third person, whereby the speaker intends to impose his will on the third party (or thing).

However, when God comes to the creation of the human race, He does not employ the impersonal, 'fiat' phraseology, but rather uses a term which indicates that God is speaking within Himself; as though He were in consultation within Himself. Some theologians have termed this remarkable use of language 'an executive divine counsel'.

Commentators have long discussed the meaning of one God speaking to Himself in plural form. Aalders succinctly summarizes the main theories that have been offered. First, some have considered the plural form a vestige of ancient polytheism, but he rightly replies: 'But this is certainly incorrect. The entire creation account is strongly monotheistic.... It is unthinkable that such a vestige, if it did indeed exist, would not have been carefully removed when this could so easily be done. The fact that it was allowed to stand clearly indicates that some other meaning was definitely intended.'[5] Others have suggested that God was taking counsel with the angels, but as Cassuto points out, this idea 'conflicts with the central thought of the section that God *alone* created the entire world...'[6] Still others have claimed that the plural form indicates royalty or majesty. Aalders, however, denies this as impossible, 'because the Hebrew does not have such a use of the plural. There are a few references in Ezra which may have a use of this kind of plural (Ezra 4:18; 7:24), but these are written in Aramaic and not in Hebrew.'[7]

The Church Fathers seem to be right in considering this plural form of the verb to indicate, albeit vaguely and 'through a glass darkly', a reality about the one God that must wait until the New Testament for its clear revelation: that there is a richness of interpersonal life within the Godhead, which Christians came to call 'the Trinity.' It is important not to overstate the case here, as though Moses and the original readers of Genesis could have grasped, from this verse alone, the doctrine of the Trinity. That of course is not the case, for as B. B. Warfield once wrote:

> '... the times were not ripe for the revelation of the Trinity in the unity of the Godhead until the fullness of the time had come for God to send forth His Son unto redemption, and His Spirit unto sanctification. The revelation in word must needs wait upon the revelation in fact ...'[8]

So then, this verse alone cannot, in simplistic fashion, be used as a 'proof' of the Trinity, but looking back from the vantage point of the incarnation of Christ and outpouring of the Holy Spirit from the Father and the Son at Pentecost, this pivotal verse literally shines with

---

5. Aalders, *op. cit.*, 69.
6. Cassuto, *op. cit.*, 55.
7. Aalders, *op. cit.*, 70.
8. B. B. Warfield, *Biblical Foundations*, 91.

fullness of meaning. And this meaning will help us understand the significance of mankind as God's own image bearer in a richer, more personal way.

The Image of God in Mankind

Genesis 1:26 gives us the theme of 'the executive divine counsel': 'Let us make man in our image, after our likeness.' Calvin is right that in the original Hebrew, there is no real distinction between 'image' and 'likeness', 'for it was customary with the Hebrews to repeat the same thing in different words. Besides, the phrase itself shows that the second term was added for the sake of explanation...'[9] Athanasius in the fourth century also understood 'image' and 'likeness' to be parallel rather than distinct realities.[10] Augustine, however, made a distinction between 'image' and 'likeness', according to which 'image' (or holiness and righteous relationship to God) was lost, while 'likeness' (or metaphysical mental capacity) remained.[11] This distinction was carried on in the theology of St. Thomas Aquinas.[12] In the thought of Aquinas, however, 'image' is ontological and thus cannot be lost, whereas 'likeness' refers to grace which could be lost. thanasius and Calvin seem to be correct in terms of the Hebrew text that image and likeness are synonyms, while Augustine and Aquinas properly note the marring effects of sin on the image (or likeness) of God in fallen mankind. Precisely what the divine image in humankind involves takes us up to the Triune God Himself.

The astonishing teaching of this verse is that for man to be in the image of God is to be like Him in certain definite respects. That is, mankind is made on a heavenly, indeed, divine pattern, which is not true of any of the other creatures. In the biological sense mankind is also like the animals in many respects. The physical structure of humanity is similar to that of the animals because they were designed by the same Creator to share a common natural environment. On the basis of this similarity to the animal kingdom, Darwinism has explained man solely as a higher sort of animal, a more highly evolved 'primate', with no further spiritual or transcendent significance. But Genesis teaches otherwise. Mankind has the highest possible spiritual, transcendent reference: likeness to God Himself. That is the clear meaning of the word 'image' (Gen. 1:26).

---

9. Calvin, *op. cit.*, 94.
10. See Regis Bernard, *L'image de Dieu d'après Saint Athanase* (Paris, 1952), 25-9.
11. Augustine, *The Literal Meaning of Genesis, Vol. I, No. 41*, Book Six, Chapters 27 and 28 (206-207).
12. Thomas Aquinas, 1 *Sent.* d. 3, q. 4, a. 1, ad 4m; p.38.

The root of the Hebrew word for 'image' (*tselem*) appears to have meant 'to carve' or 'to cut off.'[13] Perhaps this idea is best conveyed by the Latin (Vulgate) rendering: '*ad imaginem nostram*' (literally, 'to our image'). In other words, man was shaped or formed to fit into the image of God. He was created in such an exalted fashion that he and she would fit into fellowship with God, in a way totally surpassing that of any other earthly being. This high fellowship would be possible only because humankind literally *is* the image of God, for as Saint Paul indicates in 1 Corinthians 11:7, man '*is* the image and glory of God'.

The content of 'the image or likeness of God' could probably safely be summed up in the post-biblical term, 'personal'. That is, because he is in the image of God, man is personal or has personality. The contemporary usage of 'person' as synonymous with 'individual' and 'personality' with a collection of particular 'traits' does not fully express the Biblical meaning of the concept of 'image of God' nor the Christian reflection of it in the development of 'personal' terminology. The origin of the concept 'person' is discussed in *Technical and Bibliographical Notes for Chapter Eleven*. It may be sufficient to note here that the 'likeness or image' of God (or the term 'personal') bears the idea of mind, will, affections, and especially *relationship* with other similar persons. That is to say, a single person does not exist without other persons to give him or her meaning. That is the concept that may be hinted at by the plural usage of Genesis 1:26, 'Let us make', and 'our'. As Cardinal Joseph Ratzinger has written:

> Thus the image of God means, first of all, that human beings cannot be closed in on themselves. Human beings who attempt this betray themselves. To be the image of God implies relationality. It is the dynamic that sets the human being in motion toward the totally Other. Hence it means the capacity for relationship; it is the human capacity for God. Human beings are, as a consequence, most profoundly human when they step out of themselves and become capable of addressing God on familiar terms.[14]

What we learn from the full revelation of the New Testament is that God Himself has never existed as a single, lonely, solitary or 'cut-off' individual. Rather, He has always existed in the fullness of family-like being (cf. Eph. 3:14, 15: 'Father ... of whom the whole family in heaven and earth is named'). Or, as the great Saint Athanasius used to say in the fourth century, 'the Father has never been without His Son.' The amazing mystery of the origin of personality is that the one God exists as three persons in one being or 'substance' (or 'reality').

---

13. Leupold, *op. cit.*, 88.
14. Joseph Ratzinger, '*In the Beginning...*' *A Catholic Understanding of the Story of Creation and the Fall* (William B. Eerdmans Publ. Co.: Grand Rapids, MI, 1986), 47, 48.

The one 'substance' or being of God inherently involves personhood, for as the Greek Orthodox theologian, Dr John Zizioulas, says, the early Christian theologians 'transformed the idea of substance'.[15] By meditating on the Scriptural testimony concerning the relationship of Christ, the Son, to His heavenly Father, they came to understand that when used of the God of the Bible, 'substance possesses almost by definition a relational character.'[16]

Certainly, as we noted with the full concept of Trinity, Genesis does *not* teach what we learn from the later revelation about the richness of God's inner-personal life. However, to refuse to take this later light into consideration would be to impoverish our understanding of 'image' and 'personhood'. All the New Testament and Christian theological development of the implications of Genesis 1:26 should help us apprehend the noble significance of human persons being created in the image of God.

Furthermore, in that fuller light, Ephesians 4:24 and Colossians 3:10 show that the original image of God in man can only be grasped by looking at Christ, the incarnate Son of God, who manifested not only the *ontological* aspects of the image in spirit (or mind, will and affections), but also the *ethical* aspects of 'righteousness and true holiness'. Christ, in the most basic sense, shows us who Adam was before the Fall: an embodied, potentially immortal spirit, graciously granted the capacity of holy and loving fellowship with His heavenly Father. Even in our fallen state, we sinners inevitably must still dwell in the realm of conscience and morality (see Paul's discussion in Romans 1 and 2), and this indicates a continuing ethical heritage (even if tattered and twisted) that flows from our creation in the divine image.

Commentators and theologians have generally ascribed the 'likeness' mankind bears to God to spirit rather than body (since God the Father's existence is not bodily). The second century Church Father, St. Irenaeus of Lyon, however, affirmed that in some sense 'image' pertained to both body and soul,[17] while St. Augustine in the fourth century limited image to the mind or spirit: 'This [the image of God] was not, however, in his body but in his intellect...'[18] Yet Augustine adds: 'Man's body, then, is appropriate for his rational soul not because of his facial features and the structure of his limbs, but rather because of the fact that he stands erect, able to look up to heaven and gaze upon the higher regions in the corporeal world.'[19] John Calvin stated that it may not be possible totally to exclude man's body from all relationship to the image of God, at least in the sense that 'there was

---

15. See John Zizioulas, *Being as Communion*, 95.
16. *Ibid*.
17. Irenaeus, *Adversus Haereses*, 5.6.1.
18. Augustine, *The Literal Meaning of Genesis, Vol. I, No. 41*, Book Six, Ch. 12. 22 (193).

no part of man in which some scintillations of the Divine image did not shine forth... and in the body there was a suitable correspondence with this internal order [i.e. of one's sense obeying one's reason].'[20]

Thus, while the image of God is not corporeal as such, yet man's body does correspond to that divine image in a way not true of even the highest animals. Koenig summarizes these corresponding features of man's body to the divine likeness: 'a) man's countenance which directs his gaze upwards; b) a capacity for varying facial expressions; c) a sense of shame expressing itself in the blush of man; d) speech.'[21]

The irreducible fact of human speech tells us much about their creation 'to the image of God', for as John's Gospel teaches us, 'the Word (Logos) was God' (John 1: 1). We have already noted with Athanasius that God has never been without His Son, which therefore means that God has never been without Logos (or Word or reason).[22] Within the eternal Godhead there has always been Word or communication, and to be a human person ('in His image') is to communicate by means of words. This means that God created us to talk to us and we to Him. The mystery of human language systems can never be accounted for by the evolutionary hypothesis; they testify to our having been made in God's likeness, not to evolution from an impersonal, 'mute slimepit'.

Linguistic studies demonstrate, as Oller and Omdahl have stated, that 'apparently human beings, and only humans, are specifically designed to acquire just the range of language systems that we see manifested in the world's five thousand-plus languages'.[23] And the great Jewish linguist, Noam Chomsky, has shown that the ability to learn language is a 'given' in being human: 'The rate of vocabulary acquisition is so high at certain stages of life, and the precision and delicacy of the concepts acquired so remarkable, that it seems necessary to conclude that in some manner the conceptual system with which lexical items are connected is already substantially in place.'[24]

Chomsky demonstrates that even the higher apes are unable to deal with the number system or with abstract properties of space, or in general with an abstract system of expressions.[25] Chomsky speaks elsewhere of 'initially given structures of mind'[26] and 'deep

19. *Ibid.*, 193, 194.
20. Calvin, *op. cit.*, 95.
21. Koenig as quoted in Leupold, *op. cit.*, 89, 91.
22. Athanasius, *Contra Arianos*, IV. 2.
23. See their chapter, 'Origin of the Human Language Capacity: In Whose Image?' in Moreland, ed., *op. cit.*, 255.
24. Noam Chomsky, *Rules and Representations* (New York: Columbia University Press, 1978), 139, quoted in Moreland, *op. cit.*, 255.
25. Chomsky, *op. cit.*, 38-39, quoted in Moreland, *op. cit.*, 256.
26. Chomsky, *Problems of Knowledge and Freedom* (New York: Vintage Books, 1971), 23.

structures'[27], which give rise to 'universal grammar, invariant among humans.'[28] His research on the uniqueness of the human species as regards language has not been welcomed in some evolutionist circles, who have labeled him as 'a creationist' (which he denies).[29]

Unlike apes and other living creatures, humanity's capacity for language is a door into 'that eternal, unseen realm'[30] (of Logos or Word), and a standing witness that we were created on a heavenly pattern for communication with the One who made us in His image. Oller and Omdahl are surely to the point in writing that 'our capacity for language cannot have originated within the narrow confines of any finite duration of experience.... If all the eons of the space-time world could be multiplied clear to infinity, the material world would still fail to account for the abstract conceptions that any human being can easily conceive of through the gift of language.'[31] Only a speaking God could have made speaking persons.[32]

Human Dominion over the Rest of Creation

Only because mankind was created in the image of God was it appropriate to grant him the awesome responsibility of dominion over the entire created order. Genesis 1:26 records this grant of dominion over all the other creatures, and Genesis 2:19 indicates that it involved 'naming' (or, as some have suggested, the scientific task of 'classifying' in an appropriate manner) the animals, and Genesis 2:15 shows that it also involved 'dressing and keeping the Garden'. These tasks which are specified in Genesis 2, imply that the dominion mandate calls man to study (know, name or classify the created order), and then to articulate its meaning and to shape it in a direction pleasing to God.

The call to tend the garden and classify the animals provides a fine and fruitful balance in the relationship of mankind to the environment which God has placed under his derived authority. This healthy balance is not to be found outside the biblical faith. Eastern religions, such as Hinduism and Buddhism, for instance, tend to

---

27. *Ibid.*, 24.
28. Chomsky, *Reflections on Language* (New York: Pantheon Books, 1975), 29.
29. Moreland, *op. cit.*, 257.
30. Moreland, *op. cit.*, 266.
31. *Ibid.*
32. Angelo Scola's penetrating study of Von Balthasar notes that '...Man exists only through interhuman dialogue, that is, through language – the word. Why then deny the Word to being itself? Revelation thus appears as a reasonable hypothesis, which finds confirmation in the great announcement of the Prologue of John's Gospel: 'In the beginning was the Word, and the Word was with God, and the Word was God' (John l:l). Thus God can reveal himself and does reveal himself by dint of the dialogic character of being. Man himself is dialogical. If man exists so much by interhuman dialogue that he discovers *who he is* only in dialogue, can we then deny to God the capacity to enter into dialogue with man? Such a denial would be absurd.' See Scola, *Hans Urs Von Balthasar: A Theological Style* (Wm. B. Eerdmans: Grand Rapids, MI, 1991), 28.

neglect developing 'the garden' (viewing it as a sort of god, not to be tampered with), as do some forms of Christian mysticism; materialist, technological industrialism tends to destroy 'the garden' for short-sighted economic purposes, whether in the strip mines of West Virginia, the slag heaps of the English Midlands, or the dead rivers of Romania; and the ultra environmentalists or 'Greens' tend to elevate it above the legitimate needs and purposes of human society, thus losing their own significance and failing to bring to fruition what man could accomplish with the remarkable capacities of the created order. But the dominion mandate of Genesis teaches man both to respect and to subdue nature, so as to shape it in a direction that will reflect the beauty, order and glory of its Creator. Mankind was, as Gregory of Nazianzus eloquently expressed it, 'King of all upon earth, but subject to the King above...'[33]

The bearing of the dominion mandate upon man's call to shape the entirety of culture (and not just church) in a Godward direction was articulated in a fresh way by some of the sixteenth century Reformers, such as Luther, who sought to show the sacred quality of secular life[34] as well as John Calvin[35], and was fruitfully explored by Abraham Kuyper in late nineteenth and early twentieth century Holland.[36] Henry R. Van Til helpfully surveyed varying concepts of the dominion mandate and Christian culture in four theologians: Augustine, Calvin, Abraham Kuyper and Klaas Schilder.[37] Emil Brunner appositely pointed out that man's call to subdue the earth (or to create culture) is what distinguishes human society and history from the changeless beehive.[38]

The dominion mandate means that 'secular tasks', such as keeping the Garden, are of the same high 'spiritual' importance as ecclesiastical ones, such as preaching. Indeed, the traditional Western ecclesiastical dichotomy between 'sacred' or 'spiritual' and 'secular' is foreign to Genesis with its dominion mandate over the whole created order. The seventeenth century English poet, George Herbert, expressed this attitude which flows from the call to dominion beautifully, in a line from his hymn, 'Teach me, my God and King, in all things Thee to see':

---

33. Gregory Nazianzen, *Oration XXXVIII, On the Theophany, or Birthday of Christ*, section XI.
34. Martin Luther, 'The Babylonian Captivity of the Church' in *Three Treatises* (Fortress Press: Philadelphia, 1960), 202, 203, and *Luther's Works*, Vol. 3, J. Pelikan, ed. (Concordia Publ. House: St. Louis, 1961), comments on Gen. 18:15 (216-218); Vol. 28 (1973), comments on I Cor. 7:6, 7 (15-21).
35. John Calvin, *Institutes of the Christian Religion*, II. 2. 12-16.
36. See Abraham Kuyper, *Lectures on Calvinism*.
37. Henry R. Van Til, *The Calvinistic Concept of Culture* (Baker Book House: Grand Rapids, MI, 1959), 67-154.
38. Emil Brunner, *Christianity and Culture* (New York, 1948), Vol. II, 127.

A servant with this clause
Makes drudgery divine:
Who sweeps a room, as for Thy laws,
Makes that and the action fine.

Herbert's lines show that dominion (or 'the cultural mandate') is not centered either on self interest or even the created order itself as the final goal. Rather, God, 'His laws' and His glory are the only true end of all human activity, whether in daily work or worship. Along these lines, Von Rad correctly states that man's dominion is derivative, not absolute: 'Just as powerful earthly kings, to indicate their claim to dominion, erect an image of themselves in the provinces of their empire where they do not personally appear, so man is placed upon earth in God's image as God's sovereign emblem. He is really only God's representative, summoned to maintain and enforce God's claim to dominion over the earth.'[39] In other words, even at his highest dignity, man is only God's steward.

Though we need not expound it here, Psalm 8 is a meditation on the meaning of 'what is man that thou art mindful of him?' (v. 4) and of his dominion 'over the works of thy hands... (with) all things under his feet' (v. 6). Hebrews 2 places this entire Psalm with its emphasis on man and his dominion in the context of Christ, the Son of God, the Logos, the agent of creation (John 1:3), and the one who still holds the entire created order together (Col. 1:17). Hence, as Professor Colin Gunton writes: 'Because the Father created and upholds the world in being through the Son, it is ontologically appropriate, so to speak, for the Son to be the one who takes flesh. The one who holds in being the realms of time and space enters their confines in order to renew them.'[40]

None less than He 'was made a little lower than the angels' (v. 9), 'partaking of flesh and blood' (v. 14), utterly identifying with the fallen sons and daughters of Adam, who, instead of experiencing triumphant dominion, were 'through fear of death all their lifetime subject to bondage' (v. 15). By the amazing grace of God, Jesus 'tasted death' on their behalf (v. 9), so that 'through death he might destroy him that had the power of death, that is, the devil; and deliver them...' (vv. 14, 15). By His incarnate life, atoning death and resurrection, He 'brings many sons to glory' (vv. 10). In doing so, the plenitude of dominion is being restored to them *in Him*.

---

39. Von Rad, *op. cit.*, 60.
40. Colin E. Gunton, *Christ and Creation* (William B. Eerdmans Publ. Co.: Grand Rapids, MI, 1992), 84.

Humankind: Male and Female

A component part of mankind's dominion over the created order seems to be provided in God's appointment of marriage. Only creatures whose very being reflects something of God's own inner-personal richness of diversity and unity would be adequate to this high calling. Genesis 1: 27 suggests that the creation of mankind as both male and female is reflective of the rich relational life of the personal God, and thus that marital sexuality contributes to the fullness of what it means to be created in the image of God, and thus the appropriate emblem of his authority over the world. Hans Urs Von Balthasar discusses the divinely intended fruitfulness and fecundity of the male, female relationship as reflecting the blessings of God's own inter-Trinitarian relationships.[41]

Genesis 2 gives us fuller information about the creation of male and female, but what little Genesis 1 tells us about their origin agrees totally with the expanded history of the second chapter. In both places we are told that the male was created first. Genetic research confirms this, for the male has both X chromosomes (which engender females) and Y chromosomes (which engender males), whereas the female has only X chromosomes. If the female had been created first, and the male taken out of her body, then reproduction would have been impossible, for there would have been nothing but X chromosomes, in which case only females could have been reproduced. Instead, the male had the genetic material so that a female could be taken out of him, and be genetically related to him 'in the same kind', and then through relationship to her, be able to procreate both male and female. In this case, as in so many others, the scientific accuracy of the details of the Genesis account of creation can only be evaded by failing to look at reality, and the intellectual avoidance of reality severely truncates the accomplishment of dominion.

The contribution of the male/female relationship to fulfilling the dominion mandate as God's image bearers seems confirmed by the blessing placed upon the original couple in verse 28 of Genesis 1:

> And God blessed them, and God said unto them, Be fruitful, and multiply, and replenish the earth, and subdue it: and have dominion over the fish of the sea, and over the fowl of the air, and over every living thing that moveth upon the earth.

Cassuto shows the connection of this blessing of fecundity with their calling to dominion: 'Although you are only two, yet through your fruitfulness and increase, your descendants will fill the land and subdue it.' He also refers to similar expressions of increase of

---

41. See *The Christian State of Life* (Ignatius Press: San Francisco, 1983), 224-229.

progeny and vocational success in Noah, Abraham, and the children of Israel.[42]

Thus the male/female relationship would accomplish two tremendous purposes in terms of the divine image in humanity. First, by their own inter-personal relationship, they would experience some reflection of the interior relational life of the personal God Himself. This ever deepening knowledge of Who God is would enrich their life together, all the better equipping them *to be* God's image, as well as *to do* His will on earth in their own generation. And second, marriage would be the sacred channel for reproduction of those who would extend God's dominion to the ends of the earth in days to come.

'And It Was Good'

Genesis 1: 29 and 30 manifests the bounty of God in providing a wide variety of food for the sustenance and pleasure of his chosen image bearers. They could partake of all types of vegetables and fruits, as could their charges, the animals, but they were not to eat animals. As Karl Barth said, 'Just as man was created with the animals on the same day, so he has been assigned to the same table spread by God.'[43] There is a reason why flesh was not an option for the original couple. To eat meat would have entailed killing and blood shedding. 'No shedding of blood within the animal kingdom, and no murderous action by man! This word of God, therefore, also means a limitation in the human right of dominion.'[44] Evidently, man was not given permission to eat animal flesh until after the Flood of Noah, long after the Fall of Adam and the entrance of sin, evil and death into the world. Isaiah pictures the restored paradise of the Messianic age, when once again, neither mankind nor even carnivorous beasts will eat flesh. In that coming day, 'the lion shall eat straw like the ox' (see Isa. 65:25 and 11:7).

The absence of evil, killing and death is confirmed by the concluding words of Genesis 1, summarizing the remarkable work of the sixth day of creation: 'And God saw every thing that he had made, and behold, it was very good. And the evening and the morning were the sixth day' (v. 31). Cassuto appropriately comments on the difference of this concluding formula from the one used in previous days:

> Instead of the usual simple formula, we have here, at the conclusion of the story of creation, a more elaborate and imposing statement that points to the general harmony prevailing in the world of the Almighty. On the previous days the words *that it was good* were applied to a specific detail; now *God saw* EVERYTHING *that He had made*, the creation

---

42. Cassuto, *op. cit.*, 58.
43. Karl Barth, *Church Dogmatics, Vol. III, The Doctrine of Creation, Part One*, 1977.
44. Von Rad, *op.cit.*, 60.

in its totality, and He perceived that not only were the details, taken separately, good, but that each one harmonized with the rest; hence the whole was not just *good*, but *very good*.[45]

The biblical view of variety in harmony of 'everything' in the created order is profoundly different from New Age Monism, which seeks to reduce everything to one (and ultimately to the nothingness of 'Nirvana'). As Douglas Grothuis demonstrates in his critique of New Age thought, the God of Scripture loves and affirms variety and diversity.[46]

The biblical view of diversity in harmony is also different from the grim varieties of political totalitarianism, from the French Revolution, through Marxism down to the present day secularist Statism of our post-Christian Western countries (which 'legalizes' the taking of innocent life through abortion and euthanasia). The pervasive political erosion in all our countries of personal dignity, liberty and sacredness of life (called *Leftism* by Von Kuehnelt-Leddihn) seems rooted in a denial of diversity in favor of bureaucratically enforced identity ('the herd instinct' or 'egalitarianism').[47] The harmonious diversity God created and pronounced 'very good' shows us a better and true basis of thought and life; an alternative to personal meaninglessness (or 'Nirvana') and to political totalitarianism. Personal significance and political liberty are ultimately founded in God's goodness expressed in the diversity and harmony of the created order, as St. Thomas Aquinas long ago showed:

> The highest degree of perfection should not be lacking in a work made by the supremely good workman. But the good of order among diverse things is better than any of the members of an order, taken by itself .... It was not fitting, therefore, that God's work would lack the good of order. And yet, without the diversity and inequality of created things, this good could not exist.[48]

In light of this goodness pervading the freshly created order, the evolutionary theory which necessitates evil, in the form of competition, struggle, killing and death as the means of upward advance of the creatures *from the very beginning* of life on earth is ruled out by clear revelation of God Himself. Although not the subject of this brief volume, which keeps to the original creation week, Genesis 3 and the

---

45. Cassuto, *op. cit.*, 59.
46. Douglas Grothuis, *Unmasking the New Age* (InterVarsity Press: Downers Grove, Ill., 1986), see pp. 18-20.
47. Von Kuehnelt-Leddihn, op. cit., 5. His first Chapter ('Identity and Diversity') deals with the psychological and spiritual roots of the modern political enforcement of 'identity' or 'egalitarianism.' As he frequently notes, 'Egalitarianism... cannot make much progress without the use of force... Yet the use of force limits and in most cases destroys freedom' (13).

rest of the Scriptures (particularly Romans 5, 6 and 1 Corinthians 15) teach with one voice that evil and death entered the universe only after Adam sinned. The entire significance of the atoning work of Christ as the Last Adam, lies in his reversal of the sin of the First Adam, which caused all the disorders that result in death.

While secular evolutionists can easily ignore the biblical testimony on this vital point, theistic evolutionists have a much harder time coping with what God says, for it is plainly contradictory to their paradigm of origins. One of the most distinguished of them, Dr Hugh Ross has devoted major portions of a recent book attempting to evade the clear teaching of Scripture that 'by man came death' (1 Cor. 15:21).[49] While one is tempted to admire the energetic tenacity of his efforts to make Scripture say the exact opposite of what it clearly means, in the end of the day it is sad to see such talented effort spent on a futile attempt to read into Scripture what is contrary to it, rather than letting it speak for itself. There are many things in the Scripture 'hard to be understood' (cf. 2 Peter 3:16), but this is not one of them. Nothing could be more clear than the fact that the original created order was a place of holy beauty and peace, but then that '...by one man sin entered into the world, and death by sin...'[50] There can be no other sensible interpretation of Genesis 1:31.

One of the finest theological essays exploring the implications of the goodness of the original creation and the subsequent entrance of evil and death through man's sin is found in a chapter, 'Evil, Evolution and the Fall', in Dr Nigel Cameron's *Evolution and the Authority of the Bible*. He points out that in certain respects, 'Genesis 1-3 itself reads as a theodicy, a defense of the goodness of God.'[51] Referring to Genesis 1:31, he writes:

> The world which God made for man to inhabit was 'very good'. It had been prepared to receive him as its crown, and the setting was constructed so as to be ideal for the probation to which Adam and Eve were called. The world was not created with the Fall in prospect, still less with the curse already let loose.[52]

48. Thomas Aquinas, *Summa Contra Gentes, Book Two: Creation*, Translated by James F. Anderson (University of Notre Dame Press: Notre Dame, 1975), chapter 45. 8 (138).
49. Hugh Ross, *Creation And Time: A Biblical and Scientific Perspective on the Creation-Date Controversy* (NAVPRESS: Colorado Springs, Co., 1994).
50. Since Dr Ross' efforts to exegete the Scriptures are so unconvincing, I do not feel they call for a detailed refutation here. However, a recent work by Van Bebber and Taylor, *Creation and Time: A Report on the Progressive Creationist Book by Hugh Ross* (Eden Communications: Meza, AZ, 1995), deals fairly with his ideas. See especially pp.15-24 and 41-54.
51. Cameron, *op. cit.*, 61.
52. *Ibid.*, 66.

In light of this reality, Cameron speaks of the 'incoherence' of the theistic evolutionary thesis, which places evil and death in the created order *before* man's choice to sin against his Creator.[53] Therefore, with justification, he calls for a paradigm shift in the theistic evolutionary model of origins: 'the complete reconstruction of the evolutionary order of nature, and its replacement by another.'[54] This volume, building upon the work of others, has been written in hope of making a step in that direction.

TECHNICAL AND BIBLIOGRAPHICAL NOTES FOR CHAPTER ELEVEN

The Development of the Concept of 'Person'

It was only after the impact of the Gospel on the decaying classical world that the concept of person arose. Kuehnelt-Leddihn writes: '... It is well to recall that the concept of person as we know it did not exist in antiquity. It appeared in the Western world – with the advent of Christianity.'[55]

St. Augustine's fourth century *Confessions* manifest what we would call today an intense sense of inward, personal life. As a result of the spreading of the idea of 'person' in the culture, by the sixth century, the Northern Italian philosopher and theologian, Boethius attempted to define (somewhat unsuccessfully) what it meant to be a person.[56] A much more fruitful definition was provided nearly six hundred years later in France. The great twelfth-century Christian theologian, Richard of St. Victor derived an understanding of personality from meditating on the communion of love in the being of God among Father, Son and Holy Spirit, who wholly inter-penetrate and coinhere in one another in such a way that their personal distinctness as Father, Son and Holy Spirit remains inviolate.[57]

T. F. Torrance has summarized Richard's insight on the relationship of Trinity and personality:

> It was from a theological understanding of God's personal and personalizing self-communication, creating personal reciprocity between us and Himself, that the Christian concept of the person arose, which is applicable in a creaturely way to persons in relation

---

53. *Ibid.*, 65.
54. *Ibid.*, 67.
55. Von Kuehnelt-Leddihn, *op. cit.*, 34.
56. See Boethius, *De Personis et duabus Naturis*, III: 'persona est rationalis naturae individua substantia' ('a person is the individual substance of rational nature').
57. Richard defines personality in *De Trinitate* IV. 16, 22, 24: 'persona est... intellectualis naturae incommunicabilis existentia' ('a person is incommunicable existence of intellectual nature').

to one another, but which reflects the transcendent way in which the three divine Persons are interrelated in the Holy Trinity.[58]

Elsewhere Torrance states that:

... the concept of person was not found before Christianity, for it is the direct product of the way in which the Church found it had to understand Jesus Christ and the distinctive relations in the Triune God as intrinsically personal. Thus there arose the concept of person, in its supreme sense in God and in its subordinate sense in human existence, in accordance with which the relations which persons have with one another as persons are onto-relations, for they are person-constituting relations. That was a concept and a way of thinking developed through the understanding of the Holy Trinity as a Communion of Love in whom Father, Son and Holy Spirit mutually involve and coinhere in one another in the profound onto-relations of that communion, without any blurring of their hypostatic distinctions or properties as Father, Son and Holy Spirit, which would make them no more than modal aspects in an undifferentiated oneness of divine Being.[59]

With this Trinitarian background in view, having explored in its light the meaning of our creation in the image and likeness of God, we can appreciate the title of a recent book that deals with St. Thomas' teaching on the ultimate reference point of human personality; the 'model' in terms of which mankind was shaped: *To the Image of the Trinity*.[60] Thomas believed that:

... by his mind man reflects the intellectual nature of God and by the faculties of his mind he reflects the three Persons in God. Grace, which establishes its proper habits and operations in man's faculties, may depart from the soul, but man's nature remains, and with it the image of the Trinity.[61]

In an 'impressionistic', but thought-provoking way, Eugene Rosen-stock-Huessy explored what happens in society at large when numbers of people both believe and apply the implications of their *renewal* into the image of the Trinity (through the reality signified by baptism into the Name of the Father, the Son and the Holy Ghost):

For nineteen centuries, the outstanding contributors to the life we live... have worshipped the Father as the guarantor of their trust, the Son as the guarantor of their liberty, and the Spirit as the guarantor of their creativity. Thus our whole civilized inheritance has been made by men in the image of the Trinity, and we may see that image in such everyday things as pilots, whom we trust with our lives, doctors, who

58. Thomas F. Torrance, *Reality and Evangelical Theology*, 43.
59. T. F. Torrance, *The Mediation of Christ*, 58.
60. D. Juvenal Merriell, *To the Image of the Trinity: A Study in the Development of Aquinas' Teaching* (Pontifical Institute of Medieval Studies: Toronto, 1990).
61. *Ibid.*, 81.

employ the latest creations of medical science, and teachers who enjoy liberty to influence children in ways that would never happen if we merely let nature take its course. Correspondingly, we also witness what happens as modern society forsakes the Divine attributes for their opposites, mistrust, mechanization, fatalism: men are killed in wars, disintegrated by mechanical repetition, enslaved by dictators.[62]

Renewal of individuals to the image of the Trinity through union with Christ also renews society, Rosenstock-Huessy believes, in a Godward direction. In particular, he sees that it engenders qualities crucial to a wholesome 'body politic', qualities that flow from within the relationships of the three Persons of the Holy Trinity: trustworthiness, creativity and liberty.[63]

62. Rosenstock-Huessy, *op. cit.*, 111, 112.
63. *Ibid.*, 112.

QUESTIONS FOR STUDY

1. What seems to be the division of 'living creatures' into three basic sorts?

2. Discuss the shift in language when talking about the creation of mankind.

3. God employs a plural verb when speaking to Himself in Genesis 1:26. What are the different explanations of this usage?

4. Discuss the relationship between the words 'image' and 'likeness' in Genesis 1:26.

5. What is the basic meaning of the term 'personal'?

6. What does John Zizioulas mean when he writes that when used of God, 'substance poses almost by definition a relational character'?

7. Why does human speech seem to require creation rather than evolution?

8. Discuss 'the dominion mandate' and human culture.

9. In what way does human marriage seem to reflect something about the Trinity?

10. What do X and Y chromosomes indicate about the priority of the creation of the male?

11. Contrast the differing views of New Age Monism and political Totalitarianism from the biblical teaching of diversity in harmony.

12. Why did evil and death enter the world only after Adam's sin?

13. How does this differ from an evolutionary explanation of life?

Chapter Twelve

The Sabbath Day and the Orientation of the Whole Created Order towards Worship of God

FROM the summary statement of Genesis 2:1 we see that the entire work of creation was completed by the end of the sixth day, and then from verses 2 and 3, we learn that the whole sequence and rhythm of the first six days was consecrated by means of God's rest on the seventh or Sabbath day:

> Thus the heavens and the earth were finished, and all the host of them. And on the seventh day God ended his work which he had made; and he rested on the seventh day from all his work which he had made. And God blessed the seventh day, and sanctified it; because that in it he had rested from all his work which God created and made (Gen. 2:1-3).

The incomparable significance of the Sabbath day is shown in that this is the very first time the word 'holy' is used in the Bible (*qiddesh* – 'hallowed it': Gen. 2:3). The root meaning of 'holy' (*qadosh*) is believed to come from the verb 'to cut off' or 'to separate'. Cassuto explains that 'The real meaning of *q^edhusa*("holiness") is elevation and exaltation above the usual level; the seventh day was lifted up above the plane of the other days.'[1]

---

1. Cassuto, *op. cit.*, 65

Grammatical considerations indicate that two things are implied by the clause: 'he hallowed it': on the one hand, He made it holy (the *Piel* stem of the verb here implies causation), and on the other hand, He declared it to be holy, or consecrated it (for this form of the verb also carries here a declarative sense).[2] God's causing the day to be holy is directly connected to His *abstaining from work*. This is translated in most English versions as 'He rested'. This seems to imply an anthropomorphic reading back into God of human tiredness, as though the labor of the first six days had made Him weary. But the actual Hebrew text reads, 'and He abstained from work' (*wayyisboth*). Rather than conveying the idea of rest and refreshment, at this point – as Cassuto shows – 'It has a negative connotation: "not to do work".'[3] Although the concept of God Himself actually resting is used elsewhere in Scripture (as in Exod. 20:11 and 31:17):

> Nevertheless in this section, which avoids all possible use of anthropomorphic expressions in order to teach us, particularly in the account of creation, how great is the gulf between the Creator and the created, such notions would have been incongruous; hence the Bible uses only a term that signifies 'abstention from work'.[4]

Where 'rest' or 'refreshment' is applied to God in other passages, it would seem to mean that while the heavenly Father could not have been literally weary (for 'he fainteth not, neither is weary' – Isa. 40:28), still 'refreshment' is properly attributed to Him in the sense of His receiving joy and delight in the contemplation of the beauty of what He had created. We are told that a 'fruit' of the Holy Spirit (who bears the very attributes of the Father) is joy (Gal. 5: 22), and that the Son (who is the actual 'character' of the Father – cf. Heb. 1:3, 'who being... the character of his person') was 'anointed with the oil of gladness above thy fellows' (Heb. 1:9, drawing from Ps. 45:7).

God, therefore, makes the day holy by abstaining from work during it, since His creative activity has now been completed by the end of the sixth day. But Genesis 2:1 seems, at first glance, to contradict this completion of all work on the sixth day, when it states: 'And on the seventh day God ended his work which he had made...' In order to get around this difficulty, some of the ancient versions of the Old Testament, such as the Samaritan Version, the Septuagint, the Peshitta and the Book of Jubilees amended the Hebrew text to read *sixth* instead of *seventh* day.[5] Cassuto demonstrates, however, that the *seventh* day of the original Masoretic text is certainly the right reading.

---

2. Leupold, *op. cit.*, 103.
3. Cassuto, *op. cit.*, 63.
4. *Ibid.*
5. *Ibid,* 61.

He explains the meaning of this otherwise curious usage (of 'finished on the *seventh* day') by examining similar sentences elsewhere in the Pentateuch, such as 'And he finished talking with him, and God went up from Abraham' (Gen. 17: 22). 'The clause "And he finished talking with him" does not connote "And He spoke His concluding words to him," for God's final words were cited in the preceding verse; the meaning is: "Having finished talking with him, He went up from Abraham"... The [i.e. this and several other verses cited by Cassuto] clearly establish that the meaning of our verse is: "Since God was on the seventh day in the position of one who had already finished His work, consequently He abstained from work on the seventh day".'[6]

God's abstaining from work causes the seventh day to be holy. It is 'cut off' or elevated above the previous six days. Thus, it is made to be different. Cassuto states that 'the difference consists in the *novel character* of the seventh day; after a series of six days on each of which some work of creation was wrought, came a day on which God did not work or add anything to his creation; hence the remembrance of this abstinence from labor remained linked with the day on which this situation first arose.'[7]

In addition to *making* it holy, God also specifically *declares* this 'different' day to be 'holy'. He declares it to be such for the benefit of mankind, His image-bearers, in order 'to promote a special relationship to God and to His service.'[8] Therefore, this special day will always carry a divinely declared blessing with it for those who are the crown of the entire created order. Although the 'seventh day' (later termed 'the Sabbath') bears a special relationship to Israel, the covenant people of God (as in Exod. 20:8 and Deut. 5:12-14), by which they honor God and are caused 'to ride upon the high places of the earth' (Isa. 58:13, 14), in the context of Genesis 2, it clearly has a universal application to all of God's image bearers. Cassuto correctly argues:

> Every seventh day, without intermission since the days of creation, serves as a memorial to the idea of the creation of the world by the word of God, and we must refrain from work thereon so that we may follow the Creator's example and cleave to His ways. Scripture wishes to emphasize that the sanctity of the Sabbath is older than Israel, and rests upon all mankind. The fact that the name *'Elohim'* ['God'] which was current also among the Gentile nations, and not the name YHWH [E.V. 'LORD'], which was used by the Israelites only, occurs here is not without significance; the latter designation will be found in connection with the commandments concerning the proper

---

6. *Ibid.*, 62.
7. *Ibid.*, 64.
8. Aalders, *op. cit.*, 76.

observance of the Sabbath, which devolves only upon Israel. Thus in the Ten Commandments it is said, REMEMBER *the Sabbath day to keep it holy*, not 'know that there is a Sabbath in the world'; that was already known.[9]

Part of the blessing conveyed by Sabbath observance can be understood from the numerical combination of *six* days of work and *one* day of rest, providing the number used in Scripture to denote wholeness, completeness and perfection (and thus, rest): *seven*. This number seems 'writ large' in the natural order as well as in Scripture. Cardinal Ratzinger comments:

> The number that governs the whole is seven; in the scheme of seven days it permeates the whole in a way that cannot be overlooked. This is the number of a phase of the moon, and thus we are told throughout this account that the rhythm of our heavenly neighbor is also the rhythm of our human life. It becomes clear that we human beings are not bounded by the limits of our own little 'I' but that we are part of the rhythm of the universe, that we too, so to speak, assimilate the heavenly rhythm and movement in our own bodies and thus, thanks to this interlinking, are fitted into the logic of the universe. In the Bible this thought goes still further. It lets us know that the rhythm of the heavenly bodies is, more profoundly, a way of expressing the rhythm of the heart and the rhythm of God's love, which manifests itself there.[10]

The Rev. William Still, well known senior minister of Aberdeen (Scotland), has with penetrating insight explored the implications of the Sabbath rhythm for spiritual, emotional, physical and vocational health, in his *Rhythms of Rest and Work*.[11] It is no difficult task to demonstrate empirically the physical and emotional value of six days' work and one day's rest to the human race, (even apart from primary spiritual concerns). The atheistic French Revolution, for example, in order to abolish every vestige of Christianity from the land, forbade Sabbath observance by making the work week longer. But the well-being of the population suffered to such a degree, that the radical revolutionaries had to reinstate the Sabbath. And our own frenetic generation, which in most of the industrialized world has ignored the Sabbath since at least the 1960s, not surprisingly now finds itself unable to rest.[12]

9. Cassuto, *op. cit.*, 64.
10. Ratzinger, *op. cit.*, 26, 27.
11. William Still, *Rhythms of Rest and Work* (Didasko Press: Aberdeen, 1985).
12. A lead article in *Time* magazine (December 17, 1990) charted the widespread inability of many people to sleep and relax, under the title 'Too much to do, Too little rest.' It gave five suggestions to deal with stress and lack of ability to rest, but among them did not mention the one that would have been the most helpful in restoring the God-ordained balance or rhythm for human work and rest: keeping the Sabbath day holy.

It would be interesting to know how many heart attacks, strokes and emotional breakdowns could be prevented by following the creational rhythm of six days of work and one day of rest. The reason for this is that the Creator made us to exist as creatures who need to rest one day out of seven. To go against our creaturely limits tends to cause disintegration in both personality and body (and relationships). To transgress this basic rhythm which is built both into the universe and into the human soul and body is to transgress a kindly bestowed blessing of God, and is to ask for increasing personal stress and disturbance, if not breakdown.

The remarkable Jewish Christian intellectual, Eugene Rosenstock-Huessy discusses perceptively the twentieth century industrial world's changing of the weekly 'holy-day' (or 'holiday') from a communal celebration to an individualistic spending of 'leisure time'.[13] Noting that: 'Leisure is secular because it divides us; we are dragged eccentrically in this or that direction. On her holidays, the soul becomes whole',[14] he calls this turning of a holy-day into leisure 'a decay'.[15] Tragic results follow the decay of the societal 'holy-day' or Sabbath as regards professional life:

> Fifty years ago [he was writing in the 1940s], a doctor or minister or lawyer would practice fifty years with little or no time off. Now they break down after a decade, and they experiment with their daily routine nearly incessantly. Telephone, car, plane, mail have enabled them to do as much, in mere quantity, within ten years as formerly in a lifetime. No wonder that they have to cease to exist every decade. They must retire every ten years as though it was to the grave, and start a new life simply because they have crammed a whole life into a much shorter time span.[16]

He even suggests that the 'nervous breakdown' is 'the most eloquent argument' for a return to community Sabbath observance. However, within traditional, non-secularized Christianity (insofar as it is actually practiced), '... the sublime reason why Sunday is the first day of the week, instead of the last' is that within it '... we anticipate the future Kingdom of God, ahead of the week-days which carry on the patterns of organized work inherited from the past.'[17] With poetic insight,

---

13. See Chapter VIII, 'The Rhythm of Peace or Our 'Today' in *The Christian Future: Or The Modern Mind Outrun* (Harper Torchbook: New York, 1966), 198-243.
14. *Ibid.*, 202. He immediately adds: 'She [the soul] accepts her many weekday conflicts or trends because she no longer has to fear them as curses but may accept them as her wealth. She may do so because she proves to herself, on the holiday, her ultimate freedom from every one of them, by communion, by fellowship. Holidays are the mortar of society.'
15. *Ibid.*, 199.
16. *Ibid.*, 205.
17. *Ibid.*, 204, 205.

Rosenstock-Huessy adds: 'In this way, the inspiration of Sunday slowly melts the frozen forms of week-day routine.'[18]

Without denying the far-reaching benefits of 'remembering the Sabbath day to keep it holy' on mankind's physical and emotional life, the creation account seems to reach a great crescendo on the seventh day, showing that the entire creation is directed towards the Sabbath, so that something far greater than physical or even societal well-being is intended here. Ratzinger is probably right in perceiving that 'the rhythm of the seven and its cosmic significance'

> ...is itself at the service of a still deeper meaning: Creation is oriented to the sabbath, which is the sign of the covenant between God and humankind.... Creation is designed in such a way that it is oriented to worship. It fulfills its purpose and assumes its significance when it is lived, ever new, with a view to worship. Creation exists for the sake of worship.... The true center, the power that moves and shapes from within in the rhythm of the stars and of our lives, is worship. Our life's rhythm moves in proper measure when it is caught up in this.[19]

The Westminster Confession of Faith, although written in London in the 1640s, still speaks a fresh and wholesome word to guide God's image bearers in keeping the Sabbath day:

> The Sabbath is kept holy unto the Lord, when men: prepare their hearts for it; arrange for their daily affairs to be taken care of beforehand; rest the whole day from their own works and words, and from thoughts about their worldly activities and recreations; and take up the whole time in public and private worship and in the duties of necessity and mercy (Ch. 21, par. 8).[20]

As Ratzinger has proposed, the very structure of the creation week orients the entire created order to the Sabbath, and thus to the remembrance of God our Creator, and His relationship to us and purposes of blessing for us. This in itself means that the Sabbath, (remembering that *seven* is the number of final perfection), bears a profound orientation towards the future; to that final, perfect consummation of all the purposes of God in and through His creation, which has been washed clean through the blood of the Lamb (Rev. 5:9), for whose pleasure 'all things are and were created' (Rev. 4:11).

Robert Murray M'Cheyne, an eminent Church of Scotland saint of the early nineteenth century, expressed with truly devotional beauty, the God-ordained future orientation of every properly observed Sabbath day. It is fitting that his words should conclude these studies

---

18. *Ibid.*, 205.
19. Ratiznger, *op. cit.*, 27, 28.
20. *The Westminster Confession of Faith: An Authentic Modern Version* (Summertown Texts: Signal Mountain, TN, 1992 reprint), 62.

on the divine creation, which ultimately points our gaze and all our activities to a higher world, where we shall by and by enjoy endless fellowship with our Creator and Redeemer, as we enter into rest (Heb. 4:3) through belief in that One who 'made the worlds' (Heb. 1:2) and then redeemed them from sin and death (Heb. 1:3):

> It is a type of heaven when a believer lays aside his pen or loom, brushes aside his worldly cares, leaving them behind him with his weekday clothes, and comes up to the house of God. It is like the morning of the resurrection, the day when we shall come out of great tribulation into the presence of God and the Lamb, when the believer sits under the preached Word and hears the voice of the Shepherd leading and feeding his soul. It reminds him of the day when the Lamb that is in the midst of the Throne shall feed him, and lead him to living fountains of water. When he joins in the psalm of praise, it reminds him of the day when his hands shall strike the harp of God, 'where congregations ne'er break up and Sabbaths have no end.' When he retires and meets with God in secret in his closet, or like Isaac in some favourite spot near his dwelling, it reminds him of the day when he shall be a pillar in the house of our God and go out no more. This is the reason why we love the Lord's Day. This is the reason why we call the Sabbath a delight. A well spent Sabbath we feel to be a day of heaven upon earth. For this reason we wish our Sabbaths to be wholly given to God. We love to spend the whole time in the public and private exercises of God's worship except so much as is taken up in works of necessity and mercy. We love to rise early on that morning and to sit up late, that we may have a long day with God.[21]

CONCLUDING WORD

The goal of these studies has been to turn our thoughts towards the true end of our lives, the glory of God, our Creator and Redeemer, for 'this is life eternal, that they might know thee the only true God, and Jesus Christ, whom thou hast sent' (John 17:3). I have sought to argue that if we will allow our minds to fall under the compulsion of reality as it is conveyed to us in the Holy Scriptures, we shall be in a position to study, learn and in some measure articulate all the better the coherence and significance of the structures and events of the created order. Or, in the words of Sir Francis Bacon, we seek to read together and aright God's 'two books' of Scripture and Nature.

Throughout this volume, I have engaged in a running debate with the secularism of our times and its evolutionary 'paradigm', which, I believe, keeps us from understanding either Scripture or reality. Thus, it tragically turns the gaze of our culture from both God, our

---

21. Rev. A. A. Bonar, *Memoir and Remains of the Rev. Robert Murray M'Cheyne*, 539.

Creator, Redeemer and Goal (which is our very salvation), and from a realistic assessment and development of the created realm (which is part and parcel of our 'dominion mandate'). The bitter harvest of this willful blindness is being reaped with increasing swiftness in our deteriorating Western society.

There is only one way for massive intellectual, moral and cultural healing to occur, and it entails a revolutionary 'paradigm shift' from mythological evolution to a Scripturally revealed and scientifically realistic paradigm of special, divine creation. The teachings of Genesis 1 and 2 are sufficiently clear to give us our general orientation in this requisite paradigm shift, and a growing chorus of voices from operational science confirm the latter, even as they deny the former (as I have attempted to show in this volume).

As our intellectual framework is once again brought into accordance with Scriptural truth, the Psalmist promises that 'in thy light, shall we see light' (Ps. 36:9), and a world of new discoveries, interconnections and surprising meaning will open before us scientifically and culturally. Perhaps this delightful advance will be something like the beautiful bursting forth of renewed moral and cultural life, when the moribund existence of millions who lived within the decaying secularism of the late Roman Empire, was liberated in a wave of resurrection power. The spiritual, moral and cultural resurrection wrought by lifting men's eyes from blind and exclusive immersion in the secular order to the true purposes of the Creator and Redeemer has been traced by Charles Norris Cochrane in his *Christianity and Classical Culture: A Study of Thought and Action From Augustus to Augustine.*[22]

As something like this takes place again, not only will Sabbath days be a time of meditation and delight in God, but every day will more and more fulfill its ordained function for God's renewed image

---

22. Charles Norris Cochrane, *Christianity and Classical Culture: A Study of Thought and Action From Augustus to Augustine* (Oxford University Press: London, 1974). In his Preface, Professor Cochrane noted the Christians' opposition to the classical Graeco-Roman worship of the state as the final value and ultimate for human life. This classical exaltation (or deification) of the secular state, was considered by the Christians to be 'the grossest of superstitions'. According to Cochrane: 'The Christians traced this superstition to the acceptance of a defective logic, the logic of classical "naturalism", to which they ascribed the characteristic *vitia* of the classical world. In this connection it is important to notice that their revolt was not from nature; it was from the picture of nature constructed by classical *scientia*, together with its implications for practical life. And what they demanded was a radical revision of first principles as the presupposition to an adequate cosmology and anthropology. The basis for such a revision they held to lie in the *logos* of Christ, conceived as a revelation, not of "new" truth, but of truth which was as old as the hills and as everlasting. This they accepted as an answer to the promise of illumination and power extended to mankind and, thus, the basis for a new physics, a new ethic and above all, a new logic, the logic of human progress. In Christ, therefore, they claimed to possess a principle of understanding superior to anything existing in the classical world' (vi).

bearers. For, says Calvin, 'This is, indeed, the proper business of the whole life, in which men should daily exercise themselves to consider the infinite goodness, justice, power, and wisdom of God, in this magnificent theatre of heaven and earth.'[23]

TECHNICAL AND BIBLIOGRAPHICAL NOTES FOR CHAPTER TWELVE

The Christian Sabbath: A Change of Day, Not Principle

Since the fourth century AD Constantinian settlement making Christianity the established religion of the Roman Empire, most of the Western world has observed Sunday (the first day of the week), rather than Saturday (the last day of the week), as their official Sabbath day of rest and worship. While the historical details of this change are rather complex to trace,[24] the basic reason is clearly pointed out by the seventeenth-century *Westminster Confession of Faith*, which, after stating the perpetual obligation of observing 'one day in seven for a sabbath', adds that the Sabbath '... from the beginning of the world to the resurrection of Christ, was the last day of the week; and, from the resurrection of Christ, was changed into the first day of the week, which in Scripture is called the Lord's Day, and is to be continued to the end of the world, as the Christian Sabbath' (Ch. XXI.vii).

A Change of Day

Within the New Testament itself, there are already evidences of this change of day from the last day of the week to the first. Brief descriptions of early Christian worship indicate that the believers were meeting on the first day of the week to worship the risen Lord. The instructions of the Apostle Paul to the church at Corinth concerning taking up a regular collection for needy saints shows that they gathered to worship on Sunday: 'Now concerning the collection for the saints, as I have given order to the churches of Galatia, even so do ye. Upon the first day of the week let every one of you lay by him in store, as God hath prospered him, that there be no gatherings when I come' (1 Cor. 16:1, 2). Other New Testament texts bear witness to this change of day (e.g. Acts 20:7).

The apostles certainly continued to worship in the Jewish synagogue on the traditional Sabbath, especially for evangelistic purposes, for that

---

23. Calvin, *Commentary Upon Genesis*, Ch. 2, vs. 3 (105, 106).
24. Perhaps the most exhaustive discussion of this change is found in Francis Nigel Lee, *The Covenantal Sabbath: The Weekly Sabbath Scripturally and Historically Considered* (The Lord's Day Observance Society: London, 1969). See especially Chapter VII, 'The New Covenant Sabbath', pp.191-266.

is when God's people were gathered to hear the Scriptures expounded, and often the apostles were invited to preach to them. This gave them the opportunity to explain how Christ was truly their Messiah (as we see in sermons preached by Paul and Peter in the synagogues, both in Israel and in Gentile lands).[25] Apparently after the destruction of Jerusalem in 70 AD and especially after the Rebellion of Bar Kochba in 135 AD, the split between synagogue and church became complete. After this profound division, it appears that the Christians no longer visited the synagogue, and presumably worshipped exclusively on the first day of the week.

No Change of Principle

The early Christians thought of themselves as 'the new Israel', the 'Israel of God' (cf. Gal. 6:16). They understood Christ to be the fulfillment of the Old Testament, not its destruction,[26] and the God of Israel to be their God. B. B. Warfield noted how the New Testament writers did not think that their doctrine of God was alien in any way to the Old Testament:

> ... its writers felt no incongruity whatever between their doctrine of the Trinity and the Old Testament conception of God. The New Testament writers certainly were not conscious of being 'setters forth of strange gods'. To their own apprehension they worshipped and proclaimed just the God of Israel and they laid no less stress than the Old Testament itself upon His unity (John 18:3; 1 Cor. 8:4; 1 Tim. 2:5).... Without apparent misgiving they take over Old Testament passages and apply them to Father, Son, and Spirit indifferently. Obviously they understand themselves, and wish to be understood, as setting forth in the Father, Son and Spirit just the one God that the God of the Old Testament revelation is...[27]

Granted that they saw themselves as worshipping the same God and expounding the same Torah as the Jews, we would not expect to find them denying or ignoring a basic creation ordinance such as Sabbath worship and rest. And a careful reading of the New Testament text shows this, in fact, to be the case.

While, following their Lord, they did reject the burdensome 'works' righteousness' interpretation placed on the Sabbath by the Pharisaic party of their day,[28] nevertheless, they invited believers in Christ as Messiah to enter with them into the true Sabbath rest won by the risen Christ for them (see Heb. 4:1-11, which along with Heb. 3:7-19

---

25. See, for instance, such texts as Acts 13:14, 42; 14:1; 16:13; 17:2, 10; 18:4-11; 19:8-10.
26. See Christ's own words in Matthew 5:17-20.
27. B. B. Warfield, *Biblical Foundations*, p. 88.
28. See e.g. Matthew 12:1-9; Luke 13:10-17.

constitute a meditation and explication of the real meaning of the Sabbath through Ps. 95).

After careful study of numerous relevant New Testament texts, B. B. Warfield writes:

> The Sabbath came out of Christ's hands, we see then, not despoiled of any of its authority or robbed of any of its glory, but rather enhanced in both authority and glory. Like the other commandments it was cleansed of all that was local or temporary in the modes in which it had hitherto been commended to God's people in their isolation as a nation, and stood forth in its universal ethical content. Among the changes in its external form which it thus underwent was a change in the day of its observance. No injury was thus done the Sabbath as it was commended to the Jews; rather a new greatness was brought to it.[29]

Warfield shows that although:

> ... we have no record of a commandment of our Lord's requiring a change in the day of the observance of the Sabbath .... By their actions, nevertheless, both our Lord and his apostles appear to commend the first day of the week to us as the Christian Sabbath. It is not merely that our Lord rose from the dead on that day. A certain emphasis seems to be placed precisely upon the fact that it was on the first day of the week that he rose. This is true of all the accounts of his rising.[30]

After discussing various resurrection appearance texts in the Gospel of John (which occurred on *successive* first days of the week), Warfield concludes:

> The appearance is strong that our Lord, having crowded the day of his rising with manifestations, disappeared for a whole week to appear again only on the next Sabbath. George Zabriskie Gray seems justified, therefore, in suggesting that the full effect of our Lord's sanction of the first day of the week as the appointed day of his meeting with his disciples can be fitly appreciated only by considering with his manifestations also his disappearances. 'For six whole days between the rising day and its octave he was absent.' Is it possible to exaggerate the effect of this blank space of time, in fixing and defining the impressions received through his visits?[31]

There are three passages in the writings of the Apostle Paul which some have interpreted to mean an actual change of principle, thereby loosing Christians from any obligation to observe one day out of

---

29. B. B. Warfield, 'The Foundations of the Sabbath in the Word of God', chapter 35 of *Selected Shorter Writings, Vol. 1* (John E. Meeter, Ed., Presbyterian and Reformed Publishing Co.: Phillipsburg, NJ, 1980), 318, 319.
30. *Ibid.*, 319.
31. *Ibid.*, 320.

seven as a day of rest (Rom. 14: 5, 6; Gal. 4: 9-11; Col. 2: 16, 17). The last one, for instance, states: 'Let no man therefore judge you in meat, or in drink, or in respect of an holy day, or of the new moon, or of the sabbath days: which are a shadow of things to come; but the body is of Christ.'

Robert L. Dabney, nineteenth-century American Southern Presbyterian theologian, discusses these texts in careful detail.[32] As regards Colossians 2:16, for example, Dabney demonstrates that the Christian Sabbath or 'Lord's Day' was not intended in '*the sabbath days*' alluded to here by Paul:

> The word [Sabbath] was also a common name for all the Jewish festivals, including even the whole sabbatical year, with new-moons, passovers, and such like holy days.... Hence the apostle's mention of 'sabbath days' does not certainly prove that he alluded to the seventh day particularly... we know that he did not intend the Lord's day, because the early writers never apply that name to it.[33]

As to why the perpetual Sabbath did not '...pass away with the passover and the other types', he adds:

> ...The Jewish Sabbath was a sign, and also something else. Its witnessing use has passed away for Jews, so far as it was to them a sign of their exodus, their peculiar theocratic covenant and their title to the land of Canaan. But its other uses, as a means of grace and sign of heaven, remain for them and for all.... It was in full force before the typical ceremonies of Moses. It was enjoined on Gentiles, who had no business with those ceremonies. It had its permanent, moral and spiritual use before Moses came. God then placed an additional significance on it for a particular purpose. When the typical dispensation passed away, then this temporary use of the Sabbath fell off, and the original institution remains. God's day is now to us just what it was to Adam, Abel, Enoch, Noah and Abraham.[34]

Warfield says much the same concerning the indifference of Colossians 2:16 to Jewish ceremonial usages as 'the shadow of the things to come' (or that of Galatians 4:10 to the observance of 'days and months and seasons and years'):

> In thus emancipating his readers from the shadow-ordinances of the Old Dispensation, Paul has no intention whatever, however, of impairing for them the obligations of the moral law, summarily comprehended in the Ten Commandments.... He knew, to be sure, how to separate the eternal substance of these precepts from the particular form in which

---

32. Robert L. Dabney, 'The Christian Sabbath: Its Nature, Design and Proper Observance', in *Discussions: Evangelical and Theological*, Vol. I (496-550).
33. *Ibid.*, 527, 528.
34. *Ibid.*, 528, 529.

they were published to Israel.... Paul would be dealing with the Fourth Commandment precisely as he deals with the Fifth [i.e. 'Children, obey your parents in the Lord: for this is right' – Eph. 6:2], if he treated the shadow-Sabbath as a matter of indifference and brought the whole obligation of the commandment to bear upon keeping holy to the Lord the new Lord's Day, the monument of the second and better creation. That this was precisely what he did, and with him the whole Apostolic Church, there seems no room to question. And the meaning of that is that the Lord's Day is placed in our hands, by the authority of the Apostles of Christ, under the undiminished sanction of the eternal law of God.'[35]

Francis N. Lee traces the post-apostolic history of the Christian Sabbath in the Patristic, Medieval, and Reformed Church. The interested reader is referred to his volume for the details.[36]

---

35. Warfield, op. cit., 321, 323, 324.
36. Lee, op. cit., 239-266. Also Dr Joseph A. Pipa of Westminster Theological Seminary in California has written a comprehensive defence of the Lord's Day being the Christian Sabbath in his book The Lord's Day (Christian Focus Publications, 1997). Dr Pipa considers what the Old and New Testaments teach regarding the permanence of the Sabbath, before surveying the views of theologians throughout church history. In addition, he uses several chapters to give guidelines for implementing the biblical requirements of Sabbath-keeping in the modern world.

QUESTIONS FOR STUDY

1. When is the word 'holy' first used in the Bible?

2. How do you understand God's 'resting'?

3. Did the Sabbath pertain only to the Jews or to others? Why or why not?

4. What is the value of rhythms of rest and work for human life?

5. How does Rosenstock-Huessy illustrate the value of Sabbath rhythm for professional life?

6. How does Sabbath orient us to the future?

7. How could a renewal of faith in creation and in the Creator bring positive changes in the entire culture?

Select Bibliography

Aalders, G. Ch., *Genesis*, Vol. I, translated by William Heynen, Zondervan, Grand Rapids, Michigan, 1981.

Ackerman, Paul D., *It's A Young World After All: Exciting Evidences for Recent Creation*, Baker Book House, Grand Rapids, Michigan, 1986.

Allis, Oswald T., *The Five Books of Moses*, Presbyterian and Reformed Publishing Company, Philadelphia, Pennsylvania, 1947.

Ambrose, *Hexameron* in *The Fathers of the Church: St. Ambrose, Hexameron, Paradise, Cain and Abel*, John J. Savage, translator, Fathers of the Church, Inc., New York, 1962, vol. 42.

Aquinas, Thomas, *Summa Contra Gentes*, Book Two, *Creation*, Translated by James F. Anderson, University of Notre Dame Press, Notre Dame, Indiana, 1975.

Augustine, *The Literal Meaning of Genesis*, 2 Vols, translated and annotated by John H. Taylor in *Ancient Christian Writers No. 42*, Quasten et al. editors, Newman Press, New York, 1982.

Barr, James, *Fundamentalism*, The Westminster Press, Philadelphia, Pennsylvania, 1978.

Barth, Karl, *Church Dogmatics*, Vol. III, Part One, *The Doctrine of Creation*, G. W. Bromiley and T. F. Torrance, editors, T. & T. Clark, Edinburgh, 1991 reprint.

Basil, *The Nine Homilies of the Hexameron* in *Nicene and Post-Nicene Fathers, Second Series*, reprint, vol. viii, 51–107, Hendrickson Publishers, Peabody, Massachusetts, 1995.

Barnes, Thomas G., *Origin and Destiny of the Earth's Magnetic Field*, second edition, Institute for Creation Research, El Cajon, California, 1983.

Behe, Michael J., *Darwin's Black Box: The Biochemical Challenge to Evolution*, The Free Press, New York, 1996.

Blum, H. F., *Time's Arrow and Evolution*, Harper and Row Publishers Inc., New York, 1962.

Brown, Walter, *In the Beginning: Compelling Evidence for Creation and the Flood*, Sixth General Edition, Center for Scientific Creation, Phoenix, Arizona, 1995.

Calvin, John, *Genesis* (Two Volumes in One, Translated and edited by John King), The Banner of Truth Trust, London, 1975 reprint.

Cameron, Nigel M. de S., *Evolution and the Authority of the Bible*, The Paternoster Press, Exeter, 1983.

Capito, Wolfgang, *Hexameron, Sive Opus Sex Dierum*, Argentinae [Strasburg], 1539.

Cassuto, U., *A Commentary on the Book of Genesis*, Part I, From Adam to Noah, Genesis I–VI 8, Jerusalem, The Magnes Press, The Hebrew University, 1961.

_____, *The Documentary Hypothesis and Composition of the Pentateuch* English translation, Jerusalem, 1961.

Chauvin, Rémy, *La biologie de l'esprit*, Editions du Rocher, Monaco, 1985.

Cochrane, Charles N., *Christianity and Classical Culture: A Study of Thought from Augustus to Augustine*, Oxford University Press, London, 1974.

Cook, Melvin A., *Prehistory and Earth Models*, Max Parrish, London, 1966.

Darwin, Charles, *The Origin of Species*, Introduction by Thompson, Everyman's Library, E. P. Dutton & Co., Inc., New York, 1956 reprint.

Davidheiser, Bolton, *Evolution and the Christian Faith*, Presbyterian and Reformed Publishing Company, Nutley, New Jersey, 1969.

Davis, P., Kenyon, D. H. et al., *Of Pandas and People: The Central Question of Biological Origins*, Haughton Publishing Company, Dallas, Texas, 1989.

Dawkins, Richard, *The Blind Watchmaker*, W. W. Norton & Co., New York & London, 1996 edition.

Denton, Michael, *Evolution: A Theory in Crisis*, Adler & Adler, Bethesda, Maryland., 1985.

Dillow, Joseph C., *The Waters Above: Earth's Pre-Flood Vapor Canopy*, Moody Press, Chicago, Illinois, 1981.

Fields, Weston W., *Unformed and Unfilled: The Gap Theory*, Baker Book House, Grand Rapids, Michigan, 1976.

Gentry, Robert V., *Creation's Tiny Mystery*, second edition, Earth Sciences Associates, Knoxville, Tennessee, 1988.

Grassé, P.-P., *Traité de zoologie*, Tome VIII, Masson, 1976.

Gunton, C. E., *Christ and Creation*, William B. Eerdmans Publishing Co., Grand Rapids, Michigan, 1992.

Hawking, Stephen W., *A Brief History of Time: From the Big Bang to Black Holes*, Bantam Press, London, 1988.

Hooykaas, R., *Religion and the Rise of Modern Science*, William B. Eerdmans Publishing Co., Grand Rapids, Michigan, 1974.

Hoyle, Fred and Wickramasinghe, N. Chandra, *Evolution From Space: A Theory of Cosmic Creationism*, Simon and Schuster, Inc., New York, 1981.

_____ , *Archaeopteryx, the Primordial Bird: A Case of Fossil Forgery*, Christopher Davies, Ltd., Swansea, U. K., 1986.

Humphreys, D. Russell, *Starlight and Time: Solving the Puzzle of Distant Starlight in a Young Universe*, Master Books, Colorado Springs, Colorado, 1995.

Johnson, Phillip E., *Darwin On Trial*, InterVarsity Press, Downers Grove, Illinois., 1993.

_____, *Evolution as Dogma: The Establishment of Naturalism*, Haughton Publishing Co., Dallas, Texas, 1990.

Koestler, Arthur, *The Ghost in the Machine*, MacMillan Publishing Co., New York, 1968.

Kuhn, Thomas S., *The Structure of Scientific Revolutions*, University of Chicago Press, Chicago, Illinois, 1970.

Kuyper, Abraham, *Principles of Sacred Theology*, Translated from Dutch by H. De Vries, Wm. B. Eerdmans Publishing Co., Grand Rapids, Michigan, 1954.

Lee, Francis N., *The Covenantal Sabbath: The Weekly Sabbath Scripturally and Historically Considered*, The Lord's Day Observance Society, London, 1969.

Lester, Lane P. and Bohlin, Raymond G., *The Natural Limits to Biological Change*, Zondervan Publishing House, Grand Rapids, Michigan, 1984.

Roger Lewin, *Bones of Contention*, Simon and Schuster, Inc., New York, 1987.

Leupold, H. C., *Exposition of Genesis*, Volume I, Chapters 1–19, Baker Book House, Grand Rapids, Michigan, 1965.

MacLeod, Anna S. and Cobley, L. S., *Contemporary Botanical Thought*, Quadrangle Books, Chicago, Illinois, 1961.

Miller, S. L. and Orgel, L., *The Origins of Life on Earth*, Prentice-Hall, Inc., Englewood Cliffs, New Jersey, 1974.

Moorhead, Paul S. and Kaplan, Martin N., editors, *Mathematical Challenges to the Darwinian Interpretation of Evolution*, The Wistar Institute Press, Philadelphia, Pennsylvania, 1967.

Moreland, J. P., editor, *The Creation Hypothesis: Scientific Evidence for an Intelligent Designer*, InterVarsity Press, Downers Grove, Illinois., 1994.

Morris, Henry M., *The Genesis Record: A Scientific & Devotional Commentary on the Book of Beginnings*, Baker Book House, Grand Rapids, Michigan, 1976.

_____, *Biblical Cosmology and Modern Science*, Baker Book House, Grand Rapids, Michigan, 1970.

Morris, Henry M. and Whitcomb, John C., Jr., *The Genesis Flood: The Biblical Record and its Scientific Implications*, Presbyterian and Reformed Publishing Company, Philadelphia, Pennsylvania., 1967.

Polanyi, Michael, *Personal Knowledge*, Routledge and Kegan Paul, London, 1958.

Polkinghorne, John, *Science and Creation: the Search for Understanding*, SPCK, London, 1993.

Price, George McCready, *Evolutionary Geology and the New Catastrophism*, Pacific Press Publishing Association, Mountain View, California, 1926.

Proceedings of the Second International Conference on Creationism, Creation Science Fellowship, Pittsburg, Pennsylvania, 1990.

Ratzinger, Joseph (Cardinal), *'In the Beginning...' : A Catholic Understanding of the Story of Creation and the Fall*, William B. Eerdmans Publishing Co., Grand Rapids, Michigan, 1995.

Rosenstock-Huessy, Eugene, *The Christian Future or the Modern Mind Outrun*, Harper Torchbooks, New York, 1966.

Ross, Hugh, *Creation and Time: A Biblical and Scientific Perspective on the Creation-Date Controversy*, NavPress, Colorado Springs, Colorado, 1994.

Setterfield, Barry, *The Velocity of Light and the Age of the Universe*, Creation Science Association, Adelaide, Australia, 1983.

Thaxton, Charles B., Bradley, Walter L., Olson, Roger L., *The Mystery of Life's Origin*, Philosophical Library, New York, 1984.

Torrance, Thomas F., *Theological Science*, Oxford University Press, London, 1969.

_____, *Space, Time and Incarnation*, Oxford University Press, London, 1969.

_____, *Transformation & Convergence in the Frame of Knowledge*, Wm. B. Eerdmans, Grand Rapids, Michigan, 1984.

_____, *Christian Theology and Scientific Culture*, Oxford University Press, New York, 1981.

_____, *Reality and Scientific Theology*, Scottish Academic Press, Edinburgh, 1985.

_____, editor, *Belief in Science and the Christian Life: The Relevance of Michael Polanyi's Thought for Christian Faith and Life*, The Handsel Press, Edinburgh, 1980.

Verbrugge, Magnus, Alive: *An Enquiry into The Origin and Meaning of Life*, Ross House Books, Vallecito, California, 1984.

Van Bebber, Mark and Taylor, Paul S., *Creation and Time: A Report on the Progressive Creationist Book by Hugh Ross*, Eden Communications, Mesa, Arizona, 1995.

Von Kuehnelt-Leddihn, Leftism Revisited: *From de Sade and Marx to Hitler and Pol Pot*, Regnery Gateway, Washington, D. C., 1990.

Von Rad, Gerhard, *Genesis: A Commentary*, The Westminster Press, Philadelphia, Pennsylvania, 1973.

Westermann, Claus, *Genesis: A Practical Commentary, Text and Interpretation*, William B. Eerdmans Publishing Co., Grand Rapids, Michigan., 1987.

Wilder-Smith, A. E., *Man's Origin, Man's Destiny*, Telos-International, Hanssler-Verlag, Neuhausen-Stuttgart, Germany, 1974.

Wilkinson, David, *God, The Big Bang and Stephen Hawking: An Exploration into Origins*, Monarch, Tunbridge Wells, U.K., 1993.

Wysong, R. L., *The Creation-Evolution Controversy (Implications, Methodology and Survey of Evidence), Toward A Rational Solution*, Inquiry Press, Midland, Michigan, 1978.

Young, E. J., *In the Beginning: Genesis Chapters 1 to 3 and the Authority of Scripture*, The Banner of Truth Trust, Edinburgh, 1976.

_____, *Studies In Genesis One*, Presbyterian and Reformed Publishing Company, Philadelphia, Pennsylvania, 1964.

SCRIPTURE INDEX

Genesis
1   .... 38, 43, 45, 49,
         .... 54, 59, 70, 82,
         .... 84, 96, 98, 99,
         ....101, 105, 107,
         ....108, 109, 110,
         ....111, 113, 118,
         ....139, 164, 201,
         ....202, 216
1–2   .... 43, 45, 54, 84,
         .... 96, 99, 101,
         ....105, 108, 113,
         ....114, 118, 139,
         ....164, 216
1–3   .... 11, 38, 43, 47,
         .. 49, 69, 78, 114,
         ....186, 204
1–11   .... 37, 39, 40, 44,
         .... 45, 46, 47, 49,
         ....105, 114, 115,
         ....126, 141
1:1-12 177
1:1–2:3 101
1:1-5   ....58, 65, 70
1:1   .... 27, 37, 40, 41,

         .... 49, 51, 53, 54,
         .... 58, 60, 66, 68,
         .....71, 82, 85, 86
1:2   ....71, 72, 73, 74,
         .... 80, 85, 86, 87,
        162
1:2-31 41
1:3   .... 75, 76, 181
1:4 77
1:6-8 161
1:7 60
1:9 165
1:9-13 107
1:11   ....165, 174
1:11-12 ....167, 169
1:12   ....165, 166
1:14 76
1:14-19 180
1:14-23 187
1:16   ....76, 97
1:17 183
1:18 183
1:20   .....185, 186, 189
1:20-23 184
1:21 59

1:22   ....186, 189
1:24-25 191
1:26   ....191, 194, 195,
         .....196, 198, 208
1:26-28 192
1:27 201
1:28   ....86, 187
1:29 202
1:30 202
1:31   ....82, 87, 204
2   .....108,198, 201,
        211
2:1   ....209, 210
2:1-3   ....41, 209
2:2 99
2:3 209
2:4   .... 41, 42, 49, 60,
        109
2:4–3:24 43
2:4–50:26 40
2:5   .... 101, 107, 108,
         ....109, 111
2:7   ....53, 60
2:15 198
2:19 198

2:22 60
3 ....47, 203
5 125
5:1 59
6–9 93
6:7 125
6:20 168
7:14 168
7:19 164
9:1 187
9:19 155
11 125
11:10 125
14:19 71
17:16 187
17:20 187
22:17 187
24:60 187
26:3-4 187
28:3 187
30:14 96
35:9-11 187
48:3-4 187
48:15-16 187
49:25 187

Exodus
3:14 ....67, 68
20 99
20:8 211
20:9 99
20:11 ...87, 97, 98, 210
31:17 210
39:3 162

Leviticus
11:13-19 168
11:29-30 168
22 168

Deuteronomy
5:12-14 211
14:12-18 168
32:18 60
32:43 84

Joshua
17:15, 18....................59

Judges
5:20 84

1 Samuel
12:21 72

Ezra
4:18 193
7:24 193

Job
1:19 80
7:6 96
7:12 186
12:24 72
26:13 ....75, 186
27:3 75
38:4-7 84

Psalms
8 200
8:3, 4 184
33:6 ....54, 75
36:9 216
45:7 210
74:13-14 186
74:17 60
89:47 60
90:2 60
90:9 96
95 ....99, 219
97:7 84
104 ....38, 84
104:2-5 84
104:4 84
104:7-9 165
104:26 60
104:30 ....59, 75
107:40 72
119:130....................76
143:10 75
148:7 186

Proverbs
8:27 73
16:4 60

Isaiah
7:9 70

9 187
11:7 202
27:1 186
34:11 73
34:16 75
40:17 72
40:23 72
40:28 210
43:1 60
43:7 60
43:21 60
45:7 ....59, 60
45:8 59
45:12 59
45:18 ....72, 86, 184
51:9-10 186
54:16 59
55:11 77
58:13,14....................211
59:4 72
61:1 75
63:11 75
65:18 59
65:25 202

Jeremiah
4:23 73
31 77

Ezekiel
47:10 168

Daniel
8:10 84

Hosea
6:2 96

Amos
4:13 ....59, 60

Jonah
1:4 80

Zechariah
12:1 60

Matthew
1 123

2:1-10 183
5:17-20 218
12:1-9 218
13:35 .... 115, 118
19:4-6 115
19:8 116
23:35 117
24:37 117

Mark
10:6 115
13:19 115

Luke
3 123
3:34-38 117
11:50, 51 118
11:52 117
13:10-17 218
17: 26 117

John
1:1-3 27
1:1-18 53
1: 1 197
1:3 .... 115, 200
1:4 187
3 69
8:12 75
9:32 118
17 53
17:3 215
18:3 218

Acts
3:21 118
4:24 115
13:14 218
13:42 218
14:1 218
14:15 115
16:13 218
17:2 218
17:10 218
17:24 60
17:26 116
18:4-11 218
20:7 217

Romans
1–2 .... 35, 188, 196
1:21-23b 189
1:20 .... 115, 118
1:25 118
4 54
4:17 54
5 .... 86, 186, 204
5:12 116
5:14 116
5:17 116
5:19 116
6 .... 186, 204
8:19-20 116
16:25 118

1 Corinthians
6:16 116
8:4 218
11:7 195
11:8-9 116
11:9 59
15 204
15:21 204
15:21-22 116
16:1, 2 217

2 Corinthians
4:6 .... 76, 115
5:17 76
11:3 116

Galatians
4:9-11 220
4:10 220
5:22 210
6:16 218

Ephesians
1–3 59
3:9 118
3:14, 15 195
4:24 196
5:8 76
5:31 116
6:2 221

Philippians
2:5–11 105

Colossians
1:16 115
1:17 200
2:16,17 220
2:16 220
3:10 196

1 Timothy
2:5 218
2:13, 14 116
4:4 59
6:16 75

Hebrews
1:2 215
1:3 .... 210, 215
1:6 84
1:7 84
1:9 210
1:10 115
1:14 83
2 200
2:10 118
3:7-19 218
4 99
4:1-11 218
4:3 215
4:3, 4 118
4:10 118
9:26 118
11:3 .... 27, 54, 115
11:4-7 117
11:23 117
12:24 117

James
3:9 118

1 Peter
3:20 117

2 Peter
2:5 117
3:5-6 117
3:5 .... 73, 162
3:16 204

1 John
1:5 75
3:12 117

PERSON INDEX

Aalders, G. Ch. 72, 73, 77, 166,
    .... 167, 168, 182, 183, 193, 211
Ackerman, Paul D. 151, 153, 154,
    157
Allis, Oswald T. 48
Ambrose 99, 100, 111, 119
Aquinas................. 194, 203, 204, 206
Anselm.. 70
Archer, Gleason............................. 97
Aristotle 172
Armstrong, Neil 151
Athanasius......... 25, 41, 194, 195, 197
Augustine 39, 52, 69, 70, 77, 111,
    .... 112, 113, 114, 194,
    .... 196, 199, 205, 216
Austin, Steve 146, 153
Bacon, Francis 215
Bamberg, Stanley W..................... 124
Barnes, Thomas G. 151, 152
Barr, James 45, 46, 126
Barth, Karl 68, 202
Basil the Great................................ 77
Behe, Michael.. 20, 21, 33, 56 , 57, 64,
    .... 65, 66, 169, 171, 177
Bennett, Charles H. 65

Berkson, W. 30
Bernard, Regis............................. 194
Berthoud, Jean-Marc..... 12, 102, 103,
    .... 104, 124
Blocher, Henri 101, 102, 103, 106,
    111
Blum, T. H. 61, 62, 172
Boethius 205
Bonar, Andrew A. 215
Bradley, Walter L. . 18, 31, 60, 61, 62,
    .... 63, 128, 170, 178
de Bray, M. E. J. Gheury Brown,
    Robert H. 149
Brown, Walter T. ... 40, 56, 65, 91, 93,
    .... 127, 130, 131, 132, 138,
    ... 145, 148, 149, 151, 156, 163,
    .... 164, 178
Brunner, Emil............................... 199
Burdick, Clifford L. 147
Cameron, Nigel ... 43, 44, 45, 47, 204,
    205
Campbell, John Angus 20
Calvin, John.. 31, 35, 76, 82, 181, 192,
    .... 194, 196, 197, 199 , 217
Capito, Wolfgang .. 12, 17, 41, 52, 53,

.... 54, 66, 73, 74, 86
Cassuto, Umberto.. 48, 108, 109, 110,
..111, 161, 162, 165, 167, 168,
...179, 180, 181, 182, 183, 185,
...186, 187, 192, 193, 201, 202,
.... 203, 209, 210, 211, 212
Catherwood, Christopher 17
Cech, T. R. 170
Chaffi n, Eugene F. 131
Chalmers, Thomas 85
Chauvin, Rémy 177
Chomsky, Noam 197, 198
Cochrane, Charles Norris 216
Cook, Melvin A. 151
Crichton, Michael 64
Currid, John D. 12, 38, 70, 71
Custance, Arthur C. 141, 142
Cyril of Alexandria 166
Dabney, Robert L. 249
Darwin, Charles..... 18, 20, 24, 26, 31,
...32, 33, 34, 36, 44, 47, 48, 57,
...64, 89, 90, 92, 124, 138, 144,
.... 174, 178, 194
Davis, P. 170, 175
Dawkins, Richard 20, 21, 91
de Chardin, Teilhard 64
de Corte, Marcel 64, 65
Denney, James 17, 36
Denton, Michael 18, 19, 20, 26, 34,
.... 89, 177
Descartes 29, 177
Dickerson, Richard 33
Dickey 151
Dillon, Lawrence S. 172, 173
Dods, Marcus 45, 46, 99
Dooyeweerd, Herman 34, 171
Driver 45
Dryden, John 78
Dunn, J. R. 152
Duns Scotus 68
Eckelmann, Herman J. 159, 180
Eddington, Arthur 61
Einstein, Albert 23,30, 34, 55, 128,
.... 130, 133, 134
Euripides 25, 26
Farrar, F.W. 31
Faulstich, Eugene W. 137, 138
Fields, Weston W. 88
Fliermans, Carl B. 12, 62, 132, 170

Fox, Sidney 169
Fredegisius 52
Freud 34
Ganapathy, R. 151
Geisler, Norman L. 33
Gelwick, Richard 33
Gentry, Robert v. 154
Gödel, Kurt 29
Gould, Stephen J. 90, 91
Grassé, P.-P. 176
Gray, Asa 44
Gray, George Zabriskie 219
Green, William Henry 124, 125
Gregory Nazianzen 68, 199
Grothuis, Douglas 203
Gunton, Colin E. 200
Handel 79
Harned, David B. 30
Harrison, R. K. 48
Hawking, Stephen 122, 134
Heidel, A. 59
Herbert, George 199, 200
Hesiod 59
Hezekiah 38, 39
Hilary 98
Hippolytus of Rome 183, 188
Hodge, Charles 124
Hooykaas, R. 28, 31
Hoyle, Fred 33
Huse, Scott M... 91, 92, 145, 146, 152,
.... 154
Humphreys, D. Russell 131, 133,
.... 134, 139, 152, 153, 181
Hutten, E. H. 29
Hutton, James 144
Infi eld, L. 30
Irenaeus 196
Jaki, Stanley L. 28
Jeans, James 56
Johanson, D. C. 92
Johnson, Phillip E.. 24, 32, 33, 34, 44,
.... 89, 90, 91, 92, 178
Jordan, James B. 103, 125
Joyce, Gerald 171
Justin Martyr 69
Kaiser, Walter C. 124
Kant 18, 29
Kenyon, D. H. 170
Kerkut, G. A. 34

Kitchen, Kenneth A............... 48
Kitts, David B............... 90, 91
Kline, Meredith.... 100, 101, 105, 107,
.... 108, 111
Koenig............... 197
Kofahl, Robert E. 92, 142,143, 149
Kuhn, Thomas S. 19, 28, 29, 121,
.... 122, 126
Kuyper, Abraham 23, 27, 36, 106,
.... 124, 199
Laudan............... 32
Lee, Francis Nigel............... 217, 221
Leupold, H. C. 75, 180, 182, 184,
.... 185, 195, 197, 210
Lewin, Roger............... 92
Libby, W. F............... 148, 158
Lightfoot, John...... 123, 124, 125, 138
Livingstone, David N. 47
Luminet, J.-P. 133
Luther, Martin 199
Lyell, Charles............... 144
Lyttleton, R. A............... 150
Margulis, Lynn 24
Marx, Karl 15, 16, 34
Maxwell............... 136
M'Cheyne, Robert Murray.. 214, 215
Mendel, Gregor 174, 175
Merriell, D. Juvenal............... 206
Meyer, Stephen C............... 31, 32
Michelson 131
Miller 169, 170, 172
Monod, Jacques 35, 172
Moreland , J. P. 26, 27, 31, 32, 33,
.... 62, 170, 178, 197, 198
Morris, Henry M. .. 39, 40, 73, 74, 75,
..... 76, 93, 96, 97, 98, 144, 145,
.... 146, 153, 154, 155, 156,162,
... 163, 167, 168, 181, 184, 185,
.... 186, 187
Morris, John D. 152
Nebelsick, Harold P............... 29
Newman, Robert C. 159, 180
Newton, Isaac 30, 31
Noll, Mark A............... 124
Noordzij, Arie............... 100
Novatian............... 68, 77, 78
Oller 197, 198
Olsen, Roger.......... 31, 60, 61, 63, 178
Omdahl............... 197, 198

Oparin, I. A. 169, 170, 172
Orgel, Leslie............... 171
Overton, William............... 32, 33
Owen, John............... 31
Oxnard, Charles 92
Parker, Gary............... 92, 93
Pasteur, Louis 169
Patten, Donald 163
Patterson, Colin 24
Paul, Leslie 26, 27
Pearcey, Nancy 130
Pelikan, J............... 199
Pipa, Joseph A............... 221
Planck 131, 135, 136
Polanyi, Michael........... 23, 29, 30, 31
Polkinghorne, John 182
Popper, Karl............... 34
Preus, Robert D............... 97
Provine, William............... 26
Pun, Pattle P. T. 122
Rabast, Karlheinz 85, 86
Radmacher, Earl. D............... 97
Rambert, Serge............... 111
Rastall, R. H............... 148
Ratzinger, Joseph . 195, 212, 214, 243
Raup, David M. 90
Read, John G............... 147
Redi, Francesco............... 169
Richard of Saint Victor 53, 205
Roemer............... 128
Rosenstock-Huessy, Eugene...... 206,
.... 207, 213, 214, 222
Ross, Hugh....... 96, 98, 105, 111, 119,
... 122, 126, 130, 131, 152, 154,
.... 159, 204
Ruse, Michael............... 32, 33
Sagan, Carl 63
Schaeffer, Frances............... 17
Schilder, Klaas 199
Scola, Angelo 198
Scott, Thomas............... 44
Setterfield, Barry.......... 128, 129, 130,
.... 131, 132, 135, 136, 139, 142
Skiff, Frederick N. 61, 63, 64, 74,
.... 132, 135, 137, 142
Slusher, Harold S............... 153, 154
Smith, John Maynard............... 177
Still, William 212
Strangway, D. W. 152

Taylor, John H. 39, 69, 112, 113
Taylor, Paul S. 152, 169
Thaxton, Charles B. 18, 31, 60, 61,
.... 62, 63, 170, 178
Thomas, Hubert 114
Torrance, Thomas F. 18, 19, 21, 22,
... 23, 29, 30, 69, 104, 105, 205,
.... 206
Troitskii, V. S. 130, 136
Urey 169, 172
Ussher, James 123, 124, 125, 138,
.... 155
Van Bebber, Mark 152, 154, 159,
.... 204
Van Dijk, Wytse 136
Van Flandern, T. C. 132
Van Til, Henry R. 199
Van Wylen, Gordon J. 56, 60,
Verbrugge, Magnus 34, 35, 171,
.... 172, 173
Vignaux, Paul 103, 104
Von Balthasar, Hans Urs 198, 201
Von Kuehnelt-Leddihn, Baron Eric
Von 15, 16, 203, 205
Von Rad, Gerhard ... 72, 80, 181, 186,
.... 200, 202
Warfi eld, Benjamin B ... 44, 124, 125,
.... 193, 218, 219, 220, 221

Watson, David C. C. 46, 118
Weintraub, David A 153
Wells, John C 124
Westermann, Claus 80, 181
Whipple, Fred L 153
Whitcomb, John C. 93, 144, 145,
.... 156, 163
White, A. D 31
White, A. J. Monty 88
Whitehead, Alfred North 28
Whitelaw, Robert L. 45, 148, 157,
.... 158, 163, 164, 178,
Whybray, R. N. 48
Wysong, R. L. 55, 60, 63, 93, 145,
... 146, 147, 148, 149, 150, 151,
.... 152, 153, 157
Wicken, J. S. 61, 63
Wickramasinghe, N. Chandra 33
Wilkinson, David 122, 138
Willey, Basil 31
William of Occam 103, 104
Wise, Kurt P. 178
Woodmorappe, John 147
Wyatt, Stanley P. 153
Young, Davis A. 122, 159
Young, Edward J. ... 38, 48, 58, 59, 70,
..... 71, 73, 80, 86, 88, 100, 109,
Zizioulas, John 196, 208

SUBJECT INDEX

Abiogenesis 65, 166, 169-174
    see evolution
Abortion 187, 203
Adam 85, 86, 88, 110, 113, 114,
    ....115, 116, 117, 125, 138, 144,
    ....184, 186, 196, 200, 202, 204,
    ....208, 220
Angels 41, 79, 83-94, 112,
    ....113, 193, 200
Animism 171, 172
Anthropomorphism...............77, 101,
    ....210, 216
Astrology 183, 188-189
Babylonian creation story
    (Enuma Elish) 58, 59
Bacteria 41, 176, 177
Bara', Signifi cance of the Hebrew
    Verb...52, 53, 58, 59, 60, 66, 71, 80
Bible 16, 17, 18
    Divine revelation.....27, 37, 43, 70
    New Testament 39
    New Testament approach to
        Genesis 39, 40, 49
    New Testament Assumes the
        Chronological Order of

Genesis .... 1 and 2 114-119
New Testament's usage of the
    Old 86
Jesus Christ referred to Genesis
    39
Big Bang...................87, 122, 133, 134
Biotic soup 62
Black Hole 133, 134, 181
bohu   72, 73, 86
Buddhism 198
Canopy hypothesis 163
Cellular structure 62, 171
Chance ..20, 26, 35, 170, 172, 176, 178
Change
    horizontal change....................175
    vertical change................167, 175
Changing Relationship of Theology
    and Science...............................28
Chaos theory 64
    'steady state' chaos 87
Chemical evolution.........................34
Circular reasoning........147, 160, 172,
    ....173, 178
Classical pagan view of the gods
    ....25, 29

Copernican principle 133
Creation,
   absolute .. 51-66, 70, 71, 72, 80, 95
   conservative evangelical
      scholars refuse.....................46
   allusions to in New Testament
      ....39, 114, 118
   ancient cosmogonies.................59
   appearance of Age 144, 160
   canopy hypothesis 163
   chaos 72, 75, 78, 82
   ex nihilo 52, 53, 54, 114, 118
   goodness of creation........... 77-79
   intelligent design....19, 20, 26, 31,
      ....32, 56, 57, 64, 123, 170, 177,
     178
   irreducibly complex structure
      ....56, 64, 65, 66
   of angels 79
   of the land animals 191-192
   of man and woman.. 91,110, 192-
      ....194, 201, 208
   relative creation......51, 52, 53, 59,
      ....60 , 66
   series of separations..........75, 180
   without form and void......70, 72,
     85
   young earth.....122, 123, 126, 127,
      ....128, 131, 139, 149, 150, 151,
      ....152, 153, 154, 156, 160
Creationism..............24, 122, 153, 155
Culture...15, 20, 26, 64, 104, 121, 126,
   ....141, 150, 158, 165, 199, 205,
   ....208, 215, 216, 222
Cultural mandate 198-201,
   see dominian
Darwinism...20, 24, 31, 32, 33, 34, 36,
   ....44, 90, 124, 101, 140, 175,
  194,
Dating methods
   Atomic clocks 128, 132, 136
   Carbon–14 Dating... 148-150, 157
   Geological Dating 142
   Imprecise dating methods 122
   Natural Chronometers for young
      earth....................................150
   Earth's Magnetic Field 122,
      151-152
   Mississippi River Delta 152

Moon Dust 150, 156
Oil Gushers.......................151
Population Growth...154, 155
Poynting-Robertson.........153,
   ....154, 156
Radiohalos 154
Salinity and Chemical
   ...Composition of the Oceans
  152
Radioactive carbon 149, 158
Radiometric Dating 129, 142,
   ....143, 150
Deism 18, 20, 21, 36, 74, 82, 165, 178
'Day', Biblical Usage of 96-100
Day of the Lord...............................96
Death 17, 56, 69, 86, 93, 114, 116,
   ....117, 137, 138, 149, 171, 186,
   .....200, 202, 204, 205, 208, 215
Demarcationism 30-33,
   see evolution
Divine counsels 193, 194
DNA   35, 63, 64, 167, 169, 170, 175,
   ....176, 178, 187
Documentary Hypothesis...... 42, 47-
   ....49, 108
Dominion....... 115, 192 , 198-202, 208
   see image of God
Dualism 18, 20, 30, 74, 102, 166
Electromagnetic spectrum 75, 76
Empirical science....20, 22, 30, 31, 33,
   ....34, 36, 134, 177
Enlightenment 18, 48, 77, 172
Euthanasia...............................187, 203
Event horizon.........................134, 181
Evolution 18, 19, 20, 24, 25, 27, 30,
   ....32, 33, 34, 35, 36, 37, 43, 44,
   .... 57, 60, 61, 62, 64, 88, 89-93,
   .... 122-127, 167, 169, 170,
   ....173, 174, 175, 176, 177,
   ....178, 186, 203, 204, 205, 208,
a faith or dogma 20, 34, 105, 126,
   .... 168, *see* Darwinism
   impersonal fate...................26
   impersonal material 27
   theistic evolution......113, 124,
   .....126, 131, 159, 186, 204, 205
Faith, kinds of ...20, 22, 23, 24, 25, 26,
   ....27, 29, 33, 34, 35, 36, 54, 65,
   ......70, 106, 113, 115, 117, 118,

....127, 136, 144, 148, 150, 169,
............174, 177, 178, 198, 222
Fall of man..... 111, 116-117, 192, 194,
....................196, 200, 202, 204
Fiat 193
Firmament......................163, 180, 184
Flood 44, 93, 113, 114, 117, 122,
....135, 138, 145, 148, 155, 163,
............................164, 165, 202
    Global Catastrophism.... 144-148,
   164
    Hydroplate theory 164
Fossils 92-93, 141, 145-148
    Archaeopteryx..........................91
    Australopithecine.....................92
    Calavaras..................................93
    Castenedolo 93
    hominoids 91
    Homo erectus 92
    Homo sapiens...........................92
    Human and 'Pre-Human'
        Fossils 92-93
    Lucy 92
    Missing links............................89
    Neanderthal..............................92
    Peking Man...............................92
    pre-Adamic race.......................88
    Ramapithecus 92
    Sinanthropus 92
Framework Hypothesis.......103, 105,
    ....106, 108, 111, 113, 114, 118,
    ....119, 124, 179
Fruit flies...176
Gap Theory 83-88
Genesis 1:1-2 Grammatical
    Structure of .. 51, 58-59, 60, 70, 71
Genesis 2:4-25, a second
    account of creation............42, 109
Genesis, two contradictory creation
    accounts...............................42, 48
    Documentary Hypothesis.......42,
    47-48
    Liberal and Evangelical
        Interpretations of Genesis
        .... 1-3 43-47
    Mosaic authorship 48
    Parallelism 38, 99, 100, 179, 189,
   192
    Priestly' and 'Deuteronomic'

Schools...............................47
school of the Elohist.................47
school of the Yahwist 47
Non-Chronological Reading of
    Creation Week..........103, 107
Genesis, basic outline of, ...37, 49
Genesis, Liberal and Evangelical
    Interpretations of, ...43
Genesis, meaning of 'The
    generations of the heavens and
    the earth'....................................42
    subscription 41, 42, 49, 109
    superscription........41, 42, 49, 109
    a merism..............................71, 82
Genesis, type of literature ..37, 40, 43
    allegorical 39, 141
    chronological history..........37, 47
    fi gurative language.................38
    historical narrative..............38, 40
    poetic....37, 38, 39, 47, 49, 84, 101,
   105
    literal' and 'literary 39, 40, 46,
    .... 84, 96, 97, 98, 100, 101-106,
    ....108, 109, 111, 113, 114, 118,
    ....119, 124, 155, 179,
    Myth....................................24, 38
Genesis, geneologies....123, 124, 125,
    ....128, 145, 138
Genetics 167, 175, 187
    Genetic Stability of 'the Kinds'
    ....88, 89, 167, 168, 174
    Mendelian genetics..................175
    Modern genetics.......................187
Geologic column ...146, 147, 148, 160
God
    accommodates Himself............98
    eternal 25
    goodness..27, 77, 78,203, 204, 217
    immortal....................................51
    infi nite...22, 27, 29, 52, 69, 77, 81,
    ....84, 95, 98
    love..................27, 53, 67, 206, 212
    transcendent 15, 16, 21,22, 23,
    ....30, 62, 106, 166, 194
    Trinity 193, 196, 205, 206, 207,
    ....208, 218
    Holy Spirit.....27, 67, 84, 193, 205,
    ....206, 210
    brooding over chaos.................74

rather than 'Mighty Wind' of
Genesis 1:2 ....74, 80,
Son of God....76, 98, 117, 196, 200
Gödel's Theorems 29, 55,
Grand Canyon 146, 147
Gravitational forces................75, 133
Gravitational time dilation 133
Hebraic concept.............................113
Hellenic kind of thinking 108, 109
Hermeneutical dualism................102
Herring fossil bed of California ..145
Hesiod, Theogony 59
Higher critics.............42, 48, 179, 181
German Higher Criticism 47
Hinduism 198
Human beings
Concept of 'Person.......... 205-207
Creation of Man 192
Finite 53, 54
Image of God 16, 17, 192, 194-
.....................................198, 201,
Human Dominion over the Rest of
Creation....................................198
Human speech.......................197, 208
Humankind: Male and Female
.... 201-205
Karoo formation of Africa............145
Kinds, stability of the kinds ..89, 167,
.... 168, 174-177
Liberalism......43, 44, 45, 46, 126, 127,
Liberty.......................16, 203, 206, 207
Light, Sending forth of 75-77
The Speed of Light and the Age
of the Solar System ... 121-134
Decay in light speed 128, 130,
.....................132, 134,136, 142
Life 172
The Blessing of Life......... 186-187
The Creation of Life 185-186
Spontaneous generation of life
....169
Lucifer..................... 86, 87, *see* Satan
Luminaries 179-184
Macroevolution 56, 61, 123, 175,
....177
Magnetic Field 151-152
Marriage 201, 202, 208
Marxism...203
Materialism 16, 20, 169, 171, 173

materialist evolutionary monism
...................................18, 25, 174
materialist view of the Universe ...26
materialistic explanation of man's
origin.................................16, 171
Pagan materialism.........................187
Matter, eternity of 26
Mechanistic framework of the
universe 18, 20
Meteorology....................................182
Microevolution 175
Mid Oceanic Ridge........................164
Mississippi River Delta 152
Moon Dust......................................150
Mount St. Helens...................146, 160
Mutations 24, 175, 176, 177
Naturalism ..18, 19, 24, 25, 29, 31, 32,
.............33, 34, 85, 95, 119, 216
scientific.............30, 31, 32, 33, 85
philosophical 33
Neoplatonism 78, 113
New Age...................25, 78, 203, 208
New physics.................18, 19, 30, 216
Nicene Creed 41, 84
Nominalism 103, 104, 119
Oil Gushers 151
Open systems...............61, 62, 63, 178
Operational science..18, 31, 144, 172,
............................177, 178, 216
Origins of Science............................29
Paleontology 89, 90, 91
Panentheism...................................182
Paradigm shift 19, 29, 36, 121, 122,
.............126, 130, 139, 205, 216
Patriarchs........................117, 125, 138
Photosynthesis...................62, 64, 180
Planck's constant...........131, 135, 136
Platonism.......................................113
Polonium 154
Population Growth 154, 155
Positivism...........................20, 23, 32
logical positivism 29, 31
mechanistic positivism.............29
Poynting-Robertson 153, 154, 156
Process philosophy 27
Puritan 28, 31
Quantum physics 18, 29, 135, 136,
....137
Realism 104, 105, 119

Regeneration.....................................27
Relativity theory.........18, 21, 29, 130,
....134, 135
Reproducion ..167, 187, 189, 201, 202
    Reproductive systems of the
        animals 186
Rise of modern science...................28
RNA 170, 171
Royal Society....................................28
Sabbath 97-100, 119, 209-222
    A Change of Day, Not Principle
        217-221
Saltation.......................................91, 92
    Salinity and Chemical
    Composition of the Oceans
       153
Satan   85, 87, 117, 186, *see* Lucifer
Secularism 21, 25, 215, 216
Semitic way of thinking 103
Ten Commandments 16, 212, 220
Theism 31

Theology and the Rise of Science
        28-30
Theorems of Kurt Gödel 29
Thermodynamics, Laws of 55, 56,
        ....57, 60, 61, 66, 123
Tibetan Plateau 145
Time   69-72, 96-100, 123, 133-134,
       172
tohu 72, 73, 86
Totalitarianism.................15, 203, 208
Tragedy...................25, 26, 27, 36, 171
Unifi cation of ontology and
    intelligibility 21
Uniformitarianism ... 85, 93, 144-148,
        ....150, 159, 160, 164,
        .... *see* evolution
Uranium 129, 142, 143, 153, 154
Westminster Confession of Faith
       214
White Holes............................133, 134